D1210456

PARADIPLOMACY

PARADIPLOMACY

Cities and States
as Global Players

Rodrigo Tavares

OXFORD
UNIVERSITY PRESS

Oxford University Press is a department of the University of Oxford. It furthers
the University's objective of excellence in research, scholarship, and education
by publishing worldwide. Oxford is a registered trade mark of Oxford University
Press in the UK and certain other countries.

Published in the United States of America by Oxford University Press
198 Madison Avenue, New York, NY 10016, United States of America.

Library of Congress Cataloging-in-Publication Data
Names: Tavares, Rodrigo.
Title: Paradiplomacy : cities and states as global players / Rodrigo Tavares.
Description: New York : Oxford University Press, [2016] | Includes
bibliographical references and index.
Identifiers: LCCN 2016005123| ISBN 9780190462116 (hardcover : alk. paper) |
ISBN 9780190462123 (pbk. : alk. paper)
Subjects: LCSH: Subnational governments—Foreign relations. | Municipal
government—International cooperation. | Globalization—Political aspects.
Classification: LCC JZ4059 .T38 2016 | DDC 327.2—dc23 LC record available
at http://lccn.loc.gov/2016005123

9 8 7 6 5 4 3 2 1
Paperback printed by WebCom, Inc., Canada
Hardback printed by Bridgeport National Bindery, Inc., United States of America

To my father, José Francisco Tavares

Por estar sempre presente, mesmo quando ausente

Contents

Acknowledgments

No book is an island. During the time I spent writing the book, my path crossed the life of countless people who, even if unaware of it, provided data or inspiration to the endeavor. My first thanks go to my team at the Office of Foreign Affairs of São Paulo's State Government, who showed an unusual determination to make a difference in public service and in global paradiplomacy. I am also indebted to the Taubman Center for State and Local Government at Harvard University, and mainly to its director, professor Jeffrey B. Liebman, for inviting me to become a Senior Research Fellow with the mission to advance knowledge on the global competitiveness of cities and states.

The book is also a reflection of the desire of a very significant number of practitioners in having their foreign policy work critically assessed and academically contextualized. Although it will not be possible to list all scholars and practitioners who added value to the book with their views, I would like to underline the contribution of Andrey Brito, Anna Bazza, Anne Vanhollebeke, Anthony Taieb, Bruno Sarra-Bournet, Chloé Choquier, Eric Marquis, Erich Watzl, Francesca Guardiola Sala, Gala Dahlet, Hunter M. Richard, Ingrid Brachner, Jakub Eberle, Jessy Gelinas, Josep Maria Buades Juan, Joseph Alessi, Klaus Ulrich, Koen Jongbloet, Laudemar Aguiar, Laurine Platzky, Maria Luisa Zapata Trujillo, Marie-Claude Francoeur, Michael Hinterdobler, Pedro Spadale, Regina Rutenberg, Rodrigo V. Oliveira, Sun-hee Jang, Todd Barrett, Tomas Kroyer, and

Tomoya Suzuki. In this group, special thanks go to Eric Marquis who went through the manuscript with a fine-tooth comb and provided innumerable witty recommendations.

However, the two people I am most grateful to are not experts on the topic, and yet they were instrumental during the whole research process. My wife Mirna and son Gabriel stood by my side with their immense love and care. I love you too.

PARADIPLOMACY

Essentials of Paradiplomacy

No matter how far away, no matter how small in size, no matter how few competences, and indeed, no matter how poor, every single region has at least one unique jewel it can share with the others.
—VAIRA VĪĶE-FREIBERGA, *former president of Latvia*

Subnational presence on the international scene has become a fact of life in an interdependent world.
—IVO DUCHACEK, *the creator of "paradiplomacy" concept (1984)*

Global cities are increasingly driving world affairs—economically, politically, socially and culturally. They are no longer just places to live in. They have emerged as leading actors on the global stage.
—IVO DAALDER, *president of the Chicago Council on Global Affairs (2015)*

Introduction

Almost everything in nature is self-organized and a substantial part of what human beings do is organizing their behavior. Over the last centuries, we have organized the world so that sovereign states serve as the main compass. When asked what are the largest world economies, we think about countries. Who are the most powerful? A handful of sovereign states come to mind. I propose a different way of reshuffling the cards. Instead of looking at foreign affairs in a state-centric way, one should also contemplate other actors such as cities and states (or cantons, counties, departments, districts, *krays, länder, oblasts, okrugs,* prefectures, provinces, regions, republics, territories, or zones). Picking a different unit of analysis diversifies our understanding of the world, adding realism and density to our everyday life and choices. Any future institutional framework for foreign affairs should be deeply rooted in the principles of multilevel and multi-stakeholder governance in order to allow for interaction, synergy, and complementarity between all levels of governments and to encourage ownership of the challenges and the opportunities of foreign affairs.

History countersigns this view. When we look back at the last four hundred years, we notice that new actors emerge on the world stage in a cyclical way. Sovereign states, as we know them today, are a fairly recent political construction, dating back to the seventeenth century. Yet, they alone no longer monopolize the status quo of the international system, even if they still certainly play a vital role. International organizations rose as a full global actor in the late nineteenth century and were followed by multinational companies in the mid-twentieth century, international nongovernmental organizations (iNGOs) in the 1980s, and by terror groups, religious communities, a transnational civil society, or by celebrities in more recent times. All have authority and capacity to mold world dynamics and shape rules while they dispute space and resources among themselves to enlarge and protect their constituencies.

Cities and states are the brand-new international actors. If the international community has always been aware of the economic sway of some states (such as California or Texas) or of regions using foreign policy to leverage their internal autonomy (such as Quebec or Catalonia), today the phenomenon is much more widespread. The international tentacles of "mega cities" or "global cities" have also been grasped in the past, but the list of cities that are no longer nested in a national urban system only but participate directly in global governance is much wider. Virtually no state or major city in the United States, Canada, Germany, Brazil, China, Japan, Mexico, France, and several other countries in Asia, Latin America, Europe, or North America has shied away from harnessing the opportunities opened up by an international presence. North Rhine-Westphalia, Guangdong, São Paulo (state), and Île-de-France are richer than most countries in the world and have established well-staffed and dynamic structures to defend their interests abroad. Subnational entities can thus be regarded less as a territory but as a space where global flows—capital, information, people, goods, services—crisscross and solidify. The startling reality is that among the thirty largest economies in the world ranked by gross domestic product (GDP), twelve are subnational (regional or municipal) (table 1.1). A study by the McKinsey Global Institute shows that

TABLE 1.1 Ranking of top 30 national, state, and municipal GDPs (2014, unless stated otherwise)

National or Subnational state	Type	GDP (nominal) US$ million
1. United States	Country	17,348
2. China	Country	10,356
3. Japan	Country	4,602
4. Germany	Country	3,874
5. United Kingdom	Country	2,950
6. France	Country	2,833
7. Brazil	Country	2,346
8. **California (United States)**	**State**	2.310
9. Italy	Country	2,147
10. India	Country	2,051
11. Russia	Country	1,860
12. Canada	Country	1,785
13. **Texas (United States)**	**State**	1,648
14. **Tokyo Metropolitan (Japan)**	**State/City**	1,617

(continued)

TABLE 1.1 Continued

National or Subnational state	Type	GDP (nominal) US$ million
15. **New York metropolitan area**[a] **(United States)**	**City**	1,560
16. Australia	Country	1,442
17. South Korea	Country	1,410
18. Spain	Country	1,406
19. **New York state (United States)**	**State**	1,405
20. Mexico	Country	1,291
21. **Guangdong (China)**	**State**	1,103
22. **Jiangsu (China)**	**State**	1,059
23. **Shandong (China)**	**State**	967
24. Indonesia	Country	888
25. Netherlands	Country	880
26. **Los Angeles (metropolitan area)**	**City**	867
27. **Florida (United States)**	**State**	840
28. Turkey	Country	798
29. **Île-de-France (France)**	**State**	780 (2013)
30. **São Paulo (state) (Brazil)**	**State**	773 (2013)

[a] It includes the six largest cities in the state of New Jersey (Newark, Jersey City, Paterson, Elizabeth, Trenton, and Edison) and six of the seven largest cities in the state of Connecticut (Bridgeport, New Haven, Stamford, Waterbury, Norwalk, and Danbury).

Note: Subnational entities are in bold.

six hundred urban centers generate about 60 percent of global GDP (Dobbs et al. 2011).

This trend goes hand in hand with the global urbanization of the planet. Concentrated into just 2 percent of the world's surface, urban areas now hold over half of the world's population and UN-Habitat estimates that by 2050 over 75 percent of the world's population will live in cities. According to the UN agency: "The 100 years from 1950 to 2050 will be remembered for the greatest social, cultural, economic and environmental transformation in history—the urbanization of humanity. With half of us now occupying urban space, the future of the human species is tied to the city" (UN-Habitat 2008, 2). Currently, over 80 percent of global economic output is already generated by cities. This phenomenon only bears comparison to that great growth of cities that accompanied the industrial revolution in the nineteenth century. "Cities are 'our species' greatest invention" (Glaeser 2011, 6).

Aware of their economic potential and strains and faced with gridlock in the national capitals, mayors and governors have gone a long way toward filling the vacuum of effective decision-making and effective action by exercising political and economic power at their level. It is the states and cities that are the engines of growth at the ground level, where the transition from policy to practice becomes most visible. In countries around the world subnational governments have now to meet the needs of their constituencies and face constant scrutiny. Processes of decentralization of government— the downward transfer of resources, responsibilities, or authority from national to subnational governments—is a powerful global tendency (Falleti 2010; Goldsmith 2012). As pointed out by Michael Storper: "City-regions are the principal scale at which people experience lived reality. The geographical churn, turbulence, and unevenness of development, combined with the sheer scale of urbanization, will make city-region development more important than ever—to economics, politics, our global mood, and our welfare" (2013, 4). With the exception of the classical strongholds of sovereign countries—the military, border security, monetary policy, and justice—decentralization is touching all segments of power.

This offers some challenges to the practice of foreign affairs. If the international portfolio of national states is still dominated by issues of war and peace, trade matters, and monetary stability, there is a tendency and pressure for foreign ministries to diversify their agendas and to include human-scale themes such as environmental and social issues, cultural exchanges, infrastructure, education, or healthcare and epidemics. This enlargement of the field of foreign policy into nonmilitary and non-diplomatic issue areas is gradually becoming a characteristic feature of global interdependence. Yet, these are fields that usually fall under the legal competence of subnational governments. And local authorities wish not to relinquish their rights and duties. If national foreign policy is outward looking to the external environment, then subnational foreign policy looks more inward to the domestic base. A balance is possible to strike if we view the international activities of subnational governments as one element in an increasingly complex multilayered diplomatic environment wherein policy-makers seek to negotiate simultaneously with domestic as well as foreign interests (Hocking, 1993). Chinese provinces, Brazilian states, or German *länder* smoothly carry out hundreds of international cooperation programs on issues that directly relate to the welfare of their citizens.

International protocol and norms represent another barometer of the new weight that subnational actors carry in the global arena. Emblematically, when the governor of California visited China in 2013 and Mexico in 2014, he was received with pomp by Premier Li Keqiang and by President Enrique Peña Nieto, respectively. Or when Brazil's President Dilma Rousseff led a mission to the United States in 2012, she held meetings not only with President Barack Obama but also with then Governor Deval Patrick of Massachusetts. Led by economic imperatives and by constitutional rights, subnational governments have landed on the moon of foreign affairs, signaling a fundamental challenge to some of the core logics of the modern international system.

As witnessed before in ancient history, once again local spaces—cities and states—are the cradles of change, the place where new lifestyles form and new ways of organizing work, economy, and politics

are being born. But how has this situation come about? Doesn't orthodox International Relations theory claim that foreign affairs are
under the exclusive purview of central governments? Why is this
type of subnational activity becoming more prevalent and growing
at a rate that far exceeds the growth of international activity by the
traditional representatives of sovereign states? How could foreign
policy be used as an instrument to deliver domestic services, such
as healthcare, infrastructure, or better education? The international
activism of subnational governments is rapidly growing across the
world, discreetly transforming diplomatic practices and foreign
policy instruments. But the full import of this development and its
potentially far-reaching consequences is as yet not well grasped.

Although this book was written with a scholarly mind, its fundamental goal is to provide a pragmatic and critical view of the international presence of cities and states, one that can benefit both
scholars and policymakers. Drawing from a very unique pool of
experiences of close to two hundred subnational governments, the
book addresses the full spectrum of the past, present, and future of
paradiplomacy.

The Quest for the Right Word

The practice of foreign affairs by cities and states has been coined
in a multitude of different ways, which adds creativity and plural-
ity to the debate but inevitably hampers the possibility of having a
popular and universally accepted term in the foreign affairs dictionary. There are indeed too many terms to describe the "non-central
governments' involvement in international relations through the
establishment of permanent or ad hoc contacts with foreign public
or private entities, with the aim to promote . . . any foreign dimension of their constitutional competences" (Cornago 1999, 40). What
are these terms?

"Paradiplomacy," an abbreviation of "parallel diplomacy,"
first emerged in the 1980s in the writings of Ivo Duchacek[1] and
Panayotis Soldatos in the context of the academic debate around

US President Richard Nixon's "new federalism" model, a plan to turn over the control of some federal programs to state and local governments. "Para-" is an originally Greek word that means "beside," "near," "alongside," or "subsidiary," "assistant." Some scholars indeed look at paradiplomacy in reference to diplomacy and define it as a direct international activity by subnational actors supporting, complementing, correcting, duplicating, or challenging the nation-states' diplomacy (Soldatos 1990, 17). Although this is still the most commonly used term by policymakers and therefore justified in its selection for the title of this book, the term "paradiplomacy" is not immune to criticism. Some point out that the foreign affairs of subnational governments have their own nature and personality and shall not be regarded simply as complements to mainstream national diplomatic activities. Belgium's regions, for instance, have exclusive international oversight on education, culture, economy, or environment. As there is no national foreign policy on these issues, their international activities may not be regarded as complementary. In Flanders and Wallonia, the term paradiplomacy is regarded as derogatory. Others, mostly trained diplomats, question the use of the word "diplomacy" within "paradiplomacy," as the first is an activity carried out by diplomats which are representatives of sovereign states. Diplomacy is an instrument of statecraft, it is argued. For different reasons, this view is shared by some scholars who contend that employing the orthodox terminology of foreign policy helps to devalue the practice of paradiplomacy and disguises the distinctiveness of what is being examined (Hocking 1999, 21).

"Federative diplomacy" was a term popular mostly in Brazil in the 1990s and 2000s. It was first used in April 1995 by then Minister of External Relations Luiz Felipe Lampreia in his inaugural address to the National Congress (External Relations Committee). He stated that:

> It is also a policy of President Fernando Henrique that in addition to this aspect of public diplomacy, diplomacy of interaction, one should add another equally fundamental angle according to

our political system, which is *federative diplomacy*. States and even municipalities have an increasing international agenda that should be added to the external agenda of the Union, which is ultimately responsible for the foreign relations of the country (Lampreia, 1999:3; italics added).

The term was then incorporated into the Ministry's dictionary and used officially until more recent years, when the expression "decentralized international cooperation" was favored because it was believed to be more palatable as it dropped the term "diplomacy" out of the equation.

"Decentralized (International) Cooperation" was one of the innovations introduced by a legal agreement signed between the European Union (then European Economic Community) and the countries of Africa, the Caribbean, and the Pacific during the Fourth Lomé Convention of 1989. Used mostly now in countries such as Brazil and France, it puts the emphasis on cooperation and partnerships rather than on traditional diplomatic tools (such as opening offices abroad). The United Nations Development Program (UNDP) also uses the term recurrently and defines it as "a long-term partnership between communities in different cities or towns and as a mechanism for establishing a novel 'partnership' modality, which focuses on direct relationships between regional territories, as opposed to the model that promotes bilateral cooperation at the national level" (United Nations 2008, 2). The term is shared by other international bodies such as the Euro African Partnership for Decentralized Governance, supported by the United Nations Department of Economic and Social Affairs (UN-DESA).

Besides these more rooted terms, there are several other ways to coin the same phenomenon, depending on the political and academic ecosystem of their authors, such as "subnational foreign affairs," "subnational foreign policy," "substate diplomacy," "multilayered diplomacy," "constituent diplomacy," "local government external action," "local diplomacy," "local foreign policy," "regional diplomacy," "plurinational diplomacy," "pos-diplomacy," "microdiplomacy," or one may speak of "foreign policy localization."

The History of Paradiplomacy—From Past to Present

History is pregnant with examples of cities and regions that had contacts with foreign lands: from Greek city-states (Athens, Sparta, Thebes, and Corinth) or Ancient Egyptian city-states (Thebes or Memphis) to the large pre-Columbian Mesoamerican cities (Chichen Itza, Tikal, Monte Albán, or Tenochtitlan), the central Asian cities along the Silk Road or the Viking colonial cities in medieval Ireland. In a world of difficult communication and mobility, political organization was to be established in small geographical units. Cities and towns have played a central role economically, politically, and culturally in all human societies and precede nation-states by some 5,000 years (Ljungkvist 2014, 52). It is not surprising thus that the cradle of modern diplomacy can be traced back to city-states and not countries. The machinery of diplomacy began in Northern Italy in the fourteenth century and spread to the rest of Western and Northern Europe in the following hundred years. Milan played a leading role, especially under Francesco Sforza, a fifteenth-century *condottiero*, who established permanent embassies in the other city-states of Northern Italy.

Under closer scrutiny, however, these earlier foreign contacts cannot really be regarded as paradiplomacy because these political entities were independent and sovereign. Paradiplomacy, a twentieth-century invention, is a natural consequence of globalization and the perforation of the traditional notion of sovereign state. The acceleration of the global economy, the mobility of capital and communications, and transportation technology have eroded the distinction between domestic and foreign affairs and by the same token have transformed the division of responsibilities between state and subnational governments (Keating 1999, 1). The interaction between globalization and localization is now well recognized; it does not represent some unfathomable paradox but reflects the competing pressures and tensions created by a broader and more integrated global economy (Hocking 1999, 18). In this context, regions operate alongside countries, firms, multinational companies, iNGOs, trade unions, international organizations, or social movements in a way that tends to be "complex, fragmented and unstructured" (Keating 1999, 6).

The first modern attempts at fostering international exchanges of local governments were born in the late nineteenth century when Victoria (in 1857[2]), South Australia (1858), New South Wales (1864), Queensland (1869), Quebec (1882), Tasmania (1886), and Western Australia (1891)—all crown colonies under British rule—appointed their agent-generals to either London or Paris. Hector Fabre,[3] Quebec's first representative in France, was dispatched to Paris on the grounds that "the business relations between the province of Quebec and Europe are increasing constantly and that big firms, financial institutions and other enterprises, created or enhanced by French capital, [have] witnessed a considerable development" (cited in Soldatos 1990, 34). In 1911, the province opened a "commercial" office in Britain, followed by a provincial posting in Brussels in 1915. Roughly in the same period (September 1907), the state of São Paulo adopted what may be the first international agreement by a substate. Signed with Japan, it pertained to the immigrations of thousands of Japanese into Brazil (São Paulo 2014, 3) (figure 1.1). Because of this and subsequent agreements, São Paulo hosts presently the largest Japanese diaspora in the world.

Other relevant efforts arrived in the first decades of the twentieth century. The International Union of Local Authorities (IULA) was established in 1913 in the Netherlands with the intention to promote democratic local self-government—beginning with a focus on newly founded European cities. Although it was closed down twice during times of war in the early twentieth century, it has maintained its objectives and directions since its inception. The first postwar IULA congress was held in Paris in 1947 in the newly refurbished UNESCO building with representatives from twenty-three countries. During this congress, a group of French and German mayors established the Union International des Maires to foster friendly relations between the two countries and ensure peace (Vion 2007).

This was a sign of what was to come. At the end of the war, several European cities emerged from the ashes and started to engage in acts

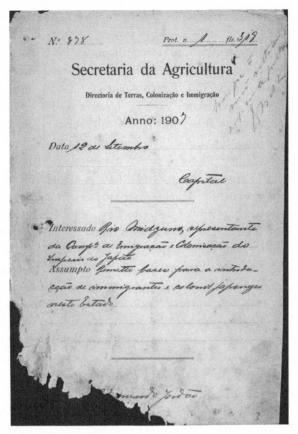

FIGURE 1.1 Agreement signed between the state of São Paulo and Japan in September 1907. The first international agreement signed by a substate

© Public Archive of the State of São Paulo

of peace and reconciliation by signing town-twinning agreements (discussed later). This led to the establishment in 1951 of the Council of European Municipalities with offices in Austria, Belgium, France, Germany, Great Britain, Ireland, Italy, Luxemburg, the Netherlands, Spain, and Switzerland, permitting that for the first time an assembly of fifty European mayors would get together to establish standards and guidelines and negotiate twinning contracts (Weyreter 2003). This new policy was replicated in the United States in the mid-1950s and championed by President Dwight D. Eisenhower through his sponsorship of sister city agreements (discussed later).

These goodwill initiatives were paralleled by the creation of the first foreign affairs governing bodies at subnational level in the 1960s. In 1967, the Legislative Assembly of Quebec, as the National Assembly was then called, unanimously adopted an act creating the Ministère des Affaires intergouvernementales, the forerunner of the current Ministère des Relations internationales et de la Francophonie, boosting the development of Quebec's international relations. It was one of the first institutional bodies of its kind.

In the 1970s, the new globalization context nourished the composition of groups of regions, mostly in Europe, interested in leveraging their sectorial or geographical proximity. Forums such as the Association of European Border Regions (founded in 1971), the Conference of Peripheral Maritime Regions (1973), the European Regions of Industrial Technology, and the Conference and Association of Steel Territories (the latter two merged in 2002 into the European Industrial Regions Association) found a way to highlight the special problems and opportunities of border regions and to represent their common interests vis-à-vis national and international parliaments, bodies, authorities, and institutions. Another initiative that drew attention was the establishment in 1988 of the Four Motors for Europe, bringing together the leading regional economies of Baden-Württemberg, Catalonia, Lombardy, and Rhône-Alpes. The twofold aim was to bring an international dimension to these regions and their citizens while promoting the role of Europe's regions within a fledgling European Union. In the Soviet Union, paradiplomacy raised in the late 1970s with the first high-level discussions held at the 25th Congress of the Communist Party of the Soviet Union, where regional leaders expressed an unprecendented interest in foreign affairs (Hauslohner, 1981).

Despite these efforts by subnational governments to attract foreign direct investment or to use culture and identity as a lever to place themselves on the international map, these initiatives were often ad hoc and limited.

Subnational activism only started to gain attention from the international community in the 1980s and 1990s when European subnational entities, spurred by the political and economic effects of globalization and by enhanced European integration, sought new ways to relate to the state, the market, and the European Union (a phenomenon known as *new regionalism*). They were given constitutional and institutional leeway to develop external activities and could thus adopt a judicially grounded set of instruments for their own diplomatic activities (Criekemans 2010b, 37–38). In Belgium, for instance, until the 1990s the foreign policy of the regions was mostly confined to cultural activities and some initiatives regarding cooperation in the education field.[4] But in the early 1990s, a series of constitutional reforms dismantled the unitary state, culminating in the St. Michael's Agreement (September 1992), which laid the groundwork for the establishment of the federal state. In this context, the external activities of the regions were broadened to all of their internal competences.

With the dawn of the new millennium, paradiplomacy reached its golden age. Against conventional views, the international activism of substate governments is now neither exclusive to federal countries nor to firmly established democracies (Cornago 2010, 17). It is undeniably salient in the case of federal countries such as Canada, Germany, Belgium, Switzerland, Austria, or the United States, but it is also very tangible in unitary countries such as Spain or France. More notably, paradiplomacy is becoming a truly global phenomenon with substates in South Africa, China, Japan, India, Brazil, Argentina, Chile, Mexico, and Russia, to name just a few, carrying out foreign activities. Chinese provinces may provide today one of the most solid examples of vigorous and ample foreign activities carried out at the subnational level.

Local governments are also becoming better organized. Presently, there are over 125 multilateral networks and forums that gather subnational governments to discuss a myriad of issues— from sustainable development to culture and education or urban development (table 1.2). The top-notch global gatherings are, possibly, the annual World Regional Governments Summit that has

TABLE 1.2 List of multilateral arrangements of subnational governments

Name	Year foundation	Members (as of 2015)
100 Resilient Cities network	2013	100
Air Quality Initiative of Regions (AIR)	2011	12 regions from 7 EU Member States
Airport Regions Conference (ARC)	1994	35
Alliance of Energy-Intensive European Union Regions	2008	11
Alps–Adriatic Working Community	1978	19
Alps–Mediterranean Euroregion	2007	5
Arab Towns Organization	1976	More than 400 cities and towns representing 22 states
Art Nouveau Network	1999	21 cities and regions
Asian Network of Major Cities 21 (ANMC21)	2001	13
Assembly of European Fruit and Vegetable Growing and Horticultural Regions (AREFLH)	1999	23
Assembly of European Regions (AER)	1985	202

(continued)

TABLE 1.2 Continued

Name	Year foundation	Members (as of 2015)
Assembly of European Wine-Producing Regions	1988	52
Association of Alpine States (Arge Alp)	1972	10
Association of Cities and Regions for Recycling and Sustainable Resource Management (ACR +)	1994	nearly 100 entities
Association of European Border Regions (AEBR)	1971	181 border and cross-border regions
Association of European Regions for Origin Products (AREPO)	2004	27 European regions
Association of Local Democracy Agencies (ALDA)	1999	more than 150 members (municipalities, NGOs, and grassroots associations)
Association of North East Asia Regional Governments (NEAR)	1996	71 regional governments from 6 countries
Atlantic Area Transnational Cooperation Program	2007	37 European regions
Baltic Sea States Subregional Cooperation (BSSSC)	1993	162 subnational governments from the 10 Baltic States
Border Governors' Conference	1980	10 US–Mexico border states

(continued)

TABLE 1.2 Continued

Name	Year foundation	Members (as of 2015)
Cities Alliance	1999	Members of UCLG and Metropolis
Cities Climate Leadership Group (C40)	2005	82
Cities for Local Integration Policy Network (CLIP)	2006	30
Cities for Mobility	2000	Over 500
CITYNET	1987	81 cities
Climate Alliance of European Cities with Indigenous Rainforest Peoples	1990	more than 1,700 cities
Commonwealth Local Government Forum (CLGF)	1995	more than 200 members
Compact of Mayors	2014	Nearly 400
Compact of States and Regions	2014	Nearly 100
Conference of European Regions with Legislative Power (REGLEG)	2000	73
Conference of European Regional Legislative Assemblies (CALRE)	1997	74
Conference of Peripheral Maritime Regions (CPMR)	1973	150

(continued)

TABLE 1.2 Continued

Name	Year foundation	Members (as of 2015)
Conference of Presidents of Ultra-Peripheral Regions (aka as Conference of Presidents of Outermost Regions)	1994	9
Congress of Local and Regional Authorities of Europe (CLRAE)	1994	636
Council of European Municipalities and Regions (CEMR)	1951	150,000 local governments
Council of Great Lakes Governors	1983	10 (including 2 associate members)
Council of State Governments—Eastern Regional Conference (CSG-ERC)	1937	18 (from United States and Canada)
Covenant of Mayors	2008	5,594 signatories
District of Creativity (DC) Network	2004	13
Energy Cities (European Association of Local Authorities in Energy Transition)	1990	more than 1,000 local authorities
Environmental Conference of the Regions of Europe (ENCORE)	1993	more than 100 European regions

(continued)

TABLE 1.2 Continued

Name	Year foundation	Members (as of 2015)
Euro Mediterranean Partnership of Local and Regional Authorities (COPPEM)	2000	35
Eurocities	1986	140
Euro-Latin American Alliance of Cooperation among Cities (AL-LAs Project)	2013	7
European Association of Elected Representatives from Mountain Regions (AEM)	1991	10,000 municipalities and 50 regions
European Chemical Regions Network (ECRN)	2004	20
European Clusters and Regions for Eco-innovation and Eco-investments Network (ECREIN)	2007	6 European regions
European Federation of Agencies and Regions for Energy and the Environment (FEDARENE)	1990	65
European Forum for Urban Security (EFUS)	1987	250 European local authorities
European GMO-Free Regions Network	2005	62 regions

(continued)

TABLE 1.2 Continued

Name	Year foundation	Members (as of 2015)
European Local Authorities Network for the Information Society (ELANET)	1996	all members of CEMR
European Region Danube Vltava (ERDV)	2012	7
European Regions and Municipalities Partnership for Hydrogen and Fuel Cells (HyRaMP)	2008	32
European Regions Research and Innovation Network (ERRIN)	2001	90
European Strategy for the Alpine Region (EUSALP)	2013	48
European Union's Committee of the Regions	1994	353
Federation of Latin American Cities, Municipalities and Associations of Local Governments (FLACMA)	1981	All Latin American members of UCLG
Federation of European Union Local Authority Chief Executive Officers (UDiTE)	1990	professional associations which represent local government in 14 European countries
Four Motors for Europe association	1988	4

(continued)

TABLE 1.2 Continued

Name	Year foundation	Members (as of 2015)
Global Cities Dialogue	1999	190
Global Fund for Cities Development (FMDV)	2010	members of Metropolis and UCLG
Great Lakes Commission	1955	10 (including 2 associate members)
Great Lakes-St. Lawrence Cities Initiative	2003	114
Ibero-American Center for Strategic Urban Development (CIDEU)	1993	132
Ibero-American Forum of Local Authorities	2006	200
Innovating Regions in Europe Network (IRE)	1995	235 member regions
International Association for Peace Messenger Cities	1988	101
International Association of Educating Cities (AICE)	1990	470
International Association of Francophone Mayors (AIMF)	1979	254 cities and associations
International Association of Francophone Regions (AIRF)	2002	170
International Lake Constance Conference (IBK)	1972	10

(continued)

TABLE 1.2 Continued

Name	Year foundation	Members (as of 2015)
International Solar Cities Initiative (ISCI)	2003	5
International Union of Local Authorities (IULA)	1913–2004	(it was replaced by UCLG)
Latin American Organization of Intermediate Governments (OLAGI)	2004	138
Leading Cities	2011	8
Local Governments for Sustainability (ICLEI)	1990	over 1,000 cities, towns, and metropolises
Mayors for Peace	1982	Around 6,500 cities
Medcities—Mediterranean cities network	1991	33
Mercocities	1995	286
MERCOSUR Committee of Municipalities, States, Provinces and Departments	2004	Up to 100 rotational members
Most Ancient European Towns Network	1994	10
Municipal Alliance for Peace in the Middle East (MAP)	2005	4 cities and 6 associations of cities
Network of European Metropolitan Regions and Areas (METREX)	1996	50

(continued)

TABLE 1.2 Continued

Name	Year foundation	Members (as of 2015)
Network of European Regions for a Sustainable and Competitive Tourism (NECStour)	2007	28
Network of European Regions on Education for Sustainability (RES)	2005	17
Network of European Regions Using Space Technologies (NEREUS)	2008	25 full members
Network of Metropolitan Areas of the Americas (RAMA)	2014	5
Network of Regional Governments for Sustainable Development (nrg4SD)	2002	50 subnational governments
Network of South American Cities (REDCISUR)	2012	10
New England Governors and Eastern Canadian Premiers' Annual Conference (NEG/ECP)	1972	6 US states and 5 Canadian provinces
Organization of Islamic Capitals and Cities (OICC)	1980	141
Organization of World Heritage Cities	1993	250
Pacific Coast Collaborative	2008	5

(continued)

TABLE 1.2 Continued

Name	Year foundation	Members (as of 2015)
Pacific Northwest Economic Region (PNWER)	1991	10
Pact of Islands	2007	12
Peri Urban Regions Platform Europe (PURPLE)	2004	15
POLIS Network	1989	67
Pyrenees-Mediterranean Euroregion	2004	4
Red Andina de Ciudades (RAR)	2003	5
Regional Greenhouse Gas Initiative (RGGI)	2003	14 (including 4 observers)
Regional Leaders Summit	1999	7
Regions of Climate Action (R20)	2010	45 subnational governments
Regions United/Forum of Regional Governments and Global Associations of Regions (FOGAR)	2007	32
Soil & Land Alliance of European Cities and Towns (ELSA)	2000	119
Southeastern United States–Canadian Provinces Alliance (SEUS-CPA)	2007	13
Sustainable Cities and Towns Campaign	1994	more than 2,700 local authorities

(continued)

TABLE 1.2 Continued

Name	Year foundation	Members (as of 2015)
The Climate Group	2004	over 80 business and government organizations
The Northern Forum	1993	24
Under Two MOU	2015	127
UNESCO Creative Cities Network	2004	69
UNESCO International Coalition of Cities against Racism	2004	503
Union of Capital Cities Luso-Afro-American-Asian (UCCLA)	1985	22
Union of Ibero-American Capital Cities (UCCI)	1982	29
United Cities and Local Governments (UCLG)	2004	Over 1,000 cities
United Nations Advisory Committee of Local Authorities (UNACLA)	2000	20
Vanguard Initiative for New Growth by Smart Specialization	2013	10 European industrial regions
Western Climate Initiative	2007	11
Working Community of the Danube Countries (ARGE)	1990	38 members in 10 states bordering the Danube

(continued)

TABLE 1.2 Continued

Name	Year foundation	Members (as of 2015)
Working Community of the Pyrenees (CTP)	1983	7 regions (from Spain and France)
World Association of the Major Metropolises (Metropolis)	1985	More than 120
World Association of Cities and Local Authorities Coordination (WACLAC)	1996	6 subnational multilateral forums
World e-Governments Organization of Cities and Local Governments (WeGO)	2008	82
World Energy Cities Partnership	1995	20 cities
World Federation of United Cities and United Towns Organization (FMCU-UTO)	1957–2004	(it was replaced by UCLG)
World Regions Forum	2009 (it was unofficially dissolved in 2013)	17

been organized since 2009 by Regions United/Forum of Regional Governments and Global Associations of Regions (FOGAR) and also the World Council of the United Cities and Local Governments (UCLG) held since 2010. They bring together thousands of participants from municipal and state governments to discuss local governance in a global context. In January 2015, five multilateral networks of local and regional governments—International Association of Francophone Mayors (AIMF), Commonwealth Local Government Forum (CLGF), Council of European Municipalities and Regions (CEMR-PLATFORMA), UCLG, and UCLG Africa—signed the first strategic partnership agreement with the European Commission acknowledging the role of subnational governments as decision-makers to define policies and contribute to addressing global challenges.

Yet, there is a cleavage between the quantitative and qualitative presence of paradiplomatic activities and their acknowledgment by the international community. The new issue of paradiplomacy is sometimes regarded as a side-track. Traditionalists are wary of the fact that regions and cities often spill over their domestic competences into the international arena, eroding the borders between political science and international relations.[5] Global flows result in "a partial denationalization of global politics and thereby open up prospects for sub-national formal and informal political actors to play a role in global governance. This is our world and it includes multiple sources who exercise authority regardless of its formal assignment" (Amen et al. 2011, 2). Subnational governments increasingly enter into global and transnational networks and international associations and gain voice in global forums where subnational governments have been underrepresented in the past (Amen et al. 2011, 3). Some authors argue further that the diplomacy of subnational governments conceived in the context of multinational states is more than the external manifestations of the domestic functions of these actors. In essence, their diplomacy represents the purposeful projection of new actors on the world stage (Lecours and Moreno 2003).

Whatever the motivation, paradiplomacy is here to stay. As pointed out by Acuto:

City leaders have often acquired a positioning that is widely overlooked by students of international relations and urban studies and that, on the contrary, presents a crucial connection

> between the two disciplines. Capable of carrying out diplomatic endeavors and establishing transnational networks, while at the same time strong of powers that emerge out of often localized prerogatives such as planning, water and waste management, and transport policymaking, city leaders represent a fundamental bridge between the grand narratives of international affairs and their everyday mundanity. (Acuto 2013, 493)

This also holds for the state-level. All Chinese provinces, for instance, have very large international relations departments, with trained plurilingual staff, and most of them have established trade offices abroad. US, Canadian, or German states follow the same track. The strength of the trend has led the World Economic Forum, in its 2014 *The Competitiveness of Cities* report, to advocate that "cities should create their own [foreign] policies on trade, foreign direct investment, tourism and attracting foreign talent, and advance these globally as far as possible" (World Economic Forum 2014, 5). Strong voices have also emerged exhorting the international community to allow cities into the global stage. Acknowledging that national governments may not be moving fast enough to avert climate change, US Secretary of State John Kerry pushed in a 2015 interview for a bigger role for cities: "A lot of mayors around the world are ahead of their national governments, and a lot of local citizens are well ahead of their elected leaders," Kerry said. "I think we need to find a way to highlight that."[6] As cities continue to lay claim to major diplomatic and economic functions, the authors Michele Acuto and Parag Khanna once asked, "Should we still be talking about inter*national* relations?" (2013; italics added).

Despite the enthusiasm, paradiplomacy is presently going through its most challenging phase. From its embryonic period (starting in the late nineteenth century) and universalization (from the 1970s), we have evolved into the current context marked by a cacophony of voices, faltering global leadership, and a profusion of initiatives. There is no need for *more*, but for *better* paradiplomacy. One may have over 125 international networks of subnational governments, but only a much smaller group are able to fulfill the pledges embodied in the original foundational declarations. Wasteful overlapping (mainly in Europe), poor logistical resources, intermittent leadership, and pallid collective drive may lead to omission and disregard. One may optimistically argue that thousands of subnational governments worldwide conduct some type of foreign relations, but the substance and quality of these actions fluctuates significantly. Therefore, despite its unquestionable relevance, one has to look scrupulously at paradiplomacy, as it is shaped in different ways and led by different priorities and interests. Optimism should be grounded in realism. This book thus looks at paradiplomacy not as a precise concept, but rather as a multilayered term, which comprehends at least four phenomena: ceremonial paradiplomacy, single-themed paradiplomacy, global paradiplomacy, and sovereignty paradiplomacy.

Ceremonial Paradiplomacy

Paradiplomacy can be more steered by image than content or more by conviviality than pragmatism. In the absence of clear-cut attributed competencies in foreign policy, some regions focus very much on image-building and public relations in conducting their external relations. The most illustrative epitome of ceremonial contacts between regions or cities are the *twin towns* or *sister states* agreements that describe a form of non-binding cooperative arrangement made between subnational governments in geographically and politically distinct areas to promote cultural and commercial ties.

The earliest known town twinning in Europe was between Paderborn (Germany) and Le Mans (France) in 836. The first city in North America to establish a sister city relationship was Toledo (United States), which sistered with Toledo (Spain) in 1931. Town-twinning was revived in 1947 as a way to promote mutual understanding when Bristol Council sent five "leading citizens" on a goodwill mission to Hanover, resulting in a town-twinning agreement. Oxford and Bonn were next in tying the knot, Reading and Düsseldorf followed suit, and the first German–French twinning, between Montbeliard and Ludwigsburg, came about in 1950

(Weyreter 2003). Presently, Europe is estimated to have more than 10,000 friendship agreements.

The town-twinning process is supported by the European Union through its "Europe for Citizens" program. Established in 2006, the program aims to put into place the legal framework to support a wide range of activities and organizations promoting "active European citizenship" and therefore the involvement of citizens and civil society organizations in the process of European integration. In 2015 alone, the program supported 240 town-twinning initiatives and invested €3.9 million. On the EU website, the process is defined in very laudatory terms:

> Town twinning is a reality in today's Europe, as an important number of municipalities are linked to each other through a formal town twinning agreement. Such partnership aims at encouraging cooperation between the towns and mutual understanding between their citizens. The Town twinning movement has developed after the Second World War, in parallel to the progress made by the European integration process. One of the major developments was the establishment of new town twinning links between EU Member States and countries from Central or Eastern Europe after the fall of the Berlin Wall, anticipating and preparing their integration in the European Union.
>
> Town twinning represents a unique and dense network and therefore has a specific role to play with regard to the challenges of today's Europe, which are reflected in the objectives of this Programme.
>
> First, town twinning relies upon the voluntary commitment of citizens, in collaboration with their local authorities and local associations. It is therefore both a sign of, and an incentive to active participation. Second, it encourages exchanges of experiences on a variety of issues of common interest, thereby raising awareness on the advantages of finding concrete solutions at European level. Finally, it provides unique opportunities to learn about the daily lives of citizens in other European countries, to talk to them and very often to develop friendships with

them. Thanks to the combination of those elements, town twinning has a real potential to enhance mutual understanding between citizens, fostering a sense of ownership of the European
Union and finally developing a sense of European identity.

In order to make the best possible use of this potential, it
is necessary to provide an appropriate vehicle to the various
actors involved in town twinning and to adapt to the variety of
potential projects. (European Commission, EACEA - Education,
Audiovisual and Culture Executive Agency) [7]

In the United States and Japan, the first sister-city agreement
was adopted in 1955 between Saint Paul (Minnesota) and Nagasaki
to promote "the cause of peace." Even today, a Saint Paul–Nagasaki
Sister City Committee is dedicated to advancing the agreement. The
accord predated the sister-city program that formally began in 1956
when President Dwight D. Eisenhower proposed a citizen diplomacy
initiative. Originally a program of the National League of Cities, the
process was later led by Sister Cities International, which became
a separate entity in 1967. Eisenhower envisioned an organization
that could be "the hub of peace and prosperity" by creating bonds
between people from different cities around the world. Whereas in
Europe town twinning was bottom-up, originating in local leader-
ships (as we saw earlier), in the United States the process was top-
down, straight from the White House.

Presently, twining agreements are fading in importance, although they are still determinately pursued by Asian countries,
especially China and Japan, whose local governments still have a
very diligent policy favoring these types of agreements with foreign
counterparts. In 2009, President Gloria Macapagal-Arroyo of the
Philippines made a speech before the Third Philippine International
Sisterhood and Twinning Association calling for town twinning as a
way to improve the economy of participating communities through
the exchange of ideas, technology, services, and manpower. Asian
paradiplomacy has a somehow ceremonial and ornamental dimension. If you are mayor or a governor of a city or state that signed a
twinning agreement with an Asian local government, you have to be

ready to receive frequent letters (in English) that simply celebrate "traditional bonds of friendship and close cooperation" or inform you whenever there is a change of staff in their governments. Delegations will also visit you frequently, more to laud the importance of cooperation than to execute it. And often those local Asian governments also assign direct interlocutors who speak your native language and have fake Western first names "to facilitate communication," as a local mayor told me once. Chinese subnational governments have established over 2,100 sister agreements.[8]

But the tendency is otherwise. Although these agreements carry historical importance, subnational governments nowadays that confine themselves primarily to the symbolic aspects of sister-city relationship tend not to seriously consider themselves in the role of conducting international relations, since they have very little opportunity, motivation, precedent, political willingness, or know-how to do so. That is why most governments refrain from signing these types of agreements. For instance, New York City decided in 2006 not to sign any additional sister agreements and proposed, instead, that its linkages with foreign cities should be galvanized through New York City Global Partners, Inc., a network of over one hundred cities that meets annually and is led by the Mayor's Office for International Affairs. São Paulo state is frequently contacted by foreign partners to sign sister-state agreements, but a new policy in 2011 urges the government to negotiate and adopt only international cooperation agreements that carry political substance and commitments. Several small cites have followed a similar route. In 2015, the mayor of the City of Casey (suburb of Melbourne) indicated that sister relations with Springfield (Ohio, United States) and Berwick-upon-Tweed (United Kingdom), had been virtually nonexistent in recent years and therefore the municipal sister program would be abandoned.

Succinctly, town twinning is probably the most prolific and the least successful instrument available to subnational governments in their foreign activities. Since the end of World War II, tens of thousands of these agreements have been signed. Virtually, all major cities in the developed world are twinned with at least one other city.

But its relevance should be questioned. Agreements tend to be short (two to four pages), non-binding (they simply convey the purpose or the intention to do something), and generalist ("we shall foster cooperation envisioning the welfare of our populations"). Most of the action is composed of reciprocal visits by high-ranking officials and politicians, producing the handshakes, public pronouncements, and photo opportunities that press advisors like. On the positive side, they may create a positive atmosphere for cooperation and create an open channel of communication between cities or states. Indeed, very often we may find landmarks in city centers or at the entrance of a city displaying the list of twin cities. Regular exchange of visits and courtesy calls may also occur. But concrete results—expressed in specific cooperation programs or projects—are the exception and not the rule. Follow-up falls behind.

For that reason, future bilateral city agreements may end up mimicking national bilateral agreements, which are more binding and robust in nature. An indication of what may come was the 2014 Global Cities Economic Partnership signed between Chicago Mayor Rahm Emanuel and Mexico City Mayor Miguel Mancera. The first-of-its-kind city-to-city agreement, it established a series of joint initiatives in trade, innovation, and education to increase employment, expand advanced industries, and strengthen overall global competitiveness.

Single-Themed Paradiplomacy

In contrast to the informality of ceremonial paradiplomacy (with its brief outbursts of formality during the mayoral or gubernatorial summits), some cities and regions are more high-reaching, despite the fact that their foreign policy may be dictated by a narrow set of issues. This is particularly the case when local governments are brought together by their wish to discuss transborder issues or are guided by the aim to promote trade and attract foreign investments.

As the fragmentation of international relations takes place, and as provinces are more and more involved internationally on sectorial issues, neighboring provinces and states become increasingly aware of the benefits of transborder cooperation. Although there does not seem to be any set pattern, and the organizational responses vary considerably depending on the circumstances, several provinces signed memoranda of understanding with neighboring states, starting in the 1980s: Alberta with Montana (1985), Manitoba with Minnesota (1988), British Columbia with Washington State (1992), Ontario with New York (2001) and with Michigan (2002), Quebec with New York (2002). Earlier, these understandings addressed specific issues, such as the environment, but recently they have tended to be more encompassing, mostly calling for general economic cooperation.

Gradually, bilateral transborder connections were multiplied and led to the creation of multilateral bodies to enhance cross-border cooperation. One striking example is the Pacific Northwest Economic Region, established in 1991 and which includes British Columbia, Alberta, Yukon, and the states of Alaska, Idaho, Montana, Oregon, and Washington. Regional cooperation in the Pacific Northwest is special because the region is strategically located both as a gateway between North America and the Asia Pacific and as a cross-border community between Canada and the United States. A parallel agreement is the Conference of New England Governors and Eastern Canadian Premiers, which dates back to 1973. In the Great Lakes region, Ontario and Quebec are associate members of the Council of Great Lakes Governors and of the Great Lakes Commission. The first has, in recent years, spearheaded a noteworthy regional effort on maritime transportation (first results were presented in a summit in June 2015). There are other regional initiatives such as the Great Lakes-St. Lawrence Cities Initiative, which has its secretariat in Chicago, or the memoranda of understanding between Ontario and New York and Michigan.

Other examples are still worth mentioning. The lack of federal reaction to the effects of two consecutive oil slicks along the Pacific coast led the governments of British Columbia, Alaska, Washington, Oregon, and California to create in 1988 a special unit or Task Force to bring together human, technical, and financial resources to tackle the ecological disaster along their coasts (Cornago 1999, 51). A similar cooperation has developed between New York, Pennsylvania, Ohio, Illinois, Wisconsin, Minnesota, Ontario, and Quebec—due to the lack of interest on the part of the federal governments—to give impetus to the adoption of measures of control against acid rain and the general ecological deterioration of the Great lakes. In Europe, the Conference of Peripheral and Maritime Regions traces its origins to the 1970s and is today the largest territorial lobby on the continent, with over 160 regions represented. The track record of these cross-border bodies varies. While some are talk-shops or only have a peak of activity when mayors and governors meet annually, others take a more political stance against the responses of their central governments to specific concerns, especially where they feel the national government has made only a half-hearted agreement for maximum publicity while only meeting the lowest common denominator. Quantitative research conducted on the strategy behind US governors' participation in foreign policy revealed that "border states' governors are . . . much more likely to be involved in foreign policy" in order to deal with issues such as immigration and border security (McMillan 2008, 244).

There are other examples of single-themed paradiplomacy, beyond transborder issues. In several other cases, and mainly in the United States or Australia, that one issue is trade and investment promotion. As we shall see in detail later, all US states conduct foreign activities to boost investment and trade opportunities. As the US government is not directly involved in attracting foreign direct investment (FDI), it is left to states. Foreign activities aim at providing local companies with know-how, key in-country contacts, and international opportunities to make business. In Australia, states such as Queensland, New South Wales, Victoria, or Western Australia frequently undertake trade missions and all have investment and trade policies. Politics is not part of the subnational agenda. For instance, Trade & Investment Queensland, the government's global business agency, has one of Australia's largest international networks with trade and investment representatives in fourteen locations.

Global Paradiplomacy

A very significant number of subnational governments—mostly in China, Germany, Canada, Brazil, or France—have a larger portfolio and engage internationally with manifold interests and agendas. They are not monovocal and tend to participate in international debates or adopt cooperation agreements in a wide range of areas, from environment to culture or from infrastructure to R&D and trade. If a regional government is competent internally for a material domain, then it also automatically becomes competent externally. The adjective "global" is therefore used here in both a functional and a geographical sense.

In Canada, although Quebec has been the leader of the paradiplomacy movement (Levesque 1976; Balthazar 1999; Michaud 2008), all ten provincial governments maintain either an international office or a separate international ministry to handle their external relations. These states are mostly led by their size and by their need to rely on their own apparatus and policies to defend their interests. California, for instance, is the eighth largest world economy, on top of Russia, Italy, India, or Canada. Texas, the thirteenth largest, has an economy larger than Australia's. The largest regional economy in the Southern Hemisphere, the state of São Paulo, has the second largest GDP in South America (after Brazil with São Paulo included) (see table 1.1). It is therefore difficult for economies of this size to operate exclusively within the confines of a state and to rely on national ministries of foreign affairs to conduct their own foreign relations.

Subnational diplomacy in these cases should not be equated with more autonomy. The case of France is paradigmatic. In contrast to other European countries, ethno-regionalist parties have had very little political impact in France (Pasquier 2006). Although several French regions are like regions of Belgium, Spain, or Italy in terms of the strength of their cultural and linguistic identity, until now the organization and the development of autonomist parties in France has remained very limited. Except in Corsica, which has had a specific statute since 1991, ethno-regionalist parties have not really developed with the decentralization process. Two main factors explain this French exception: the relatively easy cohabitation between regional identities and the national one and the electoral regime (Pasquier 2006). In France, the relationship between national and regional identification is not really conflicting (Pasquier 2006, 12).

In the United States, although most states have a single-themed diplomacy (fostering trade and investment), the government of California, the richest subnational entity in the world, has also engaged in a sort of "climate diplomacy" as a direct result of its global leadership in reducing air pollution, protecting human health, and acting aggressively to address climate change. While international action has basically stalled, California is charging ahead with its landmark suite of climate policies. California's "climate diplomacy" started with Governor Arnold Schwarzenegger (2003–2011) and has continued under Governor Jerry Brown. When Brown embarked on a much-publicized visit to China in 2013, with the goal of encouraging a long-term economic partnership between the Pacific Rim neighbors, California's leadership on climate issues was properly recognized by the Chinese government. The governor met with China's environmental protection minister, Zhou Shengxian, to discuss and sign a non-binding agreement to reduce smog and greenhouse gas emissions. During the trip, China also requested the help of experts at the California Air Resources Board to help it address its urgent air pollution problem. The agreement signed in September 2013 by California and Québec to link their carbon emissions is also a good paradigm. It allows regulated emitters in both regions to buy and sell carbon emissions allowances and offsets in either jurisdiction. This is a significant step toward the development of a North American carbon market.

Sovereign Paradiplomacy

Not all political entities that hold a diplomatic apparatus are, or wish to become, independent countries, but all independent countries hold a diplomatic apparatus. Paradiplomacy is not a cause but a consequence of statehood. Although the overwhelming majority of states that carry out external activities have no statehood expectations, for a long time the debate on paradiplomacy was still confined to the handful of states that in different ways and in different periods of their history flirted with more autonomy or sovereignty. And when we look at the reality now on the ground, it is fair to say that the best practices in global paradiplomacy, to a large extent, still originate in those regions. Quebec (Canada), Catalonia and the Basque Country (Spain), Flanders and Wallonia (Belgium), the Free State of Bavaria (Germany), Scotland (United Kingdom), Tatarstan (Russia), Transnistria (Moldava), Puntland and Somaliland (Somalia) are on the top of the list. Consequently, some of these regions also dominate the academic literature on paradiplomacy.

In these cases, paradiplomacy should be coined as "protodiplomacy," a term that refers to "the conduct of international relations by a noncentral government that aims at establishing a fully sovereign state." Protodiplomacy "represents diplomatic preparatory work for a future secession and for the international diplomatic recognition of such an occurrence" (Duchacek 1988, 22). While paradiplomacy is considered a normal activity, reflecting the degree of autonomy given to a subnational government, protodiplomacy is often seen as illegitimate or at least dangerous for the integrity of the state.

Quebec is a natural leader in protodiplomacy. During the Quiet Revolution in the 1960s, a period of intense sociopolitical and sociocultural change, the emergence of a foreign affairs apparatus was regarded as an important module of the modernization of the state, along with the effective secularization of society and the creation of a welfare state (état-providence). Presently, whenever the Parti Québécois is elected to power in Quebec City, the province puts itself back on the route of statehood and adopts a conflicting position vis-à-vis the Canadian central government (box 1.1). It is interesting to notice that Canada may be the only country in the world that recognizes the right to secede from the federation, since under certain conditions, as indicated by the Federal Supreme Court, the separation of a province and its independence from the Federation might be acceptable (Murgadas and Rico 2011, 20).

BOX 1.1 Address by the Minister of International
Relations, La Francophonie and External Trade

Address by then Minister of International Relations, La
Francophonie and External Trade, Jean-François Lisée, to the
Montreal Council on Foreign Relations (CORIM) (Excerpts)
Quebec's Global Ambitions

Montréal, February 11, 2013

. . .

Quebec's other primary interest is preserving its ability
to decide its own national destiny. We are not an independent nation. However, the choice to become one belongs to
us. Lucidity—some would call it realpolitik—imposes an in-
evitable conclusion: the stronger Quebec becomes, the more
tools it will have to exercise this choice without hindrance.

What is Quebec's strength? The sum of all its assets. At
home: its democratic health and robust institutions, the skills
of its citizens, its economic weight and natural resources,
and the quality of its products, services, research and creativity. Abroad: its political, economic and cultural clout.

. . .

Quebec's international actions, their role and relevance,
have become increasingly important in recent years because
Quebecers are less and less comfortable with the policies
of the Canadian government. It isn't that we are changing.
We remain true to ourselves. It is Canada that is taking a
different path.

. . .

If we were independent, we could double in a few months
the number of young French people coming from France to
discover Quebec, stay and work for a while, then settle here
for good. But as a province, we can only wait on the goodwill
of others. And we are sorely in need of these skilled, French-
speaking workers.

. . .

It is the great paradox of Quebec's international personality. We are more active on the international scene than many sovereign states. And, while it's true that we generally work closely with friendly, cooperative members of the Canadian diplomatic corps, we still have to routinely ask for permission to meet with ministers, sign agreements and invite diplomats to visit. We are at the mercy of Canada's goodwill in a number of areas and, even in the best of cases, this additional obligatory step saps our effectiveness. And when the goodwill disappears, as was the case when Jean Chrétien's Liberals were in power, our international actions resemble an obstacle course.

We are thus condemned to excel in international matters, despite the obstacles that our status imposes on us. At least for now.

Similarly to Quebec, Scotland, Wallonia, Catalonia, the Basque Country, or Flanders have all laid claims toward independence and, consequently, toward having an independent foreign policy. In 2014 and 2015 alone, a Scottish independence referendum was held, Catalan regional parliament voted to start the secession process, and Flemish Minister-President Geert Bourgeois used his speech on the national day of the Flemish Community (July 11) to claim that the region should become responsible for its own foreign policy.

Why Do Subnational Governments Engage in Paradiplomacy?

Seize Global Opportunities

The solution for an urban problem in the Canadian province of Manitoba could be found in the capital Winnipeg, in Manila, or in

Munich. Cities and provinces do not need to invent the wheel every time there is a new challenge and in isolation from other partners that have faced similar challenges. According to Tim Campbell, author of *Beyond Smart Cities*, the world's "learning cities" value the "deliberate and systematic acquisition of knowledge" and actively build transnational partnerships to adapt policy innovation from elsewhere (2012, 4). Leonardo Barchini, who headed São Paulo city's international affairs department, stated accordingly that "for almost everything we are doing that is new, we try to look outside."[9] Over the last two decades, globalization has allowed for a truly global movement of people, goods, and services, opening up new windows of opportunity for the subnational governments that have the ability to seize them. This is particularly true in the case of economic development. Subnational governments look for "investment, markets for their products, and technology for modernization" (Keating 1999, 4). The greater the level of GDP of a federal unit, the more internationalized its economy should be and larger diplomatic credentials the state may hold. In an era when economics commands foreign relations, this does not mean embassies and armies, but it does mean putting in place aggressive policies to foster trade and attract investment. Through marketing, trade missions, and foreign affairs, state and local governments seek to promote exports of their products and to attract foreign investment and tourists. As most subnational entities are to some extent responsible for the economic conditions in their locality, so they are keen to pursue commercial and other arrangements that will enhance the economic climate of their region or city and ideally bring jobs, commercial operations, and technology.

Provide Citizen Services

Foreign policy at the local level is generally not an end in itself but a means to strengthen local competences and local programs (such as on healthcare, education, or public safety) by having an arm outside. Paradiplomacy is therefore Janus-faced—facing inward and outward at the same time. There are endless examples of how paradiplomacy is directed at citizens' welfare. For instance, the São Paulo (state) governmental plan on foreign affairs, adopted in 2012, states as one of its three main goals to "promote sustainable development in the state of São Paulo, harmonizing economic, social, and environmental concerns and thus ensuring the well-being of future generations." The state runs a large number of cooperation programs to achieve that goal. The Chiapas region provides another good example. While it has been at the center of an ongoing armed conflict between the indigenous people of the Ejército Zapatista de Liberación Nacional and the Mexican federal government, the state government created in 2001 a Coordination of International Relations to promote local development. By 2002, Chiapas had established relations with forty-three countries (Schiavon 2010, 85).

Promote Decentralization

Often subnational leaders criticize the central government as big, dehumanized, and "over-bureaucratized" as well as far too distant when it comes to issues concerning local and regional difficulties. Some states recognize that there is a necessity to have a central government for such reasons as a national currency and to be able to negotiate and deal with other countries for trade and security reasons. But they argue that a centralized and monopolizing government is often ineffective and expensive and therefore power should be delegated to individual states, thus avoiding Big Government.

Personal Interests

Some people are able to shape institutions and policies. With the exception of a handful of large cities and states, the foreign affairs apparatus of subnational governments is embryonic and sensitive to the ambition and dedication (or lack of) of some leaders. The establishment of the Four Motors of Europe in the late 1980s was very much the result of the ambition of Baden-Württemberg premier, Lothar Späth. The president of the French region of Provence-Alpes-Côte d'Azur, Michel Vauzelle, was also instrumental in promoting subnational organizations such as the Network of Regional Governments for Sustainable Development (nrg4SD) or Regions United/FOGAR. Both looked at increased international presence as a way to gain political fuel. In a similar fashion, Indian states have recently begun to show a new international ambition, but their effort depends largely on the personal leadership and political interests of Indian chief ministers. The growing international relevance of West Bengal and Gujarat, for instance, was largely dependent on the personal ambition of the Chief Ministers Mamata Banerjee and Narendra Modi (now the prime minister), respectively. New York City also provides a very paradigmatic case. During Michael Bloomberg's administration (2002–2013), the city showed tremendous leadership in foreign affairs, either through New York City Global Partners, Inc. or the Cities Climate Leadership Group (C40), but when he stepped down the flame somehow faded away. The same happened when Rob Ford succeeded David Miller as mayor of Toronto. In France, without the intervention of Lyon's Mayor Raymond Barre (1995–2001), it is unlikely that the city would have decided to open offices abroad and talked to Grenoble and St.-Étienne to design a common foreign policy for the entire region (Paquin and Lachapelle 2005, 88). The governor of Tokyo Metropolis, Shintaro Ishihara (1999–2012), was also known for taking action (even on foreign affairs) from an ideological perspective for decades, giving him national renown that most other local leaders cannot match. The personality of decision-makers can strongly influence the determination of a subnational government's international policies. Statistical research conducted on the rationales that lead US governors to conduct foreign affairs indicates that governors' personal interests seem to drive their involvement in international activities (McMillan 2008, 242).

Electoral Opportunism

Photo opportunities with foreign leaders generate votes and print an image of leadership and glamor. Constituencies like to regard their leaders as someone who decides according to international references and has global penetration. At the subnational level, where foreign affairs institutions are less traditional and more prone to internal and external influences, very often mayors and governors play the international card to attract more political attention to themselves. Examples abound. Arturo Montiel Rojas, for instance, right after being elected governor of the state of Mexico took an official trip to South America in 2000, where he met with the president of Argentina, Fernando de la Rúa, and the president of Chile, Ricardo Lagos. By then Arturo Montiel harbored presidential expectations. In 2013, Rio de Janeiro Mayor Eduardo Paes succeed New York City Mayor Michael R. Bloomberg as C40's chair. To some extent, the move was intended to boost his international image and consequently his internal political credentials. From 2011 to 2015, Mayor Mauricio Macri went into great lengths to develop the international policy of the city of Buenos Aires, which served as a stepping stone for his political ambitions (he was elected president of Argentina in 2015).

Address Local Claims

Paradiplomacy may be regarded as a concession by federal states to local communities, allowing them to express their voice abroad. In the view of some capitals, allowing regional autonomous groups some oxygen and providing them with some new political tools and agendas, decreases their claims to independence. This was the rationale that led Russia to allow Tatarstan to develop its own international relations in certain fields through a 1994 bilateral agreement. The same model was then applied in Chechenia, aiming at ending the war. The arrangement with Tatarstan was successful but with Chechenia, although it did halt the war at a first moment, was not enough to bring a definite settlement for the conflict. As Wolff pointed out, "rather than seeing paradiplomacy as a threat, it should be embraced as a necessity and an opportunity in the process of managing and ultimately resolving what might otherwise be protracted self-determination conflicts" (2007, 141). In another case, the Mexican government accepted that the subnational state of Chiapas signed an agreement in 2004 with the European Union, through which it received €15 million to support indigenous people living in the Lacandon Jungle to move out of poverty. Chiapas has been in the spotlight for several decades due to the uprising of the Zapatista Army of National Liberation. In China, Beijing allowed the mostly Muslim Xinjiang Uyghur Autonomous Region to sign protocols of cooperation in the 1980s with the then Soviet republics of Kazakhstan, Tajikistan, Kyrgyzstan, and Turkmenistan. This had a great symbolic value for local Uyghurs.

Cultural Distinctiveness and Nationalism

Regions with their own language or cultural identity seek support and resources in the global arena, especially when their native country is unsympathetic or fails to protect the uniqueness of the regional culture. According to André Lecours, nationalism "is the single most important variable conditioning paradiplomacy" (cited in Albina 2010, 102). Since nationalism is a form of identity politics, it entails power struggles, and political and territorial mobilization, which can also be extended to the field of international relations. In the process, building national or regional identity and an international presence are mutually constitutive. When the distinct cultural heritage is not exclusive to a region but shared with other constituencies across borders, subnational governments may engage in foreign actions to protect the heritage collectively. In 1991, Baden-Württemberg set up a Joint Commission with the state of Hungary based on the strong ethnic ties of the Danube Swabian people (*Donauschwaben*), whereas the French region of Brittany has a partnership with Wales in order to promote their common Celtic culture (Blatter et al. 2008).

Diaspora

Cities and states that have large communities living abroad may use foreign policy to maintain a link between native and hosting lands. For instance, the Mexican states of Michoacán, Guanajuato, Puebla, and Zacatecas have established representation offices in states like California, Illinois, New York, or Texas, where a large number of Mexican migrants live. These offices organize social and cultural events and provide logistical and consular assistance. With a similar purpose in mind, the city of Los Angeles has strong political links with different spheres of governance in Mexico. Not surprisingly, Los Angeles Mayor Eric Garcetti's first trip abroad was to Mexico, where he was received by President Enrique Peña Nieto in March 2014. Around 7 million Mexicans live in the five-county Greater Los Angeles Area. The autonomous Portuguese region of the Azores also puts its international focus on promoting trade, tourism, and mainly cultural links with foreign states that host Azorean communities, such as Rio Grande do Sul in Brazil or Rhode Island in the United States.

Geography

The geographic location of border states favors the establishment of contacts with the territorial units of countries with which they share a border, as discussed earlier. It could therefore be argued that federal states that are located at international borders should have higher levels of foreign affairs than those with no foreign borders. The establishment of a high number of multilateral forums of sub-state governments that have geographical proximity as the main driver—such as the Association of European Border Regions or the Border Governor's Conference (in the United States)—is indicative. This is also associated with the new trend of creating "development corridors" or "regional corridors" that connect economic agents along a defined geography and turn this subregion into a gateway for trade, investment, and tourism. The Maputo Development Corridor, which links the landlocked and northernmost of South Africa's nine provinces to Maputo, Mozambique's capital, is a good case study.

Overcome Isolationism

When countries are under fire by the international community, they may sponsor the foreign activities of their local governments

to avoid insularity. After the Tiananmen crisis, the Chinese government adopted a new diplomatic strategy—*zhoubian diplomacy*—
seeking to elude its international isolation through the deploy-
ment of new objectives and policy instruments (Hsiung, 1995).
In this new framework, subnational involvement in foreign affairs
was welcomed by Beijing. The inverse sequence also holds. When
subnational governments are politically secluded within their own
countries, they may look externally for oxygen and legitimacy for
their efforts. Mauricio Rodas, one of the staunchest opponents to
Ecuador's President Rafael Correa, launched an international career
soon after being elected mayor of Quito in 2014. Just a few months
after taking office, he was elected co-president of UCLG and was
entrusted to strengthen the presence of the organization in Latin
America. He also announced Quito's commitment to the United
Nations Global Compact.

Responses to Paradiplomacy

Countries

If some decades ago the issue of paradiplomacy raised some eyebrows in national capitals, presently it is faced either with plain
tolerance (often with a grain of condescension) or with explicit
support. There have been cases when paradiplomacy created tensions between the central government and the subnational government as the former holds that foreign policy has historically been
in its preserve. National governments firmly resist relinquishing
what they regard as the dedicated national turf of foreign policy,
which is a vital source of their representative capacity and authority over the nation. Historically this turf generally involved national
defense and security and other areas of explicitly national interest
(Jain 2005, 31). But in more recent times, federal governments
tend to react well to the paradiplomacy of its subnational governments as the phenomenon is likely to be interpreted as a symptom
of the process of decentralization of modern federal states. And as
subnational governments operate only within the confines of their

constitutional prerogatives, and as their goal is to adopt public policies in the areas of their competence, the division of labor is clear. Indeed, state foreign policy has been transformed away from classical diplomacy, and foreign ministries have themselves lost their monopoly over external action as large areas of domestic policy have been internationalized (Aldecoa and Keating 1999, i). And even when national governments decide to share some of their sovereignty with their internal regions, their scope of power can actually grow and not decrease (La Palombara 1994, 89–99). The growth of clusters of regional innovation—such as in California or Karnataka—have strengthened US and Indian power, not threatened it. Moreover, in the same way that Ministers of Foreign Affairs generally do not engage with issues such as education, sanitation, or transportation, foreign affairs leaders at the subnational level also refrain from voicing an opinion on hardcore external issues. As one complements the other, intergovernmental mutual trust has been the rule in most countries. Paradiplomacy is only conflicting when a subnational government puts in place initiatives and activities through which it aspires to establish itself as a fully sovereign state. The initiatives and activities may also be part of the preparatory work toward a future secession and international recognition of such a status.

In this general context, ministries of foreign affairs have recognized "that subnational involvement in external affairs is not a matter of transient fashion but does represent a change in the practice of diplomacy" (Aldecoa and Keating 1999, iii–iv). And in an attempt to respond to this new situation, sovereign states all over the world have, during recent decades, established different legal and institutional mechanisms in order to acknowledge a new and more active role by substate government in their foreign policy designs and diplomatic machineries (Cornago 2010, 29). Hence, collaboration and not conflict epitomizes relations between both levels of government.

In 2015, France had, according to the Ministry of Foreign Affairs, close to 14,000 international cooperation projects run by close to 5,000 French local authorities. Unequivocally, the ministry's website stated that the French government "supports the implementation of this decentralized cooperation"[10] and has adopted a couple of guiding documents that support paradiplomacy. In 2006 an initial document entitled Orientations for Decentralized Cooperation was drafted, upon the initiative of the prime minister, and subsequently brought to the attention of the associations of local elected officials represented in the National Commission of Decentralized Cooperation. To reinforce internal coordination, the French Ministry of Foreign Affairs published in 2010 the "French Guidelines for the International Action of Local Authorities," a state strategy carrying orientations for decentralized cooperation. France is also the first country to come up with an Atlas of Decentralized Cooperation,[11] which lists the various initiatives undertaken by its local and regional authorities around the world.

In Mexico, the federal and the state governments hold regular meetings to enhance cooperation and cohesion. International involvement by local governments is a growing and dynamic trend in the country. In an event held in July 2013, the then Foreign Minister José Antonio Meade announced that "in recent years, the Foreign Ministry has assisted with and registered more than 500 international agreements signed by local governments in Mexico with their counterparts abroad, either for specific cooperation projects or as sister cities, which 80 percent of the time have a direct impact at the municipal level on issues related to educational and cultural cooperation, trade and technical assistance."[12] Further south in the continent, in Brazil, the Ministry of External Relations opened "representation offices" (*Escritórios de Representação do Itamaraty*) in eight states that collaborate with local governments on foreign affairs (first office was established in 1997) and the country has in place a program—run by the Presidency and the Ministry of Foreign Affairs—to identify and finance international cooperation projects that will be implemented by Brazilian states and municipalities with other developing countries. In federal countries like Australia and Germany, federal and *länder*/state governments jointly participate in a variety of foreign policy decisions.

In the United States, internal cooperation and joint decision-making is less visible but the support the US federal government has been giving to paradiplomacy since the 1950s has been well reported:

> Beginning with the administration of Dwight D. Eisenhower (1953–1961), presidents have often encouraged state international activity. The long-standing Pearson Fellowship Program, for example, allows about 14 foreign-service officers to spend a year working with a state or local government. Under John F. Kennedy's administration (1961–1963), the US Department of Commerce encouraged states to become invested in international economic affairs. Commerce was then headed by Luther Hodges, former governor of North Carolina, who had led one of the states' first trade missions to Europe in 1959. Presidents Lyndon Johnson, Richard Nixon and Jimmy Carter also encouraged states to seek out foreign investment and promote exports, At the request of President Carter, the National Governor's Association formed a new standing committee in 1978 on International Trade and Foreign Relations. (Kincaid 1999, 122)

It is also worth noticing that in 1988 the Intergovernmental Policy Advisory Committee to the Office of the US Trade Representative was created to advise the president on state and local government concerns in international trade and trade arrangements. In more recent times, under President Obama, the State Department has shown keenness in supporting paradiplomatic activities. Secretary Clinton and Chinese Foreign Minister Yang Jiechi signed in January 2011 a Memorandum of Understanding supporting US–China subnational cooperation and the establishment of the US–China Governors Forum (more later). The following year, Clinton and then Foreign Minister of Brazil Antonio Patriota signed a Memorandum of Understanding to support state and local cooperation. The Memorandum of Understanding affirms the resolve of the United States and Brazil to strengthen and deepen cooperation between their respective subnational entities and encourages peer-to-peer exchanges between subnational officials. In a 2013 article, Robert Hormats, then Under Secretary of State for Economic, Energy, and Agricultural Affairs argued that the US State Department is playing a key role in enlarging the multilevel, subnational dimension of the country's international economic policy. Yet, he underlines that "we know that the most dynamic part of this effort will not come from Washington. Instead, the broadest and deepest engagement will come from intensified interaction between leaders of America's cities and states and their counterparts in emerging countries" (Hormats 2013). He was only partially right. The support of the federal government to paradiplomacy has been made clearer as time went by. For instance, the Department of State's 2015 Quadrennial Diplomacy and Development Review stressed the need for the department to build stronger relationships with cities given the "era of diffuse and networked power" in which we live (US Department of State 2015).

To sponsor subnational diplomacy, the State Department established in 2010 the Office of the Special Representative for Global Intergovernmental Affairs, which was first led by Reta Jo Lewis.[13] In a speech she gave in Brazil in March 2012 under the title "Subnational Engagement as a 21st Century Foreign Policy Tool," she observed that:

Building peer-to-peer relationships between state and local elected officials has a tremendous effect on foreign policy that often goes unrecognized. Still, building these relationships and encouraging this engagement at the subnational level has limitless potential. Peer-to-peer relationships provide state and local leaders around the globe with an intimate glance into the American way of life, and more importantly, into our democratic institutions and system of governance. Even at a more basic but equally important level, these interactions develop trust—an attribute essential to developing strong bilateral ties. Secretary Clinton has made it a priority to engage our subnational leaders and utilize them as an extraordinary source of innovation, talent, resources, and knowledge. After all, it is the states and cities that are the engines of growth at the ground level where the transition from policy to practice becomes most visible. Secretary Clinton has stated time and time again that 21st century global challenges require us to work with new partners to collaborate and innovate globally. At the Department of State, this has meant making a transition to 21st Century Statecraft, a strategy for creating partnerships for achieving modern diplomatic goals by engaging all the elements of our national power and leveraging all forms of our strength.

Several other countries have established offices with similar objectives. Brazil counts with the Special Bureau on Federative and Parliamentary Issues (*Assessoria Especial de Assuntos Federativos e Parlamentares*) in the Ministry of External Relations, headed by an ambassador-ranked diplomat; whereas, the French foreign ministry created in 2009 a Directorate General for Global Affairs, Development and Partnerships with a Delegation for the external action of local and regional authorities attached to it. In South Korea, the Ministry of Security and Public Administration established in 1965 a Local Government Officials Development Institute (LOGODI) to train senior level officials from South Korean local governments. In 1996, LOGODI started to offer programs not only for Koreans but also for foreign government officials. By late 2014, approximately 3,000 local government officials from eighty-four countries had been trained. The support of the South Korean government toward local governance and paradiplomacy has been of vital importance to generate a consensus in the country over the importance of subnational powers.

These institutional changes serve as an indication that traditional diplomats are getting more prepared to handle the challenges of paradiplomacy. The scope of diplomacy has broadened from traditional state-to-state relations to also include nonstate actors, thereby resulting in a multitude of new challenges for Ministries of Foreign Affairs and traditional diplomats. Learning new skills and acquiring new knowledge has become an absolute necessity for today's diplomat. In Brazil, for instance, as early as 1995 the

Foreign Service Officer's Exam included questions on subnational diplomacy.

In Japan and China, subnational diplomacy is often supported by the national government as it may provide a bypass to controversial issues. In April 2014 Yoichi Masuzoe, Tokyo's governor, visited Beijing for a visit he hoped would help improve the frosty relationship between China and Japan. "I think it would be good if our city-to-city diplomacy could lead to an improvement in relations between Japan and China."[14] Although then Tokyo Governor Shintaro Ishihara visited Beijing in 2008 for the Olympics, it had been eighteen years since a Tokyo governor was specifically invited for a visit by Beijing's government. The visit was supported by Japan's Prime Minister Shinzo Abe, who also expressed his hope that Masuzoe's visit would help thaw tensions between China and Japan. China's Foreign Ministry also had positive comments about the visit. "We have always been supportive and positive about civil and local exchanges between China and Japan."[15]

In the past (and occasionally even in the present), the Japanese Ministry of Foreign Affairs tended to recognize subnational foreign activities as an intrusion on its ministerial terrain and wanted to regulate subnational activities as much as it could to protect its own jurisdiction. But it now accepts that subnational governments constitute an important part of the overall Japanese foreign policy largely because their status and practical ability relieves them of much of the diplomatic baggage and official implication that usually attached to national government actions abroad. For instance, despite the fact that tensions between Japan and the Soviet Union, and now present-day Russia, flare from time to time, relations between Hokkaido and neighboring Sakhalin Island, a former Japanese territory that was handed over to Russia after World War II, remain particularly amiable (Shen 2014).

In addition, because of the potential economic benefit that Japan can enjoy from intimate global–local networks, participation of local governments in global issues was encouraged by the central government (Shen 2014). Back in 1986, the Ministry of Foreign Affairs established the Internationalization Consultation Center (*Kokusaika*

Sodan Sentaa), within its Domestic Public Relations Section, offering assistance to subnational officials in charge of international exchanges. The support of the Ministry of Home Affairs, which is responsible for managing subnational governments, has been less cyclical and more effusive. According to Jain, the Ministry of Home Affairs is "the strongest advocate and most active promoter of subnational governments in their international pursuits" (2005, 42).

China has also been very vocal about the importance of subnational cooperation. In addition to supporting the creation of the US–China Governors Forum in 2011, President Xi Jinping has attended or met with delegates from the first three gatherings (2012, 2013, and 2015) showing his full support for the initiative. At the third forum in 2015, after underlining somehow unimaginatively that "without successful cooperation at the sub-national level, it would be very difficult to achieve practical results for cooperation at the national level," he highlighted that "31 Chinese provinces/regions/cities have established 43 sister province/state relations and 200 sister-city relations with 50 American states."[16] China's national government has realized that key policy decisions in the country are formulated and implemented by local governments: states, provinces, and fast-growing cities (Antholis 2013a, 2013b).

Slightly away from this general tendency, the United Kingdom's Foreign Office has not yet established internal capacities to handle paradiplomacy even if Scotland, London (the capital of the United Kingdom), and the City of London (the financial center and a county) carry out international activities. Despite this, the Foreign Office's Policy Unit (that serves as an internal think tank) held meetings in 2014 with subnational foreign affairs officials in Latin America and elsewhere to collect information on what paradiplomacy is all about. And it is fairly common that when the UK prime minister and other senior members of the cabinet visit other countries they end up meeting with city and state officials. In September 2012, David Cameron met the governor of São Paulo when he visited Brazil. Results-based pragmatism and respect for the local political culture have driven the United Kingdom's foreign affairs.

International Organizations

Within international bodies, support to subnational governments has been even more vocal. Probably the most clear-cut example was the establishment in 1994 of the Committee of the Regions (CoR)—the European Union's assembly of local and regional representatives that provides subnational authorities with a direct voice within the European Union's institutional framework. The CoR was set up to address two main issues. First, about three-quarters of EU legislation is implemented at the local or regional level, so it made sense for local and regional representatives to have a say in the development of new EU laws. Second, there were concerns that there was a widening gap between the public and the process of European integration; involving the elected level of government closest to the citizens was one way of closing the gap. The key Treaty of Lisbon of 2007 enhanced the role of the CoR and reshaped the principle of subsidiarity in a way which implies stronger consideration for subnational entities. In May 2013, the "Empowering Local Authorities in Partner Countries for Enhanced Governance and More Effective Development" that articulates the European Commission's view on the need to empower local authorities in developing countries around the world. To give flesh to the communication, in January 2015 the Commission adopted a strategic partnership with five large networks of subnational governments—AIMF, CLGF, CEMR-PLATFORMA, UCLG, and UCLG Africa (see table 1.2), marking a new phase in the acknowledgment of local governments in European policy.

Still in the European context, the Council of Europe, an organization founded in 1949 with currently forty-seven member states, has also put in place several programs to support local authorities. As early as in 1985, the Council adopted the European Charter of Local Self-Government, which stated that "the entitlement of local authorities to belong to an association for the protection and promotion of their common interests and to belong to an *international* association of local authorities shall be recognized in each State" (Art. 10(2); italics added). The Council of Europe is mostly an advisory international organization, but the charter is an important milestone in drawing attention to the political, administrative, and financial autonomy of local authorities.

Various UN programs, funds, and specialized agencies have also absorbed the idea that global issues should be handled with the contribution of local and regional governments. The first door was opened back in 1992 during the United Nations Conference on Environment and Development in Rio de Janeiro (Earth Summit or Rio Summit) when the concept of "major groups" was first developed. Major Groups are nine overarching categories through which all citizens could participate in the UN activities on achieving sustainable development. "Local Authorities" is one of the groups (the others are Women, Children and Youth, Farmers, Indigenous Peoples, NGOs, Trade Unions, Science and Technology, and Business and Industry). Twenty years later, the weight of local governments became more salient. The final document ("The Future We Want") of the Rio + 20 United Nations Conference on Sustainable Development that took place in Rio de Janeiro in 2012 stated that the signatories acknowledged "efforts and progress made at the *local and subnational levels*, and recognize the important role that such authorities and communities can play in implementing sustainable development, including by engaging citizens and stakeholders and providing them with relevant information, as appropriate, on the three dimensions of sustainable development" (italics added).[17] The overall outcome of the summit was lame as it did not produce any breakthrough agreements or commitments. What Rio + 20 achieved, however, was bringing attention to the fact that the path to a green economy lies at the subnational and local level. There was a general understanding that local and subnational governments left the summit with higher recognition than when they arrived.

Another good example of United Nations' support is the United Nations Conferences on Human Settlements (Habitat). Habitat I was held in Vancouver in 1976, Habitat II was organized in Istanbul in 1996, and Habitat III in 2016. Whereas a First Assembly of Local Authorities was organized in Istanbul during Habitat II, a

Global Taskforce of Local and Regional Governments for Post-2015 Agenda toward Habitat III gathers local and regional government leaders and their global organizations in order to build a joint strategy to contribute to the international policymaking debates toward Habitat III. If the participation of subnational governments in the Habitat conferences was shy in 1976, it is likely to be central forty years later.

With strong presence in the Habitat Conferences, it was natural that subnational governments played an important role in the UN program aimed at human settlements and sustainable urban development (UN-Habitat). UN-Habitat is the UN gateway for cities and states, with a Local Government and Decentralization Unit in its headquarters in Nairobi to improve communication with subnational governments. In addition, the United Nations Advisory Committee of Local Authorities was formed in 2000 as a formal channel to enable local authorities to influence the work program of UN-Habitat. It is a high-level group of selected mayors and representatives of local authority associations especially chosen on the basis of their local, national, and international commitment to engage in the implementation of the Habitat Agenda.

Other UN bodies also have highlighted the role of local governments. The UN-DESA has also shown support for paradiplomacy through the Euro-African Partnership for Decentralized Governance, whose purpose is to support decentralization and decentralized governance in Africa, by means of partnerships between European and African local institutions. The initiative has had minor achievements, but they have been able to carry out some activities for the promotion of exchange of experiences, information, and best practices with regard to decentralization. Most notably, the Partnership may be credited for shedding light upon decentralization efforts in African countries. Without this platform, these local African initiatives would likely go unnoticed.

Also interestingly, in 2014 UN Secretary General Ban Ki-moon invited world leaders, from government, finance, business, and civil society to the Climate Summit 2014 to galvanize and catalyze climate action. Among the invitees were subnational governmental leaders, and the UN Secretary General stated in the individual invitation letters that:

> World leaders today have an unprecedented opportunity to reach a meaningful agreement and take actions on the ground that can put us on a path to sustainable prosperity. Governments have agreed to reach such a universal legal agreement in 2015. It is up to leaders *from all levels of government*, civil society and private sector, to scale up their actions and commitments to make this possible. This is the task before us at the Summit in September. (italics added)

In the South American context, Mercosur has also gone a long way to promote local international activities. In 2004, the Consultative Forum of Cities, States, Provinces and Departments of Mercosur (FCCR) was created to encourage dialogue and cooperation among local governments. In the foundational document, Mercosur recognized that "the development of the integration process has an increasing political dimension, which requires systematic and coordinated actions of *all* actors involved" (italics added). Over the years, FCCR gained institutional density and a fair amount of recognition in the Mercosur countries, but its deliverables are still not impressive, despite the regular meetings of subnational leaders and the vocalization of ambitions and expectations. This has led the strongest regional economies in the Mercosur space, such as São Paulo state, to stay away from the Forum and invest instead in other international forums.

The World Bank has also been instrumental in sponsoring foreign activities by subnational governments. The Bank supports efforts to improve subnational finances and policies, institutions, and public services with analytic work, technical assistance, financial support through investment lending, and development policy lending. The first ever direct subnational loan by the Bank dates back to 1997, when a US$125 million loan supported the process of privatization in the state of Rio Grande do Sul in Brazil. Currently, all major subnational governments in the developing world have access to World Bank's assets. In the context of past economic crises, the Bank directly offered substantial loans to various Brazilian, Indian, and Argentinean provinces, facilitating their internationalization (Cornago 2010, 22). Although these relationships were for technical reasons and were initially facilitated by federal governments, their consequences were far-reaching. Nowadays, however, the Bank's relations with subnational states are more based on transparency and economic stability rather than sparked only in periods of economic crises.

Rankings on Paradiplomacy

To conclude this chapter with the essential background information on paradiplomacy, it is also important to know the major rankings of cities and states. Global rankings are a powerful force to compare cities and states in the way they stand vis-à-vis global forces, to induce internal changes in policy design and decision-making and to market in the media the ones that rank at the top. They are therefore an important instrument for policymakers to search for references and to draw strategic conclusions. Several attempts have been made by think tanks, universities, consulting firms, or the media to define, categorize, and rank global cities, of which stand out:

Globalization and World Cities (GaWC) Research Network. Created in 1998 at Loughborough University, this network focuses upon research into the external relations of world cities. It is best known for its categorization of world cities into alpha, beta, and gamma tiers, based upon their international connectedness through four "advanced producer services": accountancy, advertising, banking/finance, and law. It is published biennially.

Global Cities Index. Since 2008, *Foreign Policy*, in conjunction with the consulting firm A. T. Kearney and the Chicago Council on Global Affairs, has published a biennial ranking of global cities. It provides a comprehensive ranking of the leading global cities from around the world and includes the companion Emerging Cities Outlook, which measures the potential of cities located in middle- and high-income countries to become even more global.

Global Power City Index. The Institute for Urban Strategies at The Mori Memorial Foundation in Tokyo issues a comprehensive study of global cities. The ranking is based on six overall categories, "Economy," "Research & Development," "Cultural Interaction," "Livability," "Environment," and "Accessibility," with seventy individual indicators among them.

Global City Competitiveness Index. In 2012, the Economist Intelligence Unit (The Economist Group), ranked the competitiveness of the most prominent cities across the globe using a number of economic, demographic, and social variables (including indicators such as the ability to attract capital, businesses, talent, and visitors).

The World's Most Influential Cities. First launched in 2014, this *Forbes* magazine ranking quantifies cities' global influence looking at eight factors: the amount of FDI they have attracted, the concentration of corporate headquarters, how many particular business niches they dominate, air connectivity (ease of travel to other global cities), strength of producer services, financial services, technology and media power, and racial diversity.

Global Financial Centers Index (GFCI). First published by the Z/Yen Group in 2007, the aim is to examine the major financial centers globally in terms of competitiveness. Published every six months, the GFCI provides profiles, ratings, and rankings for seventy-five financial centers drawing on two separate sources of data—instrumental factors (external indices) and responses to an online survey.

South American States of the Future. Established by the fDi magazine of the Financial Times group, it ranks hundreds of South American states according to six criteria: economic potential, human capital, cost-effectiveness, infrastructure, FDI strategy, and business friendliness. The same magazine also ranks the American Cities of the Future following the same criteria.

By looking at the available rankings one can easily conclude that cities, and not states, are more frequently targeted, a phenomenon that may be explained by the "media appeal," as audiences feel more connected to cities than to a larger level of analysis such as states. In addition, there is a lack of data on paradiplomacy per se. Cities and states may be placed in a global context, but the quality or maturity of governmental policies on foreign affairs are only rarely ranked and accounted for.

Institutional Infrastructure of Paradiplomacy

Failure is not an option, because it's in our cities that many of our biggest opportunities and most potent challenges are playing out.
—VANCOUVER MAYOR GREGOR ROBERTSON (2012)

In a world where national governments are negotiating more and more trade agreements that make national borders much less relevant, it is essential for cities to have a strategy for international relations.
—FORMER TORONTO MAYOR DAVID MILLER (2015)

The Legal Framework

As stated by Yishai Blank, "localities are already assuming a greater role in the emerging global legal order and possess unique traits that make them good candidates to assume even more responsibility and significance in international governance" (Blank 2006, 277). This chapter deals primarily with two interrelated aspects of this emerging legal order: the legal internal mandate of subnational entities to act abroad, and, consequently, their capacity to sign agreements with foreign agents.

The mandate is generally born out of constitutional provisions, laid out either in the national or state constitution. Federative countries ordinarily set apart in their Magna Cartas, the internal division of powers, matters that are exclusive of the central authority. "National defense," "currency," and "external relations" are typically covered. However, as cross-border contacts become an imperative for subnational communities, diplomacy is increasingly becoming a decentralized prerogative. Some states do formally recognize the stakes their political and administrative units have in foreign affairs and have, accordingly, set the required legal basis at a constitutional level. When constitutional texts present no clear instructions on how to proceed, some states have adopted local legislation to overcome any legal vacuum. When there is simply no law to guide paradiplomatic activities, some subnational governments rely simply on practice and experience, guided by common sense and normative boundaries.

Regardless of the internal mandate a subnational government may carry to operate internationally—either explicit or absent—some common characteristics are discernible. First, no subnational government holds any exclusive prerogative connected to defense or hardcore external affairs. These competences are either restricted to the sovereign state (e.g., Brazil or the United States) or split between the national and subnational governments. Second, the foreign competencies of subnational governments are generally a spillover of their internal competence (i.e., local governments carry out their competencies both within and outside their boundaries). Foreign affairs are therefore not an autonomous competence per se but an instrument or a means to implement public policies.

Associated with the issue of internal mandate comes the treaty-making capacity of subnational governments under international law. The traditional view underlines that only national states have *ius tractatuum* as explicitly stated by Article 6 ("Every State possesses capacity to conclude treaties") and 2(a) ("'treaty' means an international agreement concluded between *States* in written form and governed by international law, whether embodied in a single instrument or in two or more related instruments and whatever its particular designation") of the 1969 Vienna Convention on the Law of Treaties. But contrary to this legal standing, the international status of the subnational states, especially as regards a concrete, a putative or a nonexistent *ius tractatuum*, remains far from undisputed. Indeed, from the traditional view of international relations, there is no clear answer as to what the legal reach of subnational governments is in the international system. To rectify this issue, governments should turn to national norms as guidelines to define acceptable state action (Daillier and Pellet 2002).

Despite this or because of this, there is an increased interest in the matter on the part of legal scholars, coupled with new and interesting developments in the area of federalism and external relations. In fact, international law does not contain any prohibition of such power on the part of a subnational unit. It may cognize a treaty-making competence on the part of the constituent state if the federal constitution (or other pertinent municipal legislation) stipulates so. It is also possible to claim that an international agreement between a federation and a foreign state bestow a treaty-making power on a constituent state of the said federation. Presently, as we shall see in detail below, only Belgium's regional governments have treaty-making capacity under international law. Since 1993, regions and communities in Belgium enjoy self-government in the field of international cooperation and are authorized to sign international treaties with foreign governments under international law on the areas where they enjoy internal competence.

But the power of subnational governments to enter into formal partnerships and sign agreements with international partners does not exhaust itself in the adoption of international treaties. In fact, the menu of options is fairly large and substates often exercise their right to engage in a variety of agreements:

Cooperation Agreement (aka as Memorandum of Agreement or Cooperative Agreement). This is a binding document outlining the cooperative terms of two entities to work in partnership on certain listed projects. Both the agreed responsibilities of the partners and the benefits of each party will be listed. As a part of the agreement, there is usually a list of binding terms that makes the partnership a cohesive unit and often there is an obligation of funds attached to certain terms in the agreement.

International Loan Agreement. This is a contract between the lender and the borrower that sets forth the terms and conditions of the loan (including its repayment) and the rights and obligations of both parties. It is common for subnational governments to sign loan agreements with the World Bank, Inter-American Development Bank (IDB), or French Development Agency (*Agence Française de Développement*, AFD), for instance.

Protocol of Intent (aka as Letter of Intent or Memorandum of Understanding (MoU)). This is a document that expresses mutual accord on an issue between two or more parties. They are generally recognized as binding, even if no legal claim could be based on the rights and obligations laid down in them. To be legally operative, an MoU must (1) identify the contracting parties; (2) spell out the subject matter of the agreement and its objectives; (3) summarize the essential terms of the agreement; and (4) must be signed by the contracting parties.

Exchange of Letters or Notes. Sent by representatives of two governments, they lay out a framework for the implementation of a partnership. Generally, the first party writes a note to the other party, setting out the content of the agreement. The other party replies in the affirmative, usually by reproducing in full the original letter of the other party and expressing its consent thereto.

Political Declaration or Statement. This is a document containing an announcement or proclamation. It is not intended to create legal obligations but to encapsulate the common view of at least two entities. The political significance of declarations tends to be implicit, as it is usually the declared object that is considered important, and not the declaration itself. It is often used as a rhetorical device. Hundreds of declarations have been signed, including the 2013 Nantes Declaration of Mayors and Subnational Leaders on Climate Change, which was adopted with the support of over fifty mayors from thirty countries, and more than twenty regional and global networks of local and subnational governments (figure 2.1).

FIGURE 2.1 Nantes Declaration (2013)—family photo

© ICLEI-Local Governments for Sustainability

Legal Framework in Specific Countries

Argentina

The 1994 Argentinean Constitution is a good reflection of the decentralization wave that ran through Latin America in the late 1980s and early 1990s (Falleti 2010; Trevisan and Bacigalupo 1998; Carbajales and Gasol 2008). In the drafting of the constitution, federalism was brought back to the core of the political discussion in the country. Paradiplomacy also gained juridical space. Even if the constitution attributes the main competence on foreign affairs to the federal government, Articles 124 and 125 allow the provinces of Argentina to celebrate agreements with foreign partners on the administration of justice (*administración de justicia*), economic interest (*intereses económicos*), international loans (*importación de capitales extranjeros*), or on common utility works (*trabajos de utilidad común*). Those treaties are "partial" (nonpolitical) and must not be "incompatible with the foreign policy of the Nation," nor "affect the powers delegated to the Federal Government or the public credit of the Nation" (Art. 124). These activities shall also be conducted "with the knowledge of the National Congress" (Art. 124). In short, Argentine provinces have international management capability when it is not incompatible with national foreign policy (Cabeza 2006).

It can be said that one of the major steps forward of the 1994 reform of the federal constitution was the acknowledgment of the direction toward paradiplomacy already enacted by provincial constitutions. Indeed, subnational involvement in foreign affairs is widely recognized in the constitutional charter of provinces such as La Rioja, Catamarca, Formosa, Jujuy, Córdoba, Tierra del Fuego, La Pampa, Salta, San Luis, or Rio Negro among others. The Córdoba Constitution of 1987 is a good case study. Article 144(4) states that the governor has the capacity to conclude agreements "with other nations, foreign public or private entities and international organizations, and encourage negotiations with them, without affecting the foreign policy by the Federal Government." On this fertile juridical ground, successive provincial governments have built their foreign policies, mostly on international education and culture. Overall, the Argentinean juridical apparatus on paradiplomacy—both federal and provincial—is one of the most advanced in the Latin American context.

Austria

The Austrian Constitution restricts the states' capacity to establish formal external ties to cross-border issues. Article 16 allows the *länder* to conclude agreements with neighboring states or with its constituent states in matters of their constitutional competence. But the *länder* should "inform the Federal Government before the initiation of negotiations about such a treaty" (Art. 16(2)) and "the Federal Government's approval must be obtained by the Governor before their conclusion (Art. 16(2)). The approval, whether express or tacit, obliges the federal president to the agreed text, which must be countersigned by a federal authority.

Paragraphs 4 and 5 of Article 16 regulate further the competencies of the *länder* and of the federal state in the implementation of treaties. The control of the central government over the paradiplomacy is so extensive that the federal level has a constitutional right to ask a *länd* to revoke any agreement even if it was concluded in accordance with the aforementioned procedure. If a *"länd* does not duly comply with this obligation [take measures for the implementation of international agreements], competence for such measures, in particular for the issue of the necessary laws, passes to the Federation" (Art. 16(4)). Such a constitutional "straitjacket" is hardly surprising for a constitutional order that has been described as "a federation without federalism" (Erk 2004).

Belgium

Belgium is a federal state comprising three communities (Dutch-speaking, French-speaking, and German-speaking) and three regions (Flanders, Wallonia, and Brussels-Capital Region). According to Article 167 of the 1993 Constitution, the Belgian king (that is, the federal government) conducts Belgium's international relations "without prejudicing the competency of the Communities and Regions to deal with international cooperation, including the conclusion of treaties, for the fields that fall within their competencies"—such as cultural and educational matters. As a result of the third state reform (1989),[1] even international trade and FDI have been regionalized. Since the communities have acquired exclusive right to develop their international relations on those exclusive matters, the king cannot sign, ratify, or denounce treaties on their behalf. The main exception to this *in foro interno in foro externo* principle is the substitution mechanism (Art. 169 of the Constitution), which stipulates that if a region or a community does not live up to an international or a European requirement, and if it gets convicted by an international court, the federal level can substitute the regional level in order to execute the internationally agreed policy (Bursens and Deforche 2010, 166).

The rigidity of Belgium's sphere of competencies has raised legal hurdles to the approval of international treaties dealing with both federal and community issues. These treaties are known as *traités mixtes* and are the object of a cooperation agreement between the federal state, the communities, and the regions, which provides for a complex mechanism of shared responsibilities. These types of treaties require about twenty different steps to complete, including approval by all of the parliaments involved (Paquin 2010, 185). Belgium's regions of Flanders and Wallonia regularly sign treaties and other agreements with sovereign states and have an international role that equals and sometimes surpasses that of the Belgian state (Paquin 2010). Given this very ample legal autonomy, it is possible to argue that "Belgium's sub-national governments are the most vigorous sub-state actors on the international stage" (Paquin 2010, 190). Belgium is probably the only country in the world where the national government has ceased to be the clearly dominant level in foreign policy (Blatter et al. 2008).

Brazil

After the demise of the development state, Latin America was the first region of the world to systematically implement decentralization policies (Falleti 2010), but in the case of Brazil the transfer of responsibilities to subnational governments fell short of addressing the issue of foreign affairs (unlike in Argentina, for example). The 1988 Constitution states clearly that the federal government shall have the power to "maintain relations with foreign states and participate in international organizations" (Art. 21), but Article 22, which lists the areas where the Union has the *exclusive* power to legislate, foreign affairs are not mentioned. There is therefore no legal mention about the legitimacy of international actions undertaken by subnational entities. In fact the federal and the state constitutions lay out the (shared or exclusive) competencies of local governments, which include issues such as healthcare, education, infrastructure, culture, or environment, and therefore Brazilian local governments only conduct their foreign affairs in these areas of their jurisdiction.

No constitutional statement forbids them from developing international activities.

In recent years, the discussion on the need to legally ordain paradiplomacy has led to an attempt to constitutionalize the matter as well as some efforts at infra-constitutional legal framing. In 2005 the Constitutional Amendment Proposal No. 475 was sent to the Brazilian Congress. It regulated the action of member states, the federal district, and municipalities internationally. It did so through an addition to the constitutional law that dealt with competencies common to federated entities (Barros 2010). But it was not approved. In spite of this, the practice of foreign interaction with states has become deeper and more widespread among the subnational governments.

As a response to the dormancy shown by the central executive and legislative powers, subnational governments are adopting their own juridical frameworks. São Paulo state enacted in law its first governmental plan on foreign affairs (in 2012) and the northeastern state of Bahia may not be very active globally, but the state's constitution lays out in Article 105(17) that one of the governor's attributes is to "contract external or internal loans and make operations or external agreements of any nature, following authorization by the Legislature, subject to the Federal Constitution." Other state constitutions have similar dispositions.

Canada

Although the Canadian Constitution does not address international matters, successive court rulings dating back to the nineteenth century have established that a federated state is not subordinate to the federal state and that the authority to enact international treaties falls within the jurisdiction of either the federal government or the provinces, according to the internal distribution of powers provided for by the constitution. Constitutional clarity on the division of other functions, such as education and social policy, means that the central government, while able to sign international treaties and agreements, is dependent on the subnational governments for implementation of those very same agreements. In 1937, after Canada became a member to the International Labor Organization (ILO) and the federal Parliament enacted legislation to implement the provision, the Judicial Committee of the Privy Council declared that federal legislation on any ILO convention which impinged on provincial legislation (labor is a provincial concern) was *ultra vires* ("beyond the powers") and therefore invalid.

The ten Canadian provinces therefore consider themselves enabled to exercise the external attributes of the functions it exercises internally. In Canada, the provinces have jurisdiction over natural resources management, health, education, culture, municipal institutions, and private law. Canada's Constitution is thus interpreted in a decentralist way, giving the provinces a great deal of responsibilities. In 2002, Quebec's National Assembly adopted a law that requires the National Assembly's approval of all international agreements concluded by Canada that involve Quebec's matters of competence. With such a law "Quebec's National Assembly became the first British-style legislature to be closely associated with the process of concluding international agreements by the central government" (Paquin 2010, 178). Curiously, the Canadian delegation to the San Francisco Convention of 1945 objected to the UN Charter making reference to full employment among the aims of the United Nations because labor is a matter of provincial jurisdiction (Paquin 2010, 181).

China

The reform process initiated in the late 1970s granted the provincial governments a wide range of responsibilities in local affairs. The administrative measures taken in this direction were formally codified in the 1982 Constitution, which provided that the provincial governments were responsible in the management of local "economy, education, science, culture, public health, physical culture, urban and rural development, finance, civil affairs, public security, nationalities affairs, judicial administration, supervision and family planning in their respective administrative areas" (Art. 107). Although the constitution makes no reference to the capacity of the provinces on foreign affairs, political practice in China indicates that the local governments may conduct international relations on their areas of domain. Over the years, one has witnessed a gradual transfer of power and autonomy to the provinces in multifold areas, including foreign relations, leading Chinese provinces to enter the group of the most proactive actors in subnational external affairs.

France

French local governments have a long history of decentralized cooperation. Since the adoption of the law on decentralized cooperation in February 1992 (orientation law 92-125), every French local authority is entitled to engage in actions of international cooperation. The law allows French local authorities to sign agreements with counterparts in foreign countries, provided these agreements are in line with central government policy. It also established the National Commission of Decentralized Cooperation (*Commission Nationale de la Coopération Décentralisée*), which acts as space for dialogue between local authorities and central government and aims to improve the coordination of international activities that are being developed by the various regions. Local authorities can also sign agreements with international organizations if the purpose of the agreement is related to decentralized cooperation activities.

In the following years, the legal framework on regional external relations has evolved further. With the passing of the Oudin-Santini law in 2005, local bodies and the clusters to which they belong can earmark up to 1 percent of their budget to international solidarity and cooperation activities. This was supplemented by a law adopted in December 2006 allowing specific decentralized cooperation programs, emergency aid, or international solidarity actions in the field of water and sanitation, electricity, or gas. Furthermore, the Thiollière law of February 2007 on the external actions of the territorial collectivities states that territorial collectivities may conclude conventions with local authorities worldwide in order to engage in cooperation actions or development aid (Duran 2011). More recently, a law enacted in July 2014 brought even more flexibility and legitimacy to the external action of local authorities, who now can "implement or support any annual or multi-year international cooperative efforts, development aid or humanitarian action" with even more technical and political autonomy.

Germany

There exists a long tradition, extending back at least as far as Bismarck's Reich, of power-sharing between federation and *länder* in German foreign relations. This tradition has been maintained in the Federal Republic. The 1957 Lindau Agreement between the German Federation and the *länder* marked the transfer of a significant amount of foreign relations power from the *länder* to the Federation (Panara 2010). The German Constitution recognizes the right of the *länder* "to conclude treaties with foreign states" but only "with the consent of the Federal Government" (Art. 32(3)), ensuring thereby that the *länder* do not exercise their *jus tractati* in conflict with federal foreign policy. Although Article 32(3) only refers to "foreign states," by implication the *länder* can conclude treaties and agreements with all international legal subjects. The *länder*'s agreements with those entities which have no international legal personality (regions or other substate entities), lie outside the sphere of application of Article 32(3). Therefore the federal government's consent is not required (Panara 2010). In the cases of non-binding agreements, federal authorization is not necessary either.

But it is not only the *länder* that have the capacity to initiate and propose international agreements. In fact, the federation can actually conclude international agreements on matters falling under the exclusive competence of the *länder*, after obtaining their consent. For example, treaties relating to sea, fishing, or the allocation of the continental shelf can only be concluded after the coastal *länder* have been consulted. The same applies to education, for instance. As federal laws are often executed at the regional level and the Federation may need to draw upon the technical knowledge of the *länder*, this point gains extraordinary relevance. Even if German *länder* have significant room to conduct their international affairs—opening offices abroad or meeting representatives of foreign governments—in what treaty-making is specifically concerned, German law establishes fairly clear and tight guidelines on how to proceed, mostly guided by the principle that the *länder* cannot depart from the fundamental guidelines of federal foreign policy.

Italy

According to Article 117 of the Italian Constitution, the state has exclusive power over the "foreign policy and international relations of the State; relations between the State and the European Union; right of asylum and legal status of non EU citizens." This could indicate that foreign affairs were to be an exclusive domain of the Italian central government, but the constitution makes a clear-cut distinction between the foreign affairs of the state (the central government) and the foreign affairs of the regions. The basic law explicitly lays out that "in the areas falling within their responsibilities, Regions may enter into agreements with foreign States and with local authorities of other States in the cases and according to the forms laid down by State legislation" (Art. 118). Hence, the international and European relations of the twenty regions, as well as foreign trade, are subject to concurrent legislation (i.e., state legislation on the principles and regional legislation on their implementation). For matters falling within their jurisdiction, regions are vested with the power to implement European legislation and to conclude international agreements with foreign states and their subnational entities. In that sense, the Italian Constitution, after being reformed in 2001, is one of the clearest on paradiplomacy in the European context. In any case, the constitution arms itself against rudimentary foreign policy actions by the regions. Article 120 states clearly that the "Government can act for bodies of the regions, metropolitan cities, provinces and municipalities if the latter fail to comply with international rules and treaties or EU legislation." This is reinforced in several Constitutional Court rulings that indicated that the regions cannot interfere with national foreign policy or jeopardize state interests, nor can they take on commitments that bind the state from the legal or the financial point of view (Palermo 2007). In 2003, a national law on the implementation of the constitutional reform was passed, somehow tightening up the scope of regional foreign affairs. For example, it limits regional agreements with foreign states to "agreements implementing international treaties" already concluded by the Italian state and to "agreements of a merely technical or programmatic nature," thus excluding all fully binding international agreements of a political nature (Art. 3, para. 3 of Law 131/2003).

Japan

The 1947 postwar constitution formally granted a degree of autonomy to local governments, enshrining a new status for Japan's subnational governments. This was "somewhat wishful thinking on the part of the American occupiers to prevent centralized militarist ideologies from taking hold again" (Shen 2014, 50). The new chapter on Local Self-Government (Chapter VIII) sets out the role and responsibilities of subnational governments, as does the 1947 Local Authority Law. The principles of this law involve a respect for local self-government, the separation of the executive and legislative branches, and the definition of local councils and their status in relation to central government. But neither legal framework mentions international competencies, leaving subnational government legally unimpeded to pursue their own interests abroad (Jain 2005, 41).

Two other often neglected pieces of legislation are worth mentioning. The first is the Local Employees Overseas Dispatch Law enacted in 1988. Under this law, subnational officials can be sent abroad to offer specialized technical knowledge, engage with overseas government organizations and other bodies, collect information and data, promote local trade and tourism, assist in natural disasters, and participate in international organizations such as the United Nations (Jain 2005, 54). The law also enables subnational governments to establish overseas offices in partnership with

Japanese national government offices. The second piece of legislation is the Omnibus Decentralization Act of 1999, which served to create a new political and administrative environment in which subnational governments are better placed to push the cause of international activities. "This act does not specifically mention subnational governments as international actors and by maintaining the legal silence, it allows subnational governments to continue their international actions without the potential constraint of national law" (Jain 2005, 54).

Mexico

Even if there is no ruling in the Mexican Constitution that gives the federal units the power to have direct participation in foreign affairs, there is no explicit prohibition. In fact, Article 124 establishes that "the powers that are not explicitly defined in the Constitution . . . are reserved for the states." Where treaty-making is concerned, the Constitution is more precise indicating that "states cannot, in any case, enter into alliances, treaties or coalitions with other States or foreign powers" (Art. 117.I). To add some guidance to paradiplomacy in Mexico, the Organic Law of the Federal Public Administration (*Ley Orgánica de la Administración Pública Federal*), a 1976 decree of the Congress of Mexico that provides the basis for the organization of the country's public administration, establishes that the Ministry of Foreign Affairs (*Secretaría de Relaciones Exteriores*, SRE) has the faculty to coordinate the external activities of all ministries and agencies of the federal executive and subnational governments, without affecting their competences. The Organic Law incorporates the figure of inter-institutional agreements, which establish the legal basis to allow subnational governments to have greater participation in the international arena (Schiavon 2010, 75).

In addition, the SRE published a non-binding "Guide for the Conclusion of Treaties and Inter-institutional Agreements," which lays out the criteria to be followed in the negotiation of these legal instruments. According to the guidelines, subnational governments are prevented from signing treaties, but they can sign inter-institutional agreements with foreign partners if the content of the agreement falls within the exclusive competence of the sub-national government.

Russia

The 1993 Constitution of the Russian Federation does not explicitly confer its non-central authorities the right to conduct foreign affairs, but one can see from Article 72 that "coordination of the international and external economic relations of the subjects of the Russian Federation" belongs to the joint jurisdiction of the Russian Federation and the subjects of the Russian Federation, and that, according to paragraph 2, this provision "shall equally apply to the republics, territories, regions, federal cities, the autonomous region and autonomous areas." In March 1996, Russia's President Boris Yeltsin signed a decree "On the Coordinating Role of the Ministry for Foreign Affairs in Conducting the Single Foreign Political Course of the Russian Federation," according to which all the regions had to inform the federal Ministry of Foreign Affairs about the international activities. This decree was reinforced in 1999 by a federal law entitled "Coordination of International and Foreign Economic Relations of the Federal Entities of the Russian Federation" aimed at bringing into line the chaotic and diverse regional legislation on external relations with the federal laws and constitution. The law did not prohibit paradiplomatic activities though. It actually did the opposite. The new legislation allowed the regions to maintain international relations and to sign certain international agreements on the basis of their own competencies under the Russian Constitution and federal laws. The regions can also establish missions abroad as well as receive official delegations from equivalent regions of foreign states (Cornago 2000, 3).

Moreover, some regions have special status. An appendix to the Russian Federation Treaty recognized the special autonomy region of Bashkortostan and permitted this republic to have independent foreign economic relations. Also, the bilateral agreement signed in 1994 between the central government and Tatarstan recognized its right to develop its own international relations in certain fields, in particular, in foreign trade.

South Africa

South Africa's 1996 Constitution includes a provision for relatively autonomous provincial and local administrations, which share responsibility with the national government for important functional areas while also exercising exclusive authority over others (Nganje 2013). Although the constitution is not explicit on the distribution of foreign policy competence, the dominant interpretation among South African policymakers is that this functional area is the exclusive domain of the national government (Nganje 2014). Nonetheless, all nine provinces and, arguably, most South African municipalities have developed a direct international presence, primarily dedicated to promoting their economic and other developmental interests in an increasingly competitive and interdependent global environment.

As the custodian of South Africa's foreign policy, the Department of International Relations and Cooperation has officially endorsed these engagements, with the caveat that provinces and municipalities should limit themselves to forging international partnerships in those areas where they have competency. Schedule 4 of the Constitution outlines the functional areas of concurrent national and provincial legislative competence, which include education, health, transport, culture, tourism, as well as regional planning and development. The central government has also indicated that the provinces should refrain from entering into legally binding agreements with international actors. Chapter 14, section 231 of the Constitution discusses international agreements. It states, for instance, that "the negotiating and signing of all international agreements is the responsibility of the national executive." Yet, it does not clearly define what an international agreement is and whether it only encapsulates binding accords. Because the law is not clearly defined, it leaves room for interpretation and gives provinces freedom to negotiate the types of agreements into which they enter. In fact, the principle of cooperative government that is enshrined in chapter 3 of the Constitution requires intergovernmental consultations on all policy areas that affect the mandate and powers of subnational governments, including in the area of international relations (Nganje 2014).

The Protocol Training Manual produced in 2005 by the then Department of Foreign Affairs is categorical when it states that:

> It is important to note that provinces are not prohibited from entering into contracts with other entities abroad, provided they have the legal competency to do so, as this would not impinge on the conduct of foreign relations and as long as it falls within the functional areas of Schedules 4 and 5 of the Constitution. . . . The other option is to enter into an informal arrangement including mutual intentions and goodwill but which does not entail a legally binding document. (Cited in Nganje 2014, 129–130)

Spain

Although according to the Spanish Constitution the central government has exclusive competencies over international relations, including treaty-making (chapter 3), and the substate level lacks powers to sign international agreements or treaties, different Statutes of autonomy have nonetheless included special provisions on the foreign promotion of culture or vernacular languages, international contacts with overseas migrant communities, and foreign aid. In fact, the Basque government has gone so far as to openly argue "for a limited understanding of the concept of international relations that reduces it to formal diplomatic representation, war and peace issues and the signing of treaties" (Lecours 2008, 11). It considers most everything else as domestic activities and thus that it is entitled to be active.

Catalonia follows the same footsteps. Chapters II and III of the Catalan Statute that came into effect in August 2006 provide for quite an ambitious list of competencies of the Generalitat of Catalonia in the international sphere, such as:

- The Generalitat and the State shall undertake the necessary measures to obtain official status for Catalan within the European Union and its presence and use in international organizations and in international treaties of cultural or linguistic content. (Art. 6(3))
- The Generalitat has exclusive power in matters of trade and trade fairs, including the regulation of non-international trade fair activities and the administrative planning of trading activity. (Art. 121)
- In order to promote the interests of Catalonia, the Generalitat may sign collaboration agreements in areas falling within its powers. For this purpose, the external representative bodies of the State shall provide the necessary support to the initiatives of the Generalitat. (Art. 195)
- The Government of the State shall inform the Generalitat in advance of the signing of treaties which have a direct and singular effect on the powers of Catalonia. The Generalitat and Parliament may address the observations that they consider relevant to these matters to the Government. (Art. 196(1))

Given this context, while the Spanish system in theory is one of symmetric devolution, in practice there is a certain degree of asymmetry that has resulted in some communities holding far more extensive powers than others.

Switzerland

Article 54(2) of the Swiss Constitution declares that "foreign relations are the responsibility of the Confederation." This does not entail that the Swiss cantons are roadblocked from engaging with international affairs. Actually, Articles 55 and 56 of the Constitution establish clearly what the role of the subnational governments are:

- The Cantons shall be consulted on foreign policy decisions that affect their powers or their essential interests. (Art. 55(1))
- The Confederation shall inform the Cantons fully and in good time and shall consult with them. (Art. 55(2))
- The views of the Cantons are of particular importance if their powers are affected. In such cases, the Cantons shall participate in international negotiations in an appropriate manner. (Art. 55(3))
- A Canton may conclude treaties with foreign states on matters that lie within the scope of its powers. (Art. 56(1))
- Such treaties must not conflict with the law or the interests of the Confederation, or with the law of any other Cantons. The Canton must inform the Confederation before concluding such a treaty. (Art. 56(2))
- A Canton may deal directly with lower ranking foreign authorities; in other cases, the Confederation shall conduct relations with foreign states on behalf of a Canton. (Art. 56(3))

Article 147 reinforces the cantons' role in Swiss foreign affairs by stating that they "shall be invited to express their views when preparing important legislation or other projects of substantial impact as well as in relation to significant international treaties." Provisions concerning mandatory and optional referenda concerning the entry of Switzerland into organizations for collective security, into supranational communities, or the implementation of some international treaties (Art. 140, 141, and 141a) may also imply cantonal participation if such referendum is proposed by the cantons.

United States

While the US Constitution delegates clear power of international competence to the federal government, it does not deny states all international prerogatives. Yet, it is difficult to specify precisely either the outer limits on federal power or the full extent of state powers because the US Constitution is vague about most of these matters and because it contains no concurrent list of federal and state powers (Kincaid 1999, 111–112). On the one hand, Article I, section 10 announced unequivocally that "no State shall, without the Consent of Congress . . . enter into any Agreement or Compact with another State, or with a foreign Power." This control was meant to assure that international commitments contracted by the states were not against the federal Law. But an expectation of state international competence is suggested in Article III: "The judicial Power shall extend to all Cases, in Law and Equity, [of controversies] . . . between a State, or the Citizens thereof, and foreign States, Citizens or Subjects." By saying that conflicts arising between US states and foreign states can be contained by the federal courts it assumes that US states may conduct international activities. Despite this simple constitutional guideline, in the US Constitution the international competencies of the US states are more implicit than explicit. Many matters were left to the political process and to the vagaries of history (Kincaid 1999, 113).

Presently, US states sign a huge volume of international business and cooperation formal and informal agreements, but there has been little federal–state conflict over such agreement-making activity as Congress does not wish to be inundated with time-consuming approval requests. Even though an unlawful act on this domain may be overruled by the Congress, experience has shown that international paradiplomatic affairs reflect a legitimate interest of local communities and that the states authorities would hardly overstep their legal competencies. To walk on the safe side, US states generally refrain from signing bilateral binding agreements and thus only go as far as signing MoUs or political declarations. They may also entrust the export and international activity of their states to a private corporation (e.g., JobsOhio) or to a public-private arrangement (e.g., Enterprise Florida, Inc.), which may be a circumspect way to avoid strains with federal laws.

In the multilateral front, however, US states seem to be keener to take one step forward in terms of commitment. In the frame of the Council of Great Lakes Governors, two key agreements were signed in recent years: the Mutual Aid Agreement on Aquatic Invasive Species, announced in 2014 to better protect the Great Lakes and St. Lawrence River and the legally binding Great Lakes Compact, which is the means by which eight US states implement the governors' commitments under the Great Lakes-St. Lawrence River Basin Sustainable Water Resources Agreement, which also includes Ontario and Quebec.

The Governing Body

Without exception, foreign actions need to be articulated by some sort of governing body located in the organizational structure of a government. This specific body may have many forms and varies widely also in terms of juridical and organizational capacity:

Ministries, Departments, or Secretariats

Most state and city governments are comprised of large ministries or departments, such as on Education, Environment, or Health. Among these can also be Foreign Affairs. The city of São Paulo (Secretariat of International and Federative Relations), the government of Quebec (Ministry of International Relations and Francophonie), Chiapas (Ministry of Tourism and International Relations), or Catalonia (Secretariat for Foreign and European Union Affairs) are cases in point. Although the establishment of a full-fledged ministry, with appropriate staff and budget, is an indication of the robustness and the priority status given to foreign activities, it may not be always the case. For instance, although the southern Brazilian states of Paraná and Santa Catarina are not considered global players and have a low-range foreign capacity, the respective governments have established international affairs secretariats. In any case, there seems to be a trend in most regions toward further professionalization and structural "bundling together" of all foreign relations competencies, generally centered on a ministry, department, or secretariat of foreign affairs.

Agencies

Other local governments prefer to locate their foreign affairs out-side the political apparatus and provide them with more autonomous scope and recruiting capacity. This is mostly the case when foreign activities are single-themed and directed at attracting foreign investment. For that purpose, investment agencies are established such as the Tatarstan Investment Development Agency or the Gauteng Economic Development Agency. They often are state-owned companies and their legal status varies from government department to stock companies with a state as a regular stockholder. In the city of Medellín, the Agency for Cooperation and Investment of Medellín and the Metropolitan Area (ACI) has a lot of leeway not only in the business sector but also to pursue international political and technical cooperation programs.

Bureaus, Offices

In the majority of cases, foreign affairs are conducted by a governing body located within the cabinet of the head of government or within any sectorial department. This is a particularly useful solution as it does not imply spending public resources to establish a full-fledged structure and, on the other hand, when they are located in the governor or mayor's cabinet, they have political legitimacy to supervise all foreign activities of the respective government. California, for instance, has a Bureau of External Affairs within the cabinet of the governor, whereas the government of the state of São Paulo established an Office of Foreign Affairs, which is located in the governor's cabinet to provide it with authority and capacity to supervise all foreign activities of the ministries (called *Secretarias*) below the cabinet. In South Australia, a unit on External Affairs within the premier's cabinet provides advice to the premier, cabinet ministers, members of Parliament, the chief executive, and government agencies in relation to matters of protocol and foreign affairs. In Japan, all prefectures and large cities have established international affairs offices or sections (*kokusai-bu*) for administrating international affairs. In Canada, Montréal divides its international activities between the Bureau des affaires internationales institutionnelles and the Equipe d'affaires économiques internationales.

Staff, not Structure

Cities and provinces less engaged globally may only rely on a foreign affairs advisor, located close to the head of government or within any sectorial department. In several cases, this person or small group of people do not conduct foreign affairs issues full-time, but only when a specific demands arises. In the New Mexico or Texas governments, for instance, this role is performed generally by the chief of staff, deputy chief of staff, or a policy director.

Internal Structure of Governing Bodies

The internal structure of each foreign affairs governing body—be it a bureau or a ministry—is obviously shaped by the interests and the resources available to each local government. But if we run a global screening on these governing bodies worldwide, we will realize that a significant number of them are composed of smaller units or teams dedicated to specific tasks:

Cooperation

This is probably the most recurrent capacity of foreign affairs bodies. As a general rule, cooperation programs are focused on the areas of municipal or provincial competence, such as education, culture, health, or economic development. Under this light, most international cooperation teams within the foreign affairs bodies are divided up either by theme (e.g., social issues, infrastructure, public safety, etc.), by geographical areas (e.g., Latin America and Caribbean, Africa, Western Europe, etc.) or by either bilateral or multilateral affairs. The international cooperation work is undertaken by internal bodies with different names. In Flanders, for instance, the work rests on the Foreign Affairs Division, within the Department of Foreign Affairs.

Investment/Trade

Virtually all national governments have created investment agencies (e.g., ProExport Colombia or Invest in Denmark). This is also the case at the subnational level. Larger cities (such as São Paulo or New York) or economically dynamic subnational states have established governmental agencies with the mission to promote foreign investments in their cities or regions and to assist international companies in finding business opportunities there. Generally, these agencies offer comprehensive, one-stop investment consultancy services, free of charge, which they claim to be always tailored to meet potential and existing investors' precise needs. Business agencies can also contribute to branding instruments to draw investor attention to their cities or regions. Smaller cities or regions may have no resources to establish a full-fledged agency but generally count on a governmental internal body whose mission is to help foreign investors to grow their businesses. Examples of subnational investment agencies include Invest São Paulo (state), Walloon Export and Foreign Investment Agency (AWEX), Macao Trade and Investment Promotion Institute, or Invest in Milan.

Communication

Most foreign affairs bodies count on a communication or information team that proactively develops public awareness of government activities and may also provide a media and public relations advisory service to other government departments. Most teams try to establish a professional relationship with the local press (national or foreign correspondents) to either raise awareness of the foreign activities of the government or to project the different policies of the government abroad. Press-related activities may go hand in hand with branding, or the systematic policy to build and manage the reputation of subnational entities. The aim is to improve their city or state's standing, as their image and reputation can dramatically influence their success in attracting tourism receipts and investment capital; in attracting a talented and creative workforce and in its cultural and political influence in the world. Subnational governments with communication teams within their foreign affairs bodies include the state of São Paulo (Unit on International Communication), Medellín (Communications Unit within ACI), or Quebec (Communication and Public Affairs Directorate). A lower number of governments conduct branding activities however. In addition, public diplomacy—the involvement of public opinion in foreign policy—may also be conducted. In Flanders, for instance, public diplomacy includes regular image-building or international promotional activities that are largely based on outsourcing policies (such as the publication of the English-speaking newspaper *Flanders Today*). Whenever a foreign affairs body cannot count on its own communication team, it generally relies on the general government's communication body.

Protocol and Events

Most foreign affairs bodies count on a protocol team whose mission is to plan and arrange incoming and outgoing visits (Box 2.1). The other main task is to maintain contacts with foreign diplomatic missions, consulates, and offices of international organizations in their countries. The Protocol Department also deals with the exequaturs (a patent which a head of state issues to a foreign consul, guaranteeing the consul's rights and privileges of office and ensuring recognition in the state to which the consul is appointed to exercise such powers) for foreign consuls as well as the interpretation of the Vienna Conventions on Diplomatic and Consular Relations. Very often this is the original function of foreign affairs governing bodies, as the exchange of foreign visits (city and regional officials) is a very common practice worldwide. Between 2011 and October 2014, São Paulo (state), for instance, received 1,595 foreign delegations. In the same period, the governor of São Paulo, Geraldo Alckmin, met with

BOX 2.1 What Makes a Good Official Meeting?

Official visits are part of the daily routine at government headquarters. And in smaller governments, official visits may end up being the epicenter of paradiplomatic work. Diplomatic meetings need, however, to follow certain parameters to ensure their success.

Preparation and Definition of Agenda. An official meeting with a foreign delegation should never represent the first contact between foreign governments. Preparatory work is of vital relevance. Each part has to do its homework, studying the issues and having the facts in hand before proposing a specific agenda. The agenda constitutes the participants' agreed-upon road map for the meeting. It provides an outline of items to be considered and usually lists them in order of priority. It is fairly common for advisers to spend one to four weeks in discussions to define what issues will be brought up by their leaders (e.g., mayors or governors). The preparatory work is fundamental to ensure that no stone is left on the road and that leaders will be ready to make all necessary commitments or announcements. The success of a meeting should be measured by the quality of its follow-up. Did it open any doors? A more results-oriented approach is not necessarily the rule of diplomacy, however. Very frequently, meetings are simply meant "to pay a visit" or to make a "courtesy call" and thus are of symbolic value and rarely involve a detailed discussion of issues. In fact, it all depends on the experience, expectations, and culture of the participants in the meeting. But even in these cases preparatory work is important to avoid skewed expectations or misunderstandings.

Briefing. At least the two top leaders in the meeting need to be thoroughly briefed. There are various types of briefing notes, depending upon the purpose of the communication. Some are for information only; others provide recommendations and seek decisions. They cannot be too long, verbose, and bureaucratic. Expect a leader to devote no more than five to ten minutes before the meeting to reading the notes. In addition, a leader will need to have speaking notes (talking points), which will be used discretely during the meeting or will assist him/her in briefing the press or media on something that has already been summarized in a press release that the audience has already received. Typically, these speaking points will be enough for a speech or press briefing lasting about five to ten minutes in length, which will normally be followed by a question period.

Protocol. Understanding the rules of protocol is essential to conducting diplomacy. Everything from knowing how to properly greet a foreign leader, understanding foreign customs, properly displaying the flags, or having suitable seating arrangements at a table plays an important role in the diplomatic process. One should bear in mind that there are different protocol schools and therefore it is important to establish open communication lines between protocol teams so that all details are accounted for.

Public Diplomacy. If the meeting has media relevance, the press officers need to be involved from the very beginning. They are the ones who will prepare the press releases and the media advisory (typically sent twice, once a few weeks before the event and then a day or so before the event as a reminder). The press team will also hand out media kits containing a description of the event/meeting, bios of senior staff, photographs of the meeting (if available), recent press releases, and clips of media coverage. Social media should also be used, such as Facebook, Twitter, and so on.

twenty-two heads of state and government, making him one of the most networked subnational leaders (see figure 4.2).

Associated Structures

External Associations

Very often, mayors and governors are connected by national associations that foster the exchange of insights and ideas to help state officials shape public policy. Cases in point include the National Governor's Association, Council of State Governments, National Conference of State Legislatures, National Associacion of Counties, US Conference of Mayors, National League of Cities, and International City Management Association—all in the United States; the Mayors National Front (*Frente Nacional de Prefeitos*) in Brazil, the National Conference of Governors (*Conferencia Nacional de Gobernadores*, CONAGO) in Mexico, and the National Association of Portuguese Cities (*Associação Nacional de Municípios Portugueses*). On average, these associations of state and local governments have institutionalized international capacities and activities, providing an extra arrangement at the disposal of local governments. CONAGO, for instance, counts with an International Affairs Committee. In other examples, the foreign affairs departments of subnational governments within the same country also join forces to coordinate the local foreign activities, both in the global arena and with the federal government. A good example is the Mexican Association of International Affairs Offices of the States (*Asociación Mexicana de Oficinas de Asuntos Internacionales de los Estados*), established in 2009. In Russia, the Consultative Council of the Subjects of the Russian Federation on International and External Economic Contacts was established in 1995 to regulate the foreign economic relations of the Russian federal and local governments. Belgium also counts with the Inter-Ministerial Committee on Foreign Policy bringing together representatives of different authorities at the highest political and administrative levels. It was conceived as an institution of permanent dialogue to avoid conflicts.

Think Tanks

Some governments have established policy-development or policy-planning bodies with the goal to develop methods and practices related to foreign policy, advance planning and monitoring systems, prepare regulations and instructions, and provide expert advice, training, and support services. They are generally viewed as the brains behind a foreign affairs team. When this ability is not generated within the mold of the institutions it could be delegated. That is, for example, what the Flemish government has done. The Leuven Centre for Global Governance Studies coordinates a Policy Research Centre on "Foreign Affairs, International Entrepreneurship and Development Cooperation" for the Flemish government. The center brings together leading Flemish universities to conduct data collection and analysis, and provide short-term policy-supporting research, fundamental scientific research, and scientific services.

Advising Councils

When demand on international relations grows, a counseling body for collective discussion of the government's objectives for foreign affairs and about how best to deliver them is important. Some examples are worth mentioning. Active from 2007 to 2014, the Flemish Foreign Affairs Council was an independent advisory body to the government of Flanders. The Council advised the regional government on its foreign policy, its policy on international trade, tourism, and development cooperation, either at the request of the government or on its own initiative.[2]

Coordinating Bodies

In order to enhance internal coordination and cohesion, some subnational governments have established multi-stakeholder bodies with executive power. In South Africa, the Gauteng International Relations Forum brings together representatives from the premier's office, the office of the speaker of Gauteng's provincial legislature, all Gauteng's sector departments, municipalities in the province, as well as the central Ministry of Foreign Affairs. The Forum facilitates information-sharing and consultation on international relations and related issues, including the signing and implementation of international cooperation agreements and the collaborative development and monitoring of the province's annual international relations program.

National Forums of Subnational Governments

As an arrangement fomented by national governments to facilitate bilateral contacts between subnational players, they generally introduce an additional layer of cooperation into a dense bilateral agenda. A good example is the China–US Governors Forum (presented in this sequence by Chinese official sources and press) or the US–China Governors Forum (as coined by the US State Department), which meets annually and it was first established through an MoU signed by Secretary Hillary Clinton and Chinese Foreign Minister Yang Jiechi in 2011.

Bilateral Commissions

The substate governments that have more robust relations with foreign partners may establish official working groups (mixed commissions, bilateral commissions, joint committees, bilateral groups, permanent commissions, bilateral cooperation committees) with the purpose of identifying areas of cooperation and pursuing joint projects and actions. As one of the main instruments of Flanders's bilateral foreign policy, mixed commissions, established by bilateral agreements, are held several times a year between Flanders and its partners. In the frame of these commissions, delegates of both governments generally design and pursue a cooperation framework laying out a set of milestones. An illustration of this is the biennial Flanders–Catalonia joint committee, which was created with representatives of the two governments to implement an umbrella accord signed in 2008. This committee is in charge of developing and endorsing the working agenda and evaluating the results. Catalonia has a similar arrangement with Quebec. In another example, the Permanent Croatian-Bavarian Commission was established in 1971 and since 1972 regular sessions of competent line ministries have been held on an annual basis, having a major role in the promotion and development of economic, cultural, and political cooperation between Croatia and Bavaria, as well as in the overall deepening of their relations. Croatia also has a similar arrangement with Baden-Württemberg. In the same way, the state of São Paulo created Working Groups with the countries with whom they established formal and bilateral relations. Thus far, these Groups that meet biannually have been established with the United States, Canada, United Kingdom, and France (Box 2.2).

BOX 2.2 Formal Bilateral Relations of the State of São Paulo

In 2012, the state of São Paulo adopted the pioneer initiative to establish "formal," "bilateral," and "direct" relations with sovereign states. Although it is not rare that subnational governments strike formal agreements with central foreign governments, it was the first time that those agreements explicitly stated that bilateral relations would be established in a formal or direct way and that a bilateral Working Group would be established. The Group has the mission to define the priority areas of bilateral cooperation, the cooperation projects to be implemented, and the chronogram and resources available. It ensures, according to the state government, a more coherent and coordinated relation between partners. With no exception, these agreements were analyzed and approved by the respective Ministries of Foreign Affairs. Although the working groups do not discuss bilateral issues between Brazil and the other countries, a representative from Brazil's Ministry of External Affairs is invited to participate with observer status.

United States. The agreement was signed in March 2013 by the governor of São Paulo, Geraldo Alckmin, and the US Consul-General in São Paulo, Dennis Hankins, in the presence of the US Ambassador to Brazil, Thomas A. Shannon Jr. The first meeting of the Working Group took place in July the same year. It was the first time the US government "formalized direct relations" with a subnational government in the Southern Hemisphere. According to both governments, the initiative fell under a Memorandum of Understanding to Support State and Local Cooperation signed in April 2012 by US Secretary of State Hillary Clinton and Brazil's Foreign Minister Antonio Patriota. US press regarded the agreement as "game-changing" (Oppenheimer 2013).

United Kingdom. In October 2013, Hugo Swire, British Minister of State for the Foreign Office came to São Paulo to sign an agreement to "formalize the bilateral relationship" with the São Paulo state government. The British Ambassador to Brazil, Alexander Ellis, was also present. The agreement, which was signed by the Chief of Staff to the Governor, Edson Aparecido, was later discussed in detail in a meeting of the governor of São Paulo with the British Foreign Minister, William Hague, held in February 2014. The first meeting of the Working Group took place in February that year.

France. In the presence of French President François Hollande, the governor of São Paulo and France's Minister of Foreign Affairs Laurent Fabius signed an agreement in December 2013 that "formalized their bilateral relations." In his speech, Hollande underlined that the agreement was "exceptional because it allowed a direct relation between France and the state of São Paulo to be established." He added that the accord "will amplify even more everything that we can do with Brazil in general and with São Paulo in particular, with more freedom, in a quicker way and with more easiness."

Canada. First discussed in the meeting between the governor of São Paulo and the Governor-General of Canada David Johnston in a meeting held in São Paulo in April 2012, an agreement was signed by São Paulo Chief of Staff and Canada's Consul General Stéphane Larue in February 2014. Adopted in the presence of Henri-Paul Normandin, Director General of the Latin America and Caribbean Bureau at the Canadian Ministry of Foreign Affairs, the agreement mentioned that both governments would formalize their "bilateral relations."

São Paulo proposed similar agreements to Germany, Spain, Japan, China, and Argentina (São Paulo's largest export market) and are being negotiated at the time of writing. According to the state government, the decision over who signs these agreements is only related to the timing of visits of senior representatives from the counterpart government and not related to varying degrees of importance attached to these agreements by foreign partners.

Representations Abroad

Either because of the symbolic nature of the nation-state or due to budget constraints, most local governments have shied away from opening offices abroad. More traditionalist policymakers often warn that "embassies are a prerogative of the federal state and not of federated states." However, an increasing number of federated states have seen the need to open representations in foreign countries to protect and advance their specific interests. For Canadian provinces, US states, or German *länder*, this is a common foreign policy instrument.

Between 1984 and 2000, the number of foreign offices operated by the fifty US states more than quadrupled to the point where they now nearly equal the number of embassies and consulates operated by the US federal government (Paul 2005, 2). In Germany, the *länder* established some 130 representative offices since 1970 (Paquin 2010, 174). The city that hosts the largest agglomeration of subnational representations is unequivocally Brussels. Although the idea of the emergence of a "Europe of the regions" did fade from both academic and practitioners' narratives, territorial authorities have continued to invest resources both at home and abroad to strengthen their involvement in the European Union's policymaking processes. Subnational governments continue to open offices in Brussels, and these offices in turn continue to grow, not only in maturity but also in number of staff and financial muscle (Tatham 2013).

The governments which take these steps have generally chosen one of the following routes:

Full Offices

These represent the government abroad in a wide range of different areas and interests. Presently, one of the most complete networks is run by the government of Quebec. It is composed of seven "general delegations" (the most important offices of Quebec abroad), four "delegations" (which offer services in some sectors of activity), eight "bureaus" (which provide services in a limited number of areas), five "trade offices" (headed by a resident of the host country), and two "representations in multilateral affairs" (at UNESCO and at the Organisation internationale de la Francophonie). In fact, Quebec runs the only subnational representation office with full diplomatic status: the Quebec Government Office in Paris, established in 1961. Often referred to as the flagship of Quebec's diplomatic network, it has been treated, since 1964, in the same way as an embassy and enjoys the same privileges and immunities as other diplomatic representations in France. Alongside the network managed by the Ministry of International Relations, the Ministry of Economy, Innovation and Exports has representatives in Quebec's offices, which are located in key trade markets. Other governments also have available a network of representations such as Wallonia (eighteen delegations in the Americas, Europe, Africa, and Asia), Catalonia (seven "Delegations" in the European Union, Germany, France/Switzerland, United Kingdom/Ireland, Austria, Italy, and United States/Canada/Mexico), Alberta (twelve offices in Asia, Europe, and the Americas), Baden-Württemberg (with one office in Brussels, see figure 2.2), or Scotland, which runs offices in Washington, Brussels, Toronto, and Beijing.

FIGURE 2.2 Baden-Württemberg's representative office in Brussels

© State of Baden-Württemberg

Theme-Oriented Offices

Other governments favor the establishment of single thematic offices abroad with well-shaped targets such as to encourage investment and trade by appropriate promotional activities and direct negotiations with foreign private and governmental institutions. For instance, the government of Ontario established a network of International Marketing Centers in key markets worldwide (eleven in total). Part of the ministry of Citizenship, Immigration and International Trade, the Centers serve to promote investment and trade opportunities in Ontario and work with companies to find investment opportunities in the province. Similarly, nearly all states in the United States fund export promotion programs which are often embodied in overseas trade offices. California, for instance, has a "trade and investment office" in China, financed by private donations and operated by the Bay Area Council—a business group that carries the state's imprimatur. Also in the United States, some overseas offices are wholly funded by a single state, but it is quite common for several states to jointly fund a single overseas office. For example, the Council of Great Lake States administers overseas offices in Australia, Brazil, Canada, Chile, China, and South Africa. The council's member states Illinois, Indiana, Michigan, Minnesota, New York, Ohio, Pennsylvania, and Wisconsin may opt in to any of these offices. Overseas offices have been in use since New York opened an office in Europe in 1954 (Blase 2003, 93) though they did not become widespread until the 1980s and 1990s. Other investment-promotion offices such as Invest in Bavaria (twenty-six offices abroad), Scottish Development International (twenty-eight offices abroad), New South Wales Department of Industry (ten offices and representatives abroad), or Jiangsu Provincial Economic and Trade (offices in twelve countries) are also worth attention. Beyond trade and investments, other subnational networks are oriented toward tourism promotion or development cooperation. Tourism Flanders-Brussels (with representatives in fourteen countries) or the Catalan Agency for Development Cooperation (three offices in Colombia, Morocco, and Mozambique) are cases in point.

Officials, not Offices

Some governments are represented by people and not by institutions. Flanders, for instance, has eleven diplomatic representatives in The Hague, Paris, London, Berlin, Warsaw, Vienna, Madrid, New York, Pretoria, Geneva (multilateral), and Brussels (EU). They are staff members of the Flemish Department of Foreign Affairs. Manitoba, in Canada, also appoints "trade representatives" to promote the province's investment opportunities to local companies while assisting Manitoba companies as they pursue business opportunities abroad. British Columbia has a similar strategy: it has "Trade and Investment Representatives" stationed in Japan, China, India, South Korea, Vancouver, Palo Alto (to cover the Americas), and London (to cover Europe). Île-de-France has representatives in Santiago, São Paulo, Haiti, Hanoi, and Antananarivo stationed in the offices of their local partners. Australia's state of Queensland counts with "trade and investment commissioners" in Latin America, Europe, North America, the Middle East, and Asia. The Walloon Export and Foreign Investment Agency (AWEX) has a worldwide network of over one hundred Trade and Investment Counsellors. This strategy is more cost-effective but the lack of diplomatic and institutional support may undermine the political strength of the representatives.

Consultancy

Very often states lighten up the costs of going abroad by hiring local consultancy companies to represent them. Run by local native-speaker staff, the consultancies are contracted generally to spark trade and investments. On the positive side, they generally have a good domain of local practices and narratives and can successfully mediate business contacts and seize opportunities not apparent to outsiders. On the down side, the fact that they are not run by natives of the states they represent somehow decreases their legitimacy and credibility confining them to bureaucratic activities. In the same fashion, local governments tend to look down at this sort of representation and question their status as official representatives of specific governments. The Council of Great Lake Governors is represented in São Paulo by a local consultancy company, as are the states of Florida or Georgia, for instance.

Joint Local Government Offices

States and cities from the same country may also join forces and establish joint representations abroad. In Japan, local governments created in 1988 the Council of Local Authorities for International Relations (CLAIR) to support their international activities. CLAIR provides assistance by keeping track of international trends and maintaining ties with local governments and organizations abroad. CLAIR's network is composed of the headquarters in Tokyo and seven overseas offices: London, Paris, New York, Sydney, Singapore, Seoul, and Beijing. CLAIR offices in New York, London, and Sydney are known locally as "Japan Local Government Centre." CLAIR is perhaps the foremost institution behind the rapid international rise of Japanese subnational government actors since the late 1980s (Jain 2005, 49).

Cooperation with Federal Diplomacy

Finally, it is also common to have local government offices within their respective countries' consulates or embassies though co-location agreements. For instance, Quebec's offices in Mumbai, Beijing, and Shanghai cohabitate with the Canadian Consulate General or Embassy. Cooperation between subnational and national foreign policies is generally better coordinated through this framework.

State officials often justify using financial resources to fund overseas offices by claiming the offices help small and medium-sized firms increase or initiate exports to a new country. But offices abroad are expensive—a factor that often leads to internal resistance. For instance, California closed its twelve foreign trade offices amid controversy in 2003. At the time, the Legislative Analyst's Office and other critics questioned their effectiveness and cost. The

one outpost that remained open for several years on private donations, in tiny Armenia, was widely mocked as less than significant.
Estimating the impact of export-promoting overseas offices on
state exports is difficult because it is not clear if the offices cause
exports to increase or if exports cause the offices to exist. Academia
diverges on this issue. In a case study, Timothy Kehoe and Kim Ruhl
(2004) suggest Wisconsin's enhanced export activity to Mexico
after the North American Free Trade Agreement (NAFTA) was due
to the presence of a Wisconsin office located in Mexico City. Other
scholars demonstrated that depending on the sample and weight of
states and countries used in the regression, the implied benefit of
having an overseas office to be in the range of $400,000–$1,000,000
per billion in exports, or 0.04–0.10% (Cassey 2014). Opening offices
has therefore to be regarded in a critical way. They can be indicative of the foreign policy ambitions of local and regional authorities, but their functions can also be limited in scope, have little to
do with foreign policy as traditionally conceived, and, in resource
terms, often amount to a very small team of nonexclusive consultants (Hocking 1999, 22).

The Staff

As a general rule, subnational foreign affairs departments have
fewer staff than national external relations ministries. If the ministry of foreign affairs of a middle-sized country may range from 500
to 1,500 people, a local government may have a handful to around
700–800 staff (as is the case of Flanders[3] and Wallonia[4]), although
30–50 should be seen as the average number. Even if less staggering than the Belgium regions, other regional governments have also
substantial human resources to conduct their foreign policies. As of
late 2014, Bavaria (230), Quebec (529[5]), Guangdong (300), and São
Paulo (120[6]) are cases in point.

Although it is a common practice at the national/federal level,
subnational governments invest less in the training of their staff
and recruitment tends also to be less demanding. At the national

level, the training of diplomats is either outsourced to universities or delivered internally through a School of Public Administration, a Diplomatic Academy attached to Ministries of Foreign Affairs, or a training unit within the Ministry of Foreign Affairs utilizing external and internal speakers and trainers. The Diplomatic Academy of the Ministry of Foreign Affairs of the Russian Federation, the Rio Branco Institute of Brazil's Ministry of External Relations, or the Istituto Diplomatico of the Italian Ministry of Foreign Affairs are good paradigms. But there is hardly any resemblance of this at subnational level. Although paradiplomats often engage in tailor-made and internal short courses, no local government has a training institution that levels up with classical national ones. This gap is generally not filled either by nongovernmental diplomacy-training bodies. Prestigious institutions such as the Diplomatic Academy of Vienna, the School of International Service of the American University, the School of Foreign Service at Georgetown University, or the Geneva School of Diplomacy and International Relations offer no courses exclusively on paradiplomacy.

Despite this unfavorable scenario, some countries count with national training centers on local governance. Besides offering the traditional programs on management skills in public policymaking and strategic leadership, some of these institutes have started to add courses on foreign policy training in their local governance training curricula. For instance, the Local Government Officials Development Institute, a government organization affiliated with the Ministry of Public Administration and Security of South Korea conducts international training programs and promotes international collaborative programs.

Acceptance into a local government's foreign affairs department is also less strict, when compared to the national sphere. In most cases, paradiplomacy does not entail a specific career in public administration leading to some internal vulnerability and less meritocracy. Career civil servants (not temporary workers or politicians) are generally hired on the basis of entrance examinations, but only rarely are foreign language skills and diplomatic competencies specifically assessed in these general competitions. To overcome some of these challenges, one may find (rare) occasions when national and subnational governing bodies "loan" functionaries. In Canada, for instance, there has been at least one case when a Canadian diplomat was lent to Quebec's Ministry of International Relations to lead Quebec's São Paulo Office. Japan's first exchange of staff took the opposite direction. In the 1990s, a project chief in the International Relations department of Sapporo City was seconded to a Japanese diplomatic mission serving as vice-consul in the Japanese Consulate in Boston.

White Papers

"Actions Plans," "White Papers," "Visions," "Strategies," or "Government Plans" are part of the political routine. They are strategic documents used as a means of presenting government policy preferences and priorities. They can either be put forward to test the climate of public opinion regarding a controversial policy issue enabling the government to gauge its probable impact or they may include quantitative and qualitative targets for government action within a specific time frame.

These types of strategic guidelines have started to become common at a national level (e.g., United Arab Emirates Vision 2021) or at sectorial level (e.g., Scotland's Digital Future—Infrastructure Action Plan). But they are less widespread in the foreign affairs field at the national level, and even less common at the subnational level. Even so, they are useful pieces of strategy as they provide a sense of integration and mission within the government and enhance ownership over activity and dialogue with the population. Thus far, the few subnational governments that have adopted foreign affairs government plans include the Western Cape, Quebec, Flanders, New South Wales, and the state of São Paulo.

Quebec's "International Policy—Working in Concert" was launched in 2006 and was followed by associated strategic and action plans. The policy states that Quebec will focus its international initiatives toward five objectives that take into account its political, economic, and cultural interests: (1) strengthening Quebec's action and influence; (2) fostering Quebec's growth and prosperity; (3) contributing to the security of Quebec and the North American continent; (4) promoting the identity and culture of Quebec; and (5) contributing to the cause of international solidarity. Despite the changes of government in the province, the basic tenets of the policy have not changed. As there is a broad consensus in Quebec on the need for a distinct international action, government rotations lead not to ideological shifts but only to adjustments in the sectors and issues that are emphasized, as well as the territories that are prioritized. Ultimately, Quebec's "International Policy" is a fairly good compromise between *Parti Quebecois*'s stalwart promotion of Quebecois culture and the Liberal Party's international economic objectives.

In 2010, Flanders announced its "Foreign Policy, International Entrepreneurship and Development Cooperation 2009–2014" to "place the federated state of Flanders on the international map and to give it a voice in global society." In order to realize this ambition, Flemish international policy focused on the following nine basic principles and strategic objectives: (1) global answers to global issues; (2) the European Union as global player; (3) subsidiarity and cultural diversity; (4) a sound licensing policy for the import, export, and transit of strategic goods; (5) increased internationalization of the Flemish economy; (6) freer and fairer world trade; (7) increased international accessibility of Flanders; (8) poverty reduction and social development; and (9) combating climate change effects. The policy was complemented by the 2014–2019 "Coalition Agreement" that sets the targets of Flanders's overall future actions, including on foreign affairs. The plan establishes several international goals under a guiding philosophy: "We will . . . strive to increase Flanders' connection to foreign countries more than ever. As an open society and open economy, we want to stand tall and self-assured in the world." Also in Belgium, the Wallonia government adopted its 2014–2019 Regional Policy Declaration, which includes policies and targets on foreign affairs.

In April 2013, New South Wales (NSW) adopted its "International Engagement Strategy" with the mission to provide a coordinated roadmap for international engagement to support the growth of the NSW economy. The new strategy built on the working relationship between the private sector and the NSW government, and provided a way forward for a centrally coordinated "whole of government" approach to help the state achieve greater trade and investment outcome. It expanded NSW's priority markets to ten and identified nine priority sectors based on NSW's competitive advantages and potential for growth. The strategy was launched publically by Deputy Premier of NSW and Minister for Trade and Investment Andrew Stoner. In his words, "To make NSW the first place to do business in Australia we need to effectively engage the global economy."[7]

For the longer term of twelve years, two legislative periods, the state of Upper Austria has a strategic corporate concept that covers all of the state administration with every directorate and department. The aims and guidelines for the state's foreign activities are part of that long-term strategic concept.[8] For the medium term of six years (i.e., one legislative period), a newly elected government of Upper Austria issues a working plan for the term, which also includes the area of foreign affairs with general aims and focal points.[9] In accordance with that document, a strategic plan for the state's foreign affairs is drawn up by the Foreign Affairs Team. It includes aims of the international activities of the state, topical points these activities should focus on, central multilateral and bilateral partnerships, and the level of cooperation they should reach.

Finally, it is worth mentioning the program launched by the state of São Paulo in 2012. Called "São Paulo in the World: International Relations Plan 2011–2014," it was established by decree and launched in a ceremony by the State Governor Geraldo Alckmin. Then Minister of External Relations of Brazil, Antonio Patriota, was the guest of honor. This plan was guided by three general goals outlining the state government's international activities. Each general goal comprised sectorial priorities as well as specific quantifiable objectives. The plan encompassed a total of sixteen priorities and fifty-four specific objectives. The general goals were (1) promote sustainable development in the state of São Paulo, harmonizing economic, social, and environmental concerns and thus ensuring the well-being of future generations; (2) enhance the state of São Paulo's participation at a time when Brazil is playing an ever greater regional and global role; and (3) contribute to democratic governance and to the development of partnerships between peoples. The plan was mimicked by other governments in Latin America and served as a great stimulus for the foreign activities of the Brazilian federated state.

The Foreign Partners

With what partners are subnational governments entitled to engage? At the national level, only rarely does the law discipline which actors sovereign states may establish international relations with. Diplomatic norms and practice serve as compasses. At the subnational level, the same philosophy applies. In practice, a city or a subnational state can sign international agreements with international organizations (namely multilateral development banks); sovereign states; other subnational governments; subnational forums, councils, and networks; private companies or foundations; and other nongovernmental institutions. Despite the multitude of possibilities, in fact, most cities or regions prefer to partner with other cities or regions as they share similar challenges and can incorporate similar solutions. For instance Quebec–Bavaria cooperation, probably the most dense for two regional governments, started in 1989 (Bavaria's Minister-President Max Streibl and Quebec's Premier Robert Bourassa signed a cooperation agreement in Munich) and has to date carried out over five hundred projects. The success of Bavaria–Quebec relations, they argue, is mainly due to a common political will, as well as to the friendship and trust that developed over the years of working together.[10]

There are two major breakaways from this general tendency: when a subnational entity establishes relations with a sovereign state and when a subnational government is able to join an international organization. The first is a complex issue. The establishment of "bilateral relations" can be interpreted in a variety of different ways as there is no universal understanding or codification of the language that should be used to account for subnational activities. In the universe of formal diplomatic relations between sovereign states, bilateral relations are generally initiated when diplomatic missions are established by mutual consent and are guided by proper international law.

When subnational actors are involved, the establishment of "bilateral relations" are pinpointed in a variety of ways: (1) as the natural reflection of a strong track record of bilateral cooperation, expressed in the signature of agreements and the development of joint projects over a significant period of time directly with the government of a sovereign country (e.g., relations between Baden-Württemberg and Croatia); (2) when a substate opens an official representation in a foreign country (e.g., Bavaria office in Belgium); (3) when a substate opens an official representation in a foreign land and is granted full diplomatic status (e.g., Quebec delegation in France), or when a sovereign state signs an agreement with a substate stating explicitly that relations between them are formal, bilateral, or direct and create a formal bilateral commission. The agreements that São Paulo state signed in 2013 and 2014 with the United States, France, United Kingdom, and Canada are the only example of this later type (Box 2.2).

The second major exception to the traditional *modus operandi* arises when a subnational government participates in an international organization. Very often cities and states sign technical cooperation agreements with global bodies such as the UNDP, UN Women, World Health Organization, or sign loans with development banks such as the World Bank, Japan International Cooperation Agency (JICA), Corporación Andina de Fomento, or the IDB. Yet, some subnational entities take one step further and join international organizations. For instance, Quebec joined the International Organization of the Francophonie in 1971 as a full-member (other regions such as the French Community of Belgium and New Brunswick are also members). In addition, in May 2006 the government of Quebec and the government of Canada signed an agreement—lauded as historic by the first—concerning UNESCO. It allowed a Quebec government representative to be stationed in the Permanent Delegation of Canada to UNESCO with the mandate to promote the interests of the government of Quebec in matters of education, culture, and scientific development within the international community. The province is also able to participate in the work of the Organization of American States (OAS) within Canadian delegations and therefore it takes part in the routine work of the OAS by attending the weekly meetings of the Permanent Council and the annual General Assembly—the Organization's highest policy decision-making body.

Other subnational governments also participate formally in multilateral bodies. Hong Kong and Macao, for instance, are members of the World Trade Organization. According to the organization, non-sovereign autonomous entities of member states are eligible for separate membership, provided that they have autonomy in the conduct of their external commercial relations. In another case, non-independent entities such as Flanders, Puerto Rico, Aruba, Hong Kong, Macao, or Madeira are associated members of the United Nations World Tourism Organization. Belgium and UNESCO provides a curious case. As the international organization deals with education and culture and these are competencies of the Belgian local governments, they take up Belgium's seat at UNESCO. If, however, UNESCO is to rule on an issue different from the competences of Belgium local governments (such as acceptance of a new member), the federal government is called back in.

When states are not juridically able to join an organization, it may happen that they get embedded into a national delegation. Catalonia, for instance, observed the 33rd and 34th UNESCO General Conference and participated in the First Intergovernmental Committee Convention on Diversity and Cultural Expressions within UNESCO as a member of the Spanish delegation.

Multilateral Arrangements

Symbolically, in 1985, the newly adopted European Charter of Local Self-Government of the Council of Europe indicated that local authorities were "entitled" to belong to an international association for the protection and promotion of their common interests (Art. 10(2)). As the creation of IULA in 1913 and the forums of mayors established in postwar Europe indicate, city networks have been characteristic for the whole twentieth century (table 1.2). Yet, it was in the 1990s that we saw a staggering growth of multilateral subnational arrangements worldwide, especially in the environmental domain (Bouteligier 2013). Globalization and the information revolution are empowering decentralized networks that challenge state-centered hierarchies. As networked actors, subnational alliances are developing the ambition and, perhaps, the capabilities to have a real impact on global governance outcomes (Curtis 2014, 28). The networks that are woven by substate entities indeed seem to capture a part of the action that sometimes seems to elude central diplomacies (Criekemans 2010b). Over 125 of these arrangements exist today (table 1.2). They serve multiple purposes. Most of them are summit-led organizations that gain a certain momentum when leaders meet but cool off in between meetings. Others are more robust and provide technical consulting, joint coordination, training, and information services to build capacity, share knowledge, and support local government in the implementation of policies at the local level (figure 2.3). They may also be used as trampolines of collective action and political lobbying, either on momentary issues (for instance, in 2014 the Sports Working Group within Mercocities issued a communiqué condemning racist abuses targeting a Brazilian soccer player in Peru) or on planetary challenges, such as climate change. They stage events where officials meet to learn from each other and establish personal relationships. This means facilitating contacts and access. For example, "through C40, member cities have gained access to multinational companies (MNCs) (e.g. ARUP), foundations (e.g., Clinton Climate Foundation), financial institutions (e.g., Citibank), and multilateral organizations (e.g., the World Bank), which provide beneficial terms of cooperation, because they gain access to a network of partnering cities" (Bouteligier 2014, 64).

FIGURE 2.3 Regional Leaders Summit (2012)—family photo

© State government of São Paulo

Participation in this type of multilateral arrangement is often the first, and sometimes the only, opportunity for cities and states to engage with foreign partners. Subnational governments came to realize that unless they participate in these external forums, they would be swept along by international agreements over which they would have no control (Hooghe and Marks 2001, 90). But there is currently a proliferation of these arrangements leading to the pursuit of overlapping or conflicting agendas. It is also common for subnational governments to be members of five to ten organizations but confine their contribution to the annual attendance of the organization's summit. Apart from a handful of subnational governments that have a more mature and strategic vision, participation in these networks is often momentary, erratic, or reactive. It is therefore vital that cities and states establish precise criteria for participation, which could include:

Financial Commitment. Several of these organizations demand annual membership fees that are used to run the organization. Does the local government have the financial means to participate?

Financial Opportunities. Other organizations have managed to create funds, available to members, to advance some of their agendas. Is the local government able to access these funds or wish to contribute to them?

Visibility. Participation in international forums may serve as a promotional tool for local governments that use them to market themselves as leaders in specific areas. Networks distribute influence and power across traditional boundaries, allowing powerful interest groups to form and reshape rapidly.

Lobbying. Any global organization may in theory provide spotlights and opportunity for participants to set the agenda, voice their concerns, and pursue their interests. Regions often try to gain access to important multilateral debates that affect their internal competences.

Best Practices. In these forums, regions may learn from other regions with similar or different experiences. The solution to a problem faced by a local government can be found anywhere on the planet. A best practice is a method or technique that has consistently shown results superior to those achieved with other means and is used subsequently as a benchmark.

Network of Contacts. "To have access" is the new mantra of international politics. Participation in networks generates personal connections that may benefit and facilitate the management of foreign policies.

Membership Variation. In the largest organizations, there may be a discrepancy between the weight and the interests of its members, which could include a small city or the richest region in a continent. Organizations that do not provide adequate interlocution should be avoided.

Awards

Cities and states have seen their efforts recognized by international awards and prizes, which have ended up serving an important instrument to catapult subnational leadership globally. The abundance of awards, along with their positive impact, inspire local leaders to direct their energy in preparing and submitting (sometimes) long applications to multiple competitions. The gains tend to outpace the risks. These prizes vary in terms of recognition and sector targeted, but the following have drawn most attention.

The United Nations Public Service Awards rewards the creative achievements and contributions of public service institutions that lead to a more effective and responsive public administration in countries worldwide. According to the United Nations, "the Awards aim at discovering innovations in governance; reward excellence in the public sector; motivate public servants to further promote innovation; enhance professionalism in the public service; raise the image of public service; enhance trust in government; and collect and disseminate successful practices for possible replication." Several local governments have won the award. In 2015 the Basque Country and the city of Seoul were recognized.

The **"Water for Life" UN-Water Best Practices Award** promotes efforts to fulfill international commitments made on water and water-related issues through recognition of outstanding best practices that can ensure the long-term sustainable management of water resources and contribute to the achievement of internationally agreed goals and targets as contained in the Millennium Development Goals, Agenda 21, and the Johannesburg Plan of Implementation. The prize is awarded yearly in two categories, one in best water management practices and another one in best participatory, communication, awareness-raising, and education practices. In 2013 the winner was the city of Kumamoto—the largest city in Japan to supply all drinking water with completely natural groundwater.

Established in 1995, the **Dubai International Award for Best Practices** recognizes best practices with positive impact on improving the living environment. These practices need to have a demonstrable and tangible impact on improving people's quality of life and are socially, culturally, economically, and environmentally sustainable. The city of Lisbon (Portugal), the emirate of Dubai (UAE), the city of Linfen (China), the city of Pontevedra (Spain), and the city of Extrema (Brazil) are some of the winners in the most recent editions.

The International Transport Forum Award recognizes an innovation that has the potential to significantly improve the transport industry. The innovation could be based on technological change, operational change (e.g., business process), or organizational change (e.g., business model), or a combination of these. Milan was the 2014 winner in recognition of its sustainable mobility and traffic regulation policies.

The Green Stars Awards recognize individuals, organizations, governments, and companies who have demonstrated achievements in prevention, preparedness, and response to environmental emergencies. A joint initiative between Green Cross International, the UN Office for the Coordination of Humanitarian Affairs, and the UN Environment Program, the Green Star Awards seeks to increase awareness of environmental emergencies by drawing attention to efforts made to prevent, prepare for, and respond to such emergencies. The mayor of the Katsurao village, Masahide Matsumoto, located 25 km from the Fukushima nuclear power plant in Japan was one of the winners of the 2013 edition.

The World Green Building Council Government Leadership Awards acknowledges local government leadership in green building and highlights policies that maximize the opportunity for buildings to mitigate environmental impact. The biennial award program is held in partnership with Local Governments for Sustainability and UN-Habitat, and aims to encourage the uptake of high-quality policies and practices worldwide. Past winners include Christchurch, Vancouver, Seoul, and Abu Dhabi.

The World Habitat Awards were established in 1985 by the Building and Social Housing Foundation as part of its contribution to the United Nations' International Year of Shelter for the Homeless in 1987. Two awards are given annually to projects from the Global South as well as the North that provide practical, innovative, and sustainable solutions to current housing needs and are capable of being transferred or adapted for use elsewhere. Several local governments have won the award, including the city of Leinefelde-Worbis in former East Germany, which carried out an innovative and sustainable urban development program in the context of the dramatic changes in eastern Germany after reunification (2007).

The Lee Kuan Yew World City Prize is a biennial international award that honors outstanding achievements and contributions to the creation of sustainable urban communities around the world. The Prize seeks to recognize cities and their key leaders and organizations for displaying foresight, good governance, and innovation "in tackling the many urban challenges faced, to bring about social, economic and environmental benefits in a holistic way to their communities." It is co-organized by the Urban Redevelopment Authority of Singapore and the Centre for Liveable Cities. The cities of Bilbao, New York, and Suzhou have been laureates.

Co-hosted by United Cities and Local Governments, Metropolis, and Guangzhou Municipal Government, the **Guangzhou International Award for Urban Innovation** aims to reward innovations to improve the socioeconomic environments in cities and regions, promote sustainability, and hence advance the livelihood of their citizens. Presented biennially, the award recognizes outstanding innovative projects and practices in the public sector. The cities of Vienna, Seoul, Kocaeli, Lilongwe, and Vancouver have been recognized.

In 2009 the South Australian government established the annual **South Australian International Climate Change Leadership Award** to recognize and encourage leadership by regional governments in response to the challenges of climate change. Winners gain international recognition and have an area of South Australian urban forest named in their honor. Past winners include the governors of California, Quebec, São Paulo, and New York, and the first minister of Scotland.

Organized by C40 and Siemens, the **City Climate Leadership Awards** are granted in ten categories and provide recognition for cities that demonstrate climate action leadership. Five award categories are open exclusively to C40 cities: urban transportation, solid waste management, finance and economic development, carbon measurement and planning, and sustainable communities. Five other categories—green energy, adaptation and resilience, energy-efficient built environment, air quality, and intelligent city infrastructure—are open to C40 cities as well as cities in the "Green

City Index," a Siemens and Economist Intelligence Unit research project. Past winners include London, Taipei, and Melbourne.

The **Mayors Challenge** is an ideas competition that encourages cities to generate innovative ideas that solve major challenges and improve city life. Sponsored by Bloomberg Philanthropies, each year focuses on a different region. Past winners include Barcelona, Athens, and Stockholm. The winning cities are selected based on four criteria: their idea's vision and creativity, potential for impact, transferability, and viability of implementation.

External Policies by Subnational Governments

We live in an increasingly interconnected, interdependent world. The local and the global are intertwined. Local government cannot afford to be insular and inward-looking.
—LOCAL GOVERNMENT DECLARATION TO
THE UN WORLD SUMMIT ON SUSTAINABLE
DEVELOPMENT (2002)

Paradiplomacy versus Diplomacy

The distinction between paradiplomacy and diplomacy is not only detectable at the level of their conceptual underpinnings or on the obvious issue of agency but also with regard to practice too. The line can be drawn on at least four matters.

On the Issues

The foreign policy of subnational governments is generally built upon their domestic competencies. Most cities or states warehouse authority on issues such as health, education, transportation, culture, tourism, or public security, demanding that they are handled within the local–global spectrum. Subnational governments are concerned with what has traditionally been defined as "low policy" as distinct from "high policy" represented by the military security agenda. In other words, paradiplomacy represents the projection abroad of the domestic competencies of subnational governments. Indeed, subnational governments rarely venture into areas where provinces and cities have no jurisdiction (exclusive or shared), and they generally refrain from voicing an official view on major world conflicts, as this is generally the role of national capitals. Examples to the contrary are rare, but we could point to the resolution on China on humanitarian grounds, related to the events in Tiananmen Square in 1989, passed by the New England Governors and Eastern Canadian Premiers.

On Participation

State and local governments rely greatly on private-sector business, nonprofit institutions, and civic organizations to help promote and protect state and local interests in the international arena. For instance, São Paulo state signed in 2012 an agreement with the Federation of the Industries of the State of São Paulo (largest federation of its kind in Latin America) and another one with the Union for Housing (Secovi-SP), both entities with international experience, to boost synergies and effectiveness.

On the Modus Operandi

It is noteworthy how easily adaptable the practices, institutions, and discourses of substate diplomacy have proven, even in the most disparate contexts. Paradiplomacy differs from state diplomacy as it is not about pursuing a defined state interest in the international arena, but rather it is more pragmatic, targeted, and opportunistic—sometimes even experimental. Subnational partnerships have the advantage of being far more flexible than nation-to-nation agreements. This makes it easier to target specific needs across national borders, largely absent from foreign policy agendas of countries. One example is the improbable agreement on regional cooperation that the Sakhalin oblast signed with the Japanese prefecture of Hokkaido, despite the serious territorial dispute between Russia and Japan over the Kurile Islands, currently administrated by Sakhalin. Subnational agreements are also better suited to policy innovation and the tackling of tough issues like climate change, because the stakes are much lower than at the international level

(Moore 2013). Subnational governments need to be less ceremonial and symbolic because that political obligation can be taken care of by the federal governments.

On the Final Goal

Paradiplomacy is more oriented toward the needs of citizens, as its ultimate objective is to perfect the tools available to local governments for adoption of policies that benefit the welfare of the population. In countries that are not directly touched by international conflicts or terrorism and enjoy stable commercial ties with other nations, it is difficult for the population to see the immediate impact of their country's foreign policy on their individual welfare. That is not the case with paradiplomacy. In the words of Mike Bloomberg, then mayor of New York: "We're the level of government closest to the majority of the world's people. We're directly responsible for their well-being and their futures. So while nations talk, but too often drag their heels—cities act" (cited in Bouteligier 2014, 77).

Ensuring Policy Quality

Managing large international projects and programs has always been complex. In a government it is not always easy to match the broader strategic planning with how each project fits in it as part of a portfolio. Failure to think through generally translates into project delays, cost overruns, and other problems. To ensure the capacity of a subnational government to deliver, paradiplomats should be able to pursue a four-step track.

The first of these steps is to establish an umbrella foreign affairs policy. Governments should have a principle or protocol to guide decisions and achieve rational outcomes. Often referred to as "white papers" or "governmental plans," they guide actions toward those that are most likely to achieve a desired outcome. In most cases, these umbrella policies may include quantitative and/or qualitative targets (see Chapter 2, White Papers).

A second step is to distinguish between programs, projects, and actions. According to the Project Management Institute, "A *program* is a group of related *projects* managed in a coordinated manner to obtain benefits and control not available from managing them individually. Programs may include elements of related work outside of the scope of the discreet projects in the program. . ... Some projects within a program can deliver useful incremental benefits to the organization before the program itself has completed" (2006, 4). *Actions*, on the other hand, are merely temporary activities that may fulfill the aims of a specific project, such as receiving a foreign delegation, organizing an event, or taking part in a summit abroad.

The third step is to create criteria for initiating projects. Subnational foreign activities tend to be fairly reactive and experimental. It is very common that projects do not come into fruition due to a lack of resources, political will, or ability to conclude them. It is therefore important that foreign affairs governing bodies devise some measurable criteria before taking up a new project. These may include:

(1) alignment with the overall governmental priorities;
(2) expected gains to the government and other impacts;
(3) existing resources to pursue the project (includes financial resources, human resources, and political will);
(4) legal components (is there enough juridical basis to proceed?);
(5) internal performance legacy (what is the performance track record of the governmental agencies that will be involved?); and
(6) external performance legacy (what is the performance track record and the motivation of the foreign partners that will be involved?).

This latter criterion is explicitly used by the Wallonia government. They look at what they call "partner attitude or the willingness to cooperate" before taking steps forward.[1] As each criterion has a varying importance, weighting factors should be incorporated into the equation.

Finally, paradiplomats must adopt project management abilities. Governments that face high international demand should engage in a process of managing several related projects, with the intention of improving the government's performance. Project management is therefore the process of planning, organizing, motivating, and controlling resources, procedures, and protocols to achieve specific goals. In a traditional approach five components of a project can be distinguished: (1) initiation; (2) planning and design; (3) execution and construction; (4) monitoring and controlling systems; and (5) completion. There are many project management software systems on the market such as PRINCE2, MITP, AceProject, Tenrox, or Microsoft Project.

International Policies

With few exceptions, the subnational government public policies that generally have a foreign component include: (1) trade and investment; (2) environment and sustainable development; (3) tourism, culture, and sports; (4) social policies; (5) economic development, industry, infrastructure, and agriculture; (6) communication and branding; (7) credit and loans; (8) international development assistance; (9) lobbying; or (10) large events.

Trade and Investment

Virtually all subnational states have adopted policies on trade and investment. Foreign direct investment (FDI) may bring much-needed capital, technical know-how, organizational, managerial, and marketing practices, and global production networks, thus facilitating the process of economic growth and development in host cities or states. At a general level, in order for a city or state to be more attractive to investors (both local and foreign), there is a need to put in place measures to ensure an enabling environment by reducing so-called hassle costs. Over and above the creation of a business-friendly environment, it may be important for a potential host city or state to actively undertake investment-promotion policies to fill in information gaps or correct perception gaps that may hinder FDI inflows. A commonly used definition of investment promotion is "activities that disseminate information about, or attempt to create an image of the investment site and provide investment services for the prospective investors" (Wells and Wint 2000, 4). With the advent of economic globalization, regions and cities offer unlimited advantages that determine the issue of development. Michael Porter, for instance, argues that "internationally successful industries and industrial clusters frequently concentrate in a city or region, and the bases for advantage are often intensely local" (Porter 1990, 158). In the same vein, when assessing the location determinants of 19,444 investment projects in the EU-25 regions over the 2003–2008 period, Crescenzi et al. concluded that even if "country-level factors exert a significant influence on the location decision of MNCs in Europe," regional factors "become significantly more important when human capital is introduced into the model. Consequently, regions with a strong human capital endowment (proxied by the percentage of employed people with tertiary education) are highly attractive for foreign investments" (Crescenzi et al. 2013, 1080). The subnational level is therefore vital to understanding global FDI dynamics.

A transversal look at initiatives carried out at the subnational level indicates that any investment promotion strategy must be geared toward the following:

(1) image-building activities promoting the country and its regions and states as favorable locations for investment;

(2) investment-generating activities through direct targeting of firms by promotion of specific sectors and industries, and personal selling and establishing direct contacts with prospective investors;

(3) investment-service activities tailored to prospective and current investors' needs; and

(4) activities that raise the realization ratio (i.e., percentage of the FDI approvals translated into actual flows).

There are currently about 160 national investment promotion agencies and over 250 subnational ones.

Many subnational governments all over the world have also set up special agencies, most of them in the public domain, to implement trade promotion policies and provide support services to domestic enterprises. This is an area, however, where national and subnational foreign policies may overlap. Provincial policies that were previously considered domestic are now often subject to international scrutiny. For example, a wide array of provincial/state government subsidies and procurement policies could be considered trade-distorting under the North American Free Trade Agreement and the General Agreement on Tariffs and Trade Uruguay Round agreement. Canadian provinces and US states (and also many municipal jurisdictions) therefore have a direct interest in the terms and implementation of international agreements (Cohn and Smith 1996).

Subnational trade and investment promotion agencies have been able to embrace groundbreaking and creative investment promotion techniques. A good mapping of these initiatives is showcased at the annual fDi Innovation Awards. Entities that stood out from the crowd in recent years include Central Alberta, Invest São Paulo, Invest in Catalonia, Invest Victoria, and Business Birmingham. Central Alberta's investment agency, called Central Alberta: Access Prosperity, has corralled what it calls "a group of bright business leaders who are active in international trade, are members of established international networks and are proud promoters of trade and investment in Central Alberta" to be its international ambassadors. The investment agency for the Brazilian state of São Paulo sends carefully selected employees on exchange programs abroad, giving them an opportunity to learn from their peers. The agency has established cooperation agreements with investment promotion agencies worldwide such as the UK Trade & Investment, Korea Trade Promotion Corporation, Japan External Trade Organization, or the Portuguese Agency for Trade & Investment. Through the Global Partnership Program, Invest in Catalonia's staff carry out active searches for business partnership opportunities and provide matchmaking assistance to foreign companies in order to facilitate joint venture and mergers and acquisitions agreements with Catalonia-based companies. Invest Victoria has adopted a private-sector-style "sales force" approach to economic development, which has allowed for a quadrupling of the number of business development managers in the department, and every company with more than twenty employees in the state is allocated a business development manager. Finally, Business Birmingham offers well-tailored and flexible incentives to investors, with a particular eye for supporting job creation. The Mobile Investment Fund provides £2,000 ($3,200) per job created by overseas investors—one of the UK's most flexible investor funding schemes.

In the field of trade promotion, regional governments are also very active, especially in North America. Georgia, for instance, has put in place the Georgia Reaching Out Worldwide program that provides new export services and reduced fees for existing export services and is designed to increase Georgia's small business exports. Quebec, which played a major role in the negotiation of a Comprehensive Economic and Trade Agreement (CETA) between Canada and the European Union, is an even more striking example. As a full participant to the negotiations in the areas covered in whole or in part by its legislative powers, Quebec was one of the principal promoters of CETA and it was present in all rounds of negotiation which were held alternatively between Quebec and Brussels. As stated by then EU Trade Commissioner Karel De Gucht: "It was essential for the EU that areas falling under their [sic] jurisdiction of the Canadian Provinces and Territories could be put on the negotiating table and that the results would be later implemented by the provinces—because this is where a lot of the real potential for a deepened economic relationship lies."[2] In our globalized and complex world, trade will increasingly be dealt with at all levels of government, from supranational to local. The intrusiveness of foreign-trade agreements into areas of domestic policy space is already a reality as commitments may include areas of subnational jurisdiction such as alcohol, procurement, services, and natural resources, as well as health, labor, and environmental standards. In the United

States, the growing importance of trade issues to subnational governments is revealed by the intensity of foreign travelling. From early 2014 to mid-2015, U.S. governors have taken or scheduled about 80 international trips, generally focused on fostering exports or attracting businesses to their states. [3] For a discussion of a successful trade mission, see Box 3.1.

BOX 3.1 A Successful Trade Mission

A trade mission is an international trip by government officials and business people that is organized by agencies of national or provincial governments for the purpose of exploring international business opportunities. These missions are a significant component of government international business development efforts. The presence of a senior government official on a trade mission facilitates access to key economic and political decision-makers for participating firms and provides a greater public profile to business participants, helping them to network with the local business community. Trade missions generally follow a structured program which includes one or more countries, spending an average of one to three days in each city. The setting up of a trade mission is not, however, an easy business, and it is not always easy to ensure that successful business deals are made. In order to increase the likelihood of success, some steps should be taken.

Before Travelling

Research. Deep market research has to be conducted before the trade mission. The research provides important information to identify and analyze the market need, market size, and competition. What is the profile of the market in the countries to be visited? What are the opportunities and the hindrances? What sectors deserve more attention?

Pre-screening. Before travelling, identify a handful of potential business opportunities and organize Business-to-business (B2B) phone conferences. Companies should have a deep knowledge of one another before meeting physically.

Briefing. The organizing government should organize a market briefing session with everyone involved, laying out the strategy, the ultimate goals, and the logistical arrangements.

While Travelling

Events. Any trade mission is composed of several types of events, such as site visits, networking receptions, general presentations or one-on-one business matchmaking appointments. All of them play their own role, but the cherries of trade missions are the one-on-one business meetings between firms that have been screened and that have already established contact before the trip. Well-organized meetings with a couple of companies may provide a better outcome than large presentations to hundreds of them at the same time.

Government-to-Government Meetings. While firms may sometimes actually appreciate some distance from government participation, in some cultures it is important for local firms to absorb the idea that visiting companies travel with full governmental support. Meetings between high-level government representatives should be arranged to discuss the economic potential of a partnership been cities, states, or countries.

Local Support The organizing government should count on the expertise of its local representatives, its Consulate or Embassy, investment and trade promotion agencies, consulting companies, or chambers of commerce. Business is a universal language that speaks local dialects and follows local rules. To rely on who knows the local practices is of fundamental importance.

Media. Trade missions or any trip abroad led by governmental officials may raise eyebrows in the public and the media due to its costs and sometimes questionable results. It is very important therefore that a government is able to publicly announce concrete results such as a major business partnership. A government should question if it is the right timing to travel if no major achievements are expected to be made. A press adviser should also follow the trade mission to ensure that there is proper media coverage, which would raise the national and international profile of the companies taking part.

After Travelling

Follow-up Is Everything. Government trade agencies should keep close contact with participating companies and assist them to keep a fluid dialogue with foreign companies. Updated market research should also be provided.

Environment and Sustainable Development

Since the Rio Summit in 1992, when stakeholders were given a voice through the establishment of Major Groups by the United Nations, subnational governments all over the world have been fully involved in sustainable development processes and have demonstrated in a number of ways that their contribution is relevant to achieving the objectives of sustainable development. The concrete initiatives of subnational governments have significantly evolved over the past years and shown that the efforts and initiatives of a country become stronger when complemented by subnational governmental stakeholders.

This view was reinforced during the World Summit on Sustainable Development held in Johannesburg in 2002 ("Earth Summit"), where "representatives of the cities and local governments of the world" presented a forward-looking "Local Government Declaration."

Although the initiative had a tenuous outreach and was not regarded as a landmark document in the frame of the Earth Summit, it played its role in marking territory in favor of local governments. Ten years later, the situation changed. The World Summit of Federated States and Regions that took place in 2012 in Rio de Janeiro, on the eve of the UN Conference on Sustainable Development (Rio + 20) had a more substantial nature. It brought together more than 110 representatives of subnational entities from across the globe to showcase the mobilization of federated states, regions, provinces, and other subnational authorities around the issues of a green economy and sustainable development. Organized by the host state of Rio de Janeiro, in partnership with Regions United/FOGAR, the Network of Regional Governments for Sustainable Development (nrg4SD), and the Climate Group, it led to a declaration from subnational governments and authorities on the green economy in the context of sustainable development and poverty eradication.[4]

One month before Rio + 20, and in a symbolic fashion, UN Secretary General Ban Ki-moon received a high-level delegation of local and subnational government representatives, conveyed by UCLG and UN-Habitat, with support of Cities Alliance. The results of the meeting in New York were the basis for participation of UCLG in Rio + 20. Around ten city mayors (including those of New York, Lisbon, Istanbul, and Montreal) conveyed their expectations to Ban Ki-moon for a global and inclusive reform of the international governance framework for sustainable development. This includes all levels of governance from international to local. The UN Secretary General's gesture was highly symbolic, as it was an important signal that he agreed with a more substantial role for subnational governments.

After Rio + 20, the United Nations preserved its support for local governments. In 2014, on the occasion of the Climate Week hosted by Ban Ki-moon, a joint statement endorsed by member organizations from eight of the nine Major Groups highlighted that an agreement between national governments will not be enough to address the issue of climate change without the commitment of all nonstate actors at local and subnational levels. Each group bears a part of the global solution and their efforts will be essential. It was the first time that subnational governments addressed such a statement to the United Nations. During the Summit, Ban Ki-moon and the UN Special Envoy for Cities and Climate Change Michael R. Bloomberg announced also the launch of a global Compact of Mayors, a global coalition of mayors and city officials committed to reducing local greenhouse gas emissions, enhancing resilience to climate change and tracking their progress transparently, and of a Compact of States and Regions, the first-ever global reporting mechanism showcasing greenhouse gas reduction contributions by state and regional governments. At the 2015 Climate Week, they launched a partnership to ensure the coherence of the two initiatives and to explore synergies between the different levels of government.

In recent times, several other summits of local governments have been instrumental in conveying a strong message toward the deeper involvement of regional and city governments in global climate negotiations, persuading therefore the United Nations to recognize that local government is an equal sphere of government, vital to the success of sustainable development and good governance. These summits and gatherings of local governments are generally held immediately before global summits on the climate and environment of national countries. A good example of this is the World Summit of Regions for Climate held in Paris in October 2014. Organized by R20 Regions of Climate Action, it mobilized regions, cities, businesses, investors, and universities around a joint declaration calling for commitment to a series of concrete actions within the framework of the Paris 21st Conference of Parties to the United Nations Framework Convention on Climate Change (COP21) held in December 2015. It was in fact in Paris that the Climate Summit for Local Leaders took place with the participation of more than 440 mayors. Hosted by Anne Hidalgo, the mayor of Paris, and Michael Bloomberg, the UN Secretary General's Special Envoy for Cities and Climate Change, it was the largest global convening of mayors, governors, and local leaders focused on climate change. The final declaration reaffirmed their commitment to tackle climate disruption through the adoption of a handful of quantitative targets, including on urban greenhouse gas emissions reductions. In comparison, the COP21 final agreement, signed by UN member states in the same week, is less vocal about the importance of cities, even if their role is properly acknowledged: "Parties recognize that adaptation is a global challenge faced by all with *local, subnational*, national, regional and international dimensions, and that it is a key component of and makes a contribution to the long-term global response to climate change to protect people, livelihoods and ecosystems" (Art. 7(2), italics added).[5]

Several less high-profile events are also worth mentioning. Through the US Mayors' Climate Protection Agreement, an initiative launched in 2005 by Seattle Mayor Greg Nickels, more than 1,000 mayors in US cities have agreed to meet or beat Kyoto Protocol targets even though the US government never ratified the Protocol (Ljungkvist 2014, 48). In 2015, the UN Environmental Program calculated that city-level climate initiatives will deliver 1.08 gigatons of carbon emissions reductions by 2020.[6]

Ever since the Rio Summit in 1992, it has become clear that the means for subnational entities to provide tangible contributions to sustainable development are widespread and include, for instance, prioritizing government investment and spending in areas that stimulate the greening of economic sectors or establish sound regulatory frameworks (Box 3.2). According to UN-Habitat, cities and urban areas consume about 75% of the world's energy and produce up to 80% of its greenhouse gas emissions.

At the bilateral level, several other initiatives have left a positive mark. For instance, in 2008 Upper Austria and the German region of North Rhine-Westphalia founded the so-called CO2 Alliance for regions with a strong focus on industrial and hence energy-intensive products. This alliance now includes eleven member regions from Austria, Germany, and the Netherlands. In another example, Kumamoto in Japan and Heidelberg in Germany both rely on groundwater as their sole source of water and the two cities have worked together on water conservation programs since 1995. Their sister-city tie was established in 1992 on the basis

BOX 3.2 Local Governments' Contribution to Sustainable Development: A View from the nrg4SD

How Subnational Governments May Contribute to Sustainable Development: A View from the nrg4SD

Establishing Sound Regulatory Frameworks. Subnational governments have regulatory competencies essential to strengthen their respective territories from the social, economic, and environmental point of view. This leads them to elaborate general economic and sustainable development strategies, as well as thematic ones on climate change, waste, or social inclusion for instance. Subnational governments have long-track experience in elaborating these strategies in close collaboration with other levels of government and with actors from academia, civil society, or the private sector.

Prioritizing Government Investment and Spending in Areas that Stimulate the Greening of Economic Sectors. Thanks to their regulatory, budgetary, and often fiscal competences, subnational governments can steer public investment to green a wide range of economic sectors and also influence the market. Competencies in the area of public procurement and public provision of services allow subnational governments to incorporate not only economic but also environmental and social parameters in this field. This can set market trends and accelerate the market penetration of certain sustainable services and goods.

Limiting Government Spending in Areas that Deplete Natural Capital. Because of the above-mentioned competencies, subnational governments can help national governments phase out subsidies with negative impacts on sustainable development or on the profitability of green investments. Also, a detailed knowledge of their respective communities is an asset in structuring subsidy reforms that do not entail negative consequences to the poorest communities.

Employing Taxes and Market-Based Instruments to Promote Green Investment and Innovation. Subnational governments are able to influence the private-sector behavior through financial incentives and disincentives and green taxation. They can also contribute significantly to internalizing the value of ecosystem services into the economy. Often they do provide incentives to the private sector and forge partnerships with it to accelerate the innovation, development, and diffusion of environmentally sound technologies. These mechanisms can encourage long-term investments in infrastructures—for instance, in the fields of sustainable mobility and renewable and efficient energy systems—that otherwise would not be viable. At the opposite end, subnational governments can discourage unsustainable industries and practices by means of restrictive authorization policies and heavier taxation.

Investing in Capacity Building, Training, and Education. Subnational governments, like national governments, are well positioned to tap into the reservoirs of engineering and manufacturing firms, as well as academic and research institutions, that are operating within their territories to encourage the sharing of scientific and technological skills and know-how with developing countries. Moreover, subnational governments can enter into cooperation agreements with private-sector companies that hold green or low-carbon technology patents and proprietary rights that can be offered to developing countries.

Awareness Raising. Subnational governments constitute social cultural entities. Their closeness to citizens and experience in working directly with other stakeholders creates a pivotal position for raising awareness, providing public information on the environmental and social costs of certain practices, giving expert advice and counselling, and involving a range of stakeholders in the complex process of changing behaviors and production and consumption patterns.

of this shared concern (Jain 2005, 92). Finally, it is important to highlight the partnership between Quebec and California that led to the first transborder carbon market in North America. In 2008, Quebec began developing a cap-and-trade system for greenhouse gas emissions—commonly referred to as the carbon market—which ended up kicking off its trade operations in January 2013. One year later, Quebec's market was linked with a similar system set up by California, creating the first transborder carbon market in North America.

Tourism, Culture, and Sports

Most regional governments have the mandate to contribute to the sustainable development of tourism and to increase economic return, employment, and welfare in their territories. Generally through an agency or a department/ministry, they promote the city or region's tourism industry, provide information to tourists on facilities, infrastructures, and services, initiate action to promote cooperation with other tourism agencies, conduct research into market trends and market opportunities, and disseminate such information and other relevant statistical data on the city or region. Flanders, for example, established in the early 1980s the Flanders Tourism Promotion Agency (it changed its name to Tourism Flanders-Brussels in 2004), whereas São Paulo state has a Secretariat of Tourism and Maharashtra created the Tourism Development Corporation (MTDC). With no exception, these subnational tourism-promotion agencies develop major campaigns and strategies to attract more tourists. Maharashtra, for instance, has since 2013 annually organized the event "Diwali at Times Square." Thousands of people gather in New York to celebrate Diwali, the most significant festival for Indians. It is also an opportunity to showcase Maharashtra's "rich culture, cuisine, pristine beaches, historical and natural heritage preserved for thousands of years" in the words of Jagdish Patil, Managing Director of MTDC.[7]

Connected to tourism comes culture and sports. Several subnational governments share the ambition to strengthen cohesion and cultural diversity in their cities, while improving public access to culture and the arts. In addition, they seek to promote cultural exchanges and create favorable conditions for those engaged in the culture sector, cultural institutions, and cultural organizations. They may also be active in promoting their creative art abroad. This is so key for some regional governments, such as Scotland, that the administration has a Cabinet Secretary for Culture and External Affairs that aims to "raise the profile of Scotland at home and abroad, and ensure that as many people as possible in Scotland and overseas are able to benefit from, be inspired by and enjoy the very best of Scotland's creative, cultural and historic wealth."[8] Even states that are less sensitive to the issue of cultural independence and distinctiveness have strong cultural policies. For instance, Ontario's Ministry of Tourism, Culture and Sport has been very active in enhancing the contribution of cultural industries, arts, heritage, archaeology, libraries, museums, and cultural agencies to Ontario's quality of life. Quebec has also advanced its cultural policies internationally. It was a key actor in the diplomatic strategy surrounding the adoption by UNESCO of the Convention on the Protection and Promotion of the Diversity of Cultural Expressions in 2005. In fact, the Canadian province was one of the first to advocate the creation of an international legal instrument that would recognize the rights of the states and governments to freely elaborate their cultural policies. At the end, it was one of the first to adopt the convention after its adoption by UNESCO.

Multilateral organizations composed of subnational states have also spearheaded the adoption of cultural policies. For instance, the Agenda 21 for Culture, a document adopted in 2004 to promote the role of culture in local policies is championed by UCLG. It starts from the idea that culture makes a great contribution to human development, because it promotes values like creativity, diversity, memory, or rituality, all of them increasingly necessary for any human being to widen his or her freedoms.

Social Policies

This is probably the area where subnational entities have more leverage. Health, education, and social development usually fall into the portfolio of cities or regions. Let us first pause on education. In an interconnected world, local governments are adopting increasingly international education policies that aim to build intercultural competency, knowledge of the international community, and a sense of global citizenship among students and education professionals. Some well-known initiatives are student exchanges, teacher exchanges, school twinning, and second-language learning programs. The benefits of international education initiatives go beyond the personal growth and skills obtained by individual participants. These initiatives also have positive cultural, political, academic and economic impacts on our society (Box 3.3). Exchange programs, for instance, are so popular in Australia, mainly at the subnational level, that the national government had to issue the *National Guidelines for the Operation of International Secondary Student Exchange Programs in Australia* that need to be complied with by all federated states. In Canada, most provinces have adopted exchange programs. Generally, programs give students the opportunity to improve their second-language skills through linguistic and cultural immersion. Participants in these exchanges alternate between hosting a partner from another culture in their home and school, and travelling to live with their partner and study at their partner's school. In Alberta, students can participate in an exchange in Germany, Japan, Spain, Mexico, or Quebec (Box 3.3). Similar options are offered by Quebec, Ontario, Manitoba, or British Columbia.

Another variant of foreign policy at the subnational level is healthcare. Even if sovereign nations are pressed to include new issues into their foreign affairs portfolio, such as healthcare, and they may have the capacity to muster funds to do so, subnational governments have an intense familiarity with these issues as the provision of human services is generally carried out by municipal and state governments. In the United States alone, combined

BOX 3.3 The Benefits of International Education According to the Government of Alberta, Canada

Cultural	By learning about different cultures and languages, Albertans not only develop a better sense of cultural understanding, they also gain greater insight into their own culture and way of life.
Political	Alberta's and Canada's ability to engage effectively with the international community and exert positive influence in world affairs requires knowledge about the culture, conditions, and aspirations of citizens in other countries.
Academic	School-based international education initiatives expose students to social and cultural differences, new educational methods and systems, and unique global perspectives. They also allow students that are studying a second or third language to interact with native speakers.
Economic	International education initiatives are critical in today's economy. They contribute to the development of an internationally and interculturally competent labor force within Alberta. In addition, the cross-border relationships that are formed during a student exchange, for instance, are sometimes life-long relationships that may become the foundation of future economic transactions or business collaborations.

Source: https://archive.education.alberta.ca/students/internationaleducation/.

healthcare expenditures by state and local governments increased by an inflation-adjusted 262% between 1987 and 2013.[9]

In November 2014, G20 leaders met in Australia and issued a call for global action to tackle the Ebola outbreak in Africa, urging action by governments that had not yet made a contribution to supplying aid, medical equipment, and personnel. They also urged greater efforts on the part of researchers, regulators, and pharmaceutical companies to develop safe, effective, and affordable diagnostics, vaccines, and treatments. But in the same month, it was a research center managed and funded by the São Paulo state government, the Butantan Institute, that announced an agreement with the US National Institutes of Health to develop a serum to fight Ebola. And a month before, the Scottish government donated £300,000 worth of medical equipment and supplies to help fight the spread of Ebola in the affected countries of West Africa.

State governments have also adopted social impact bonds (SIBs), an innovative vehicle to procure public services in a way that fosters efficiency, innovation, and measurable social impact. In an SIB structure, a public authority buys a "desired outcome," such as the reduction of reoffending rates or increases in school attainment, from a partnership of service delivery organizations and private investors, where the former deliver the contractual services and the latter provide the necessary capital. Investors are rewarded for the risk they take by the commissioning public authority, which pays their investment back (plus a pre-agreed return) as and if independently measured outcomes are achieved. In 2013, New York's Governor Andrew Cuomo announced the launch of the first state-led SIB in the United States, and service delivery has begun. Through this project 2,000 formerly incarcerated individuals who are at high risk of reoffending will be connected with the Center for Employment Opportunities to receive evidence-based employment training and job placement services over four years. Individual and institutional investors invested $13.5 million in this project and will be repaid based on the program's impact on recidivism and employment. In 2014, Massachusetts also announced a $27 million, seven-year SIB aimed at reducing the number of at-risk former inmates who go back to prison or jail. At that time, it was the country's largest investment in this new type of funding. As SIBs are a new feature in modern governance, states in different parts of the world have established contact among themselves to enable the exchange of best practices.

Economic Development, Industry, Infrastructure, and Agriculture

A large segment of the subnational foreign policy of a city or state may be accounted for by actions toward sustainable economic development. Economic opportunities create the basis for population growth, which itself is an economic stimulus to industry sectors and assists in defraying the costs of infrastructure development. A region's economic opportunities and livability advantages combine to make it a place that attracts and retains people to live and work. Subnational entities have put in place public policies to ensure that their local economies demonstrate growth, employment, and equitable opportunities.

Local governments are tasked with ensuring that the right environmental framework and initiatives are put in place to foster economic growth and job creation in the provinces and cities. The old paradigm of regional policy centered on top-down decision making by the central government or external agencies, while largely ignoring mixed, integrated, and/or bottom-up approaches, is definitely out-of-fashion (Vanthillo and Verhetsel 2012). Resulting from a diverse mix of social, cultural, economic, and political factors, there is a growing trend of decentralization of different competencies related to development fields (e.g., research policy, innovation policy, and regional development policy) in European countries (OECD 2010). Where initially the regional level adapted national policies and instruments, individual regions in various member states now have strengthened capabilities for tailor-made policies, and they have more weight in regional programming and policy coordination (Bachtler et al. 2003; Lagendijk 2011). In this context, the concept of "smart specialization" has gained significant political and analytical importance. According to the European Commission, smart specialization strategies lead to a more comprehensive set of development objectives: "tapping under-utilized potential in all regions for enhancing regional competitiveness" (OECD 2009). Rather than focusing on the dichotomy between convergence and competitiveness, these strategies enhance greater regional specialization and cooperation. In 2013, the European Union launched the Vanguard Initiative New Growth through Smart Specialization, an initiative that is driven by a regional political commitment to use smart specialization strategy for boosting new growth through bottom-up entrepreneurial innovation and industrial renewal in European priority areas. The initiative counts with the participation of economically strong regions such as Baden-Württemberg, Rhône-Alpes, Lombardy, Flanders, or Skåne.

Agriculture may also represent considerable weight in the economic structure of a subnational unit (more of states and less of cities) and therefore most regional governments have governing bodies on agriculture to develop and execute state government policy on farming, agriculture, forestry, and food. They aim to meet the needs of farmers and ranchers, promote agricultural trade and production, work to assure food safety, protect natural resources, foster rural communities, and end hunger. All this has an obvious international component as food and commodities supplies are integrated in global chains of production, distribution, and consumption. To tap on global fluxes, Georgia's Department of Agriculture works together with the state's Office of International Trade to market Georgia's agriculture products both domestically and abroad. Food and agricultural production need to work side by side with innovations in process technologies and the development of new products with higher value. This led the São Paulo Secretariat of Agriculture and Food Supply and the German Fraunhofer Institute for Process Engineering and Packaging to install in 2014 a Fraunhofer Project Center for Innovation in Food and Bioresources in the state with the mission to establish an international culture of research and development that is driven by innovation, with the aim of increasing the value added across integrated food and bioenergy production chains. Modern agriculture policies and practices, as the examples from Georgia and São Paulo indicate, have a strong international outlook.

This international component of food production is also detectable in the agendas of subnational multilateral forums. In 2003, Upper Austria, along with Tuscany, founded the European GMO-Free Regions Network. The focus of the Network is the production of GMO-free products and regional co- and self-determination in the use of GM technology in the field of agriculture. Since its foundation around sixty other regions from Croatia, Germany, Greece, Italy, France, Spain, the United Kingdom, and all other Austrian federal states have joined the network.

Communication and Branding

In today's competitive and marketing savvy world, branding is accepted as a fundamental strategy for competitive advantage and success. And countries, like companies, are beginning to use branding to help them market themselves for investment, tourism, and exports. The burden of winning the hearts and minds of foreign publics can no longer solely fall on the national government. Public diplomacy must be pursued at multiple levels, with subnational participation being most effective in building mutual understanding and relationships (Wang 2006).

China has been successful in using branding and public diplomacy at the subnational level. In a 2013 article in the *People's Daily* by Cai Mingzhao, Director of the State Council Information Office and vice-director of the Chinese Communist Party's External Publicity Office, two important players in China's public diplomacy, he suggested that the role of subnational public diplomacy in China should be expanded. In recent years, the Chinese government has encouraged provincial and city governments, in particular those in the country's western border areas, to reach out to audiences in neighboring countries with whom they are more familiar than the central government in Beijing and where ethnic minorities on both sides of the border often share language and customs, facilitating cultural exchanges. Local authorities in Yunnan, Guangxi, and Xinjiang gladly seized this opportunity to raise their profile, boost tourism, and attract foreign investment, and they are now actively involved in promoting China via local-level cultural, media, and educational cooperation projects in Southeast and Central Asia (d'Hooghe 2013).

In North America, the Massachusetts Office of Travel and Tourism contracts with destination marketing agencies in its six primary markets (United Kingdom, Germany, Japan, France, Italy, and Ireland) to implement comprehensive promotional programs. Marketing and public relations activities include, but are not limited to, ongoing proactive travel trade outreach, international travel trade and consumer shows, destination training programs, cooperative marketing with in-market travel partners, familiarization tours, media relations, and consumer promotions.

Scotland is also a very interesting case as far a public diplomacy is concerned. In July 2002 First Minister Alex Salmond announced a long-term strategy to strengthen Scotland's international image, and he outlined the Scottish government's plans for promoting Scotland more effectively overseas. Strengthening Scotland's international image was considered a priority by the First Minister in order to bring economic, social, and cultural benefits. The policy tied together internal agencies that had an international presence—Visit Scotland, Scottish Development International, and British Council Scotland (Criekemans 2010c, 56).

Credit and Loans

Loans are agreements between a bank and its clients, whereby clients agree to return to the bank, within a specified period, the sum of money borrowed for a specific purpose, plus interest, fees, and other expenses agreed between the parties. If internal legislation allows, subnational governments can access external financial resources, which includes multilateral development loans and bilateral loans. The first is normally made available by development banks, such as the World Bank, Corporación Andina de Fomento, the European Investment Bank, African Development Bank, Asian Development Bank, or the IDB. They are customarily related to loans for specific projects. Indeed, there are many large public-sector projects which require long-term financing. This financing is often not available, or affordable, through the market. A key benefit of concessional loans is the ability to mobilize large levels of upfront financial resources, with affordable terms and conditions, for these projects. Examples may include an education reform program, an electricity distribution and transmission program, or a citizen security program. Besides offering lower rates than the private sector, these development banks can offer their advice and experience in areas like the environment and infrastructure.

Some countries are also in the business of offering concessional loans, mainly focused on high-return public-sector projects which have a high impact on growth and development, and where there is a funding gap. Countries such as Japan (Japan International Cooperation Agency, JICA), Germany (KfW), France (French Development Agency, AFD), Brazil (Brazilian Development Bank, BNDES), or China (China Development Bank) provide concessional loans with potential economic benefits. They can offer advantages to donors in terms of recycling finance and leveraging additional finance; and to recipients in terms of offering a less expensive option to market loans. But for concessional loans to be effective, donors need to have the appropriate skills and expertise to ensure that loan finance works properly and is used appropriately, so that projects are fully implemented and achieve the desired development impact; that the debt sustainability of the recipient country is not threatened; and that the loan is repaid. Indeed, a key drawback of loans is the risk that they can lead to an accumulation of debt which, if not managed well, can threaten the future stability of vulnerable economies.

Most subnational states and a few cities have ample experience with foreign credit and loans. According to official sources, from 2001 to 2014 the State of São Paulo took R$8.8 billion in loans from world agencies to invest in infrastructure, sanitation, and healthcare projects. In 2010, the city of Rio de Janeiro, also in Brazil, took one of the highest loans by the World Bank to a city, worth US$1.045 billion, to improve the quality and coverage of social services, Mayor Eduardo Paes declared on the occasion that "this program with the World Bank, the first one if its kind with a municipality, is a giant step in that direction, supporting the City's investment program and bringing with it the knowledge and best practices from abroad."[10] Foreign development institutions are not only capital providers but also serve as reservoirs of international expertise.

International Development Assistance

A handful of regional governments have also entered into international development practices to "contribute to the closing of the North–South gap, to promote sustainable development in the South and to help create a just, peaceful and prosperous international community" (Flanders) or to "support the solidarity efforts of international cooperation organizations working in partnership with communities in the most disadvantaged countries of Francophone Africa, Latin America and the West Indies" (Quebec). Although these governments may be led by altruistic principles, the international community is aware that development assistance plays a fundamental role in driving the legitimacy of the source, both domestically and internationally. To put it simply, development assistance increases the global status of the donor. The regional governments that stand out in this matter are Flanders, Quebec, Scotland, Catalonia, and the Japanese provinces.

Flanders has pursued its own development cooperation policy since the early 1990s, when it created a Program for Central and Eastern Europe that tagged over €10 million to support the transition process in Central and Eastern Europe and the development of strong and healthy market economies (Criekemans 2010c, 51–52). From 2006 to 2014, development assistance was carried out by the Flanders International Cooperation Agency (FICA) which had the duty to manage bilateral cooperation with partners in the South, to develop initiatives toward awareness raising, and develop programs on emergency relief and humanitarian aid. In 2014, an internal restructuring led to FICA's dissolution and the integration of its staff and mission into the Department of Foreign Affairs.

In Quebec, the Quebec International Development Program aims to support the solidarity efforts of international cooperation organizations working in partnership with communities in the most disadvantaged countries of Francophone Africa, Latin America, and the West Indies. The first component of the program provides support to initiatives focusing on Human Rights resource training and aimed at strengthening governance capabilities in response to basic needs, whereas the second provides funding for emergency initiatives undertaken by Quebec-based international cooperation organizations in response to natural disasters and major humanitarian crises in disadvantaged countries.

The International Development Policy of the Scottish Government focused on a smaller number of identified developing countries to provide support to those in greatest need (mostly in Africa and South Asia), working through organizations in Scotland and in line with priorities of the respective countries. The delivery of the policy is supported by an International Development Fund (approximately £9 million a year). Besides this, Scotland contributes to UK efforts through the Department for International Development. Development assistance in the case of Scotland plays a fundamental role in driving the legitimacy of its autonomist agenda, both domestically and internationally (Alexander 2014).

Catalonia's development initiatives are carried out by the Catalan Agency for Development Cooperation. Although the agency is long-serving and has an interesting track record of development practices in Africa and Latin America, Catalonia's overall Official Development Assistante (ODA) disbursements have declined, from €63 million in 2008 to €19 million in 2012. Japanese subnational governments are also involved with ODA in two ways: either funded from their own budget and initiated and managed independently by them or working in partnership with the national government's ODA agencies. In the early 2000s, each prefecture carried out about ten projects annually, either through their own resources or in cooperation with central government ODA projects (Jain 2005, 98).

Lobbying

Regions may also engage in lobbying activities to influence international decisions that are strictly taken by sovereign nations in areas that do not fall into their local competencies, but that may have an impact at the local level. In 2013 and 2014, the Japanese province of Mie, led by its Governor Eikei Suzuki has strongly lobbied for a short-stay Visa Waiver program between Japan and Brazil and has persuaded Brazilian governors and Japanese federal and local authorities to embrace the cause. The reasons are simple: Brazil hosts the largest Japanese diaspora in the world and social and economic travelling between both countries needed to be facilitated. When in 2014 both countries announced the introduction of multiple-entry visas as an important first step to a possible exemption, he sent letters to various Brazilian governors to thank them for their support.

The bulk of lobbying initiatives from subnational governments is, however, on security and international human rights issues. Although these concerns are mostly associated with federal and not with local politics, subnational governments often incorporate the voice of their constituencies and take them up to higher platforms. An often mentioned example is a US case from the 1990s, where twenty local and state governments adopted international human rights laws targeting Burma (despite the fact that the US federal government had not done so), and economic sanctions were imposed by those subnational governments on companies that traded with Burma. This particular case eventually reached the US Supreme Court and was declared unconstitutional (Ljungkvist 2014, 41). Also in the United States, in June 2011 the US Conference of Mayors (USCM) passed a resolution urging President Obama and Congress to speed up the ending of the wars in Afghanistan and Iraq. As then Los Angeles mayor Antonio Villaraigosa stated in assuming the presidency of USCM: "It's time to bring our investments back home: We can't be building roads and bridges in Baghdad and Kandahar and not in Baltimore and Kansas City" (cited in Bouteligier 2014, 77).

Some of these lobbying exercises have questionable weight and may only serve to market the person who voices them, but the majority of them, primarily when they represent a large group of cities and states, may very well have the capacity to mold international agendas.

Large Events

Olympic Games, World Championships, Universal Exhibitions—all these are large events that serve to boost the economy and the infrastructure, to promote tourism, and to market a city, state, or country, and thus can be conceived as foreign policy tools. Aware of their impact, cities and states—in association with their countries—take bold steps to secure the possibility of hosting them. The impacts of the Olympic Games in Barcelona (1992), Atlanta (1996), or Sydney (2000), or the Universal Exhibitions of Lisbon (1998) or Shanghai (2010) were felt not only at the national level but particularly at the local.

Shanghai was China's first world's fair and the largest in history by size, attendance, and international participants. It not only attempted to promote China as a central player in the twenty-first century but also was very successful in showcasing the largest Chinese city as a global financial center and a major global player. It was a good opportunity for the city to transfer its economic structure from industrialization to postindustrialization, to revive the inner city, and to integrate both sides of the Huangpu River that cross the city. The Milan and Dubai World Exhibitions in 2015 and 2020, respectively, have the similar purpose to showcase the cities as global powerhouses.

The case of Barcelona is even more palpable. Before 1992, Barcelona was relatively unknown despite its rich history and first-class architecture. But the "Barcelona model" for organizing the Olympics was quite successful. It was based on large urban projects combined with small operations in the neighborhoods, the decentralization of the city into ten districts, and the modernization of public administration. The Olympics marked the opportunity to project the city as another great European city. Strategic planning has been used as an instrument of city marketing all over the world, and even today, the Barcelona Olympics is regarded as a successful case study (Tomás 2005, 54; Kenneth and Moragas 2006). The Games were indeed widely heralded as a success in the mass media, and the keys to that success have been researched and documented perhaps more than for any other Games in Olympic history (see Moragas and Botella 1995, 2002). The organizational model adopted in Barcelona affected International Olympic Committee policy (Felli 2002, 65–76) and was highly influential in the staging of the Sydney 2000 Olympic Games (Cashman and Hughes 1999) and other mega-sports events. The Olympics were also key to promoting Catalonia's identity and to injecting fuel into regional claims for more autonomy. The overriding objective for the Generalitat was the "Catalanization" of the Barcelona Games (Botella 1995, 139–148). Miquel Botella described the role of the Generalitat as participatory, seeking representation and exposure at an international level for Catalan national identity.

If in 1992 attempts were made to position Barcelona as the economic hub of Southern Europe, a vibrant, cosmopolitan city with a rich cultural heritage (Kennett and Moragas 2006), Rio de Janeiro's local authorities (the city and state) similarly wanted to use the 2016 Games as a catapult for the city's economic performance and urban revitalization. Over the last generations, a large number of urban projects were announced by local politicians and expectations were raised, but most of them were never enacted due to juridical or financial hindrances. Local authorities argued that the Olympics (and the 2014 World Cup) were used to actually erect some of these never-implemented projects, such as the Bus Rapid Transit lines, water storage and flood prevention infrastructure, and the regeneration of the Port area. By investing in urban requalification and hosting the Olympics, Rio de Janeiro wished to market itself globally.

Although there is a causal relation between the size of the events and its global impact, smaller events are also pursued by mayors and governors. For instance, Mayor Rahm Emanuel's Chicago administration has tried to heighten the city's global visibility by hosting such events as the NATO Summit and the World Summit of Nobel Peace Laureates, both in 2012, and the US–China Joint Commission on Commerce and Trade in 2014.

4

Case Studies

Subnational Governments in Action

A stronger statement is that all activity is local and that the global only comes into being through the integration of numerous locally based actors and activities.

(BEAUREGARD 1995, 242)

Paradiplomacy has quietly turned into a global phenomenon. Certainly local governments step into the world for different reasons and equipped with dissimilar resources. Surely the effectiveness of their actions and the public acknowledgment of their successes and failures varies widely. But currently hardly any large-size city or state is completely immune to global forces and opportunities. To show the universality of local foreign policy, I will dissect twenty cases from Africa (1), Asia, (3), Europe (6), Latin America (3), North America (5), and Oceania (2).

Azores (Portugal)

Paradiplomacy is a fairly unknown issue in Portugal, and there is virtually no public debate on the topic. The small and centralized nature of the country may explain why Portuguese cities and regions are internationally shy. Yet, there are some examples of foreign policy actions coming from the cities of Oporto and Lisbon and the only two autonomous regions of Portugal: the archipelagos of Madeira and the Azores. The Portuguese Constitution makes things easy. Article 227(u) states that the autonomous regions have the power to "cooperate with foreign regional bodies and to participate in organizations with the purpose to foster inter-regional dialogue and cooperation, all in accordance with the guidelines set out by the bodies that exercise sovereign power and are responsible for foreign affairs" and they are also entitled to participate in EU procedures when the topics under consideration fall into their areas of competence (Art. 227(x)).

The autonomous region of the Azores—composed of nine volcanic islands situated in the North Atlantic Ocean with a population of 250,000—has exercised its constitutional right to conduct foreign affairs and it presents the best example of Portuguese paradiplomatic efforts. The external affairs guidelines of each regional government derives from its governmental plan (*programa do governo regional*), which needs to be submitted to the Azorean Legislative Assembly at the beginning of the term. The latest one dates from November 2012 and carries thirteen pages entirely devoted to external relations establishing policy objectives in the areas of external cooperation, the European Union, diaspora, and defense. The body responsible for putting in place this mission is the Under-Secretariat for External Affairs (*Subsecretaria Regional da Presidência para as Relações Externas*) within the presidency of the government. Under its supervision, there is also the Regional Directorate of Communities (*Direção Regional das Comunidades*), which deals directly with emigration, immigration, and Azorean communities abroad. Farther away, but also with foreign policy competences, lays the vice-presidency for Employment and Business Competitiveness (*vice-presidência do Governo, Emprego e Competitividade Empresarial*), which handles trade and investment-related issues, along with the EU structural funds and the cohesion fund (the financial instruments of the European Union's regional policy, which are intended to narrow the development disparities among regions and member states). Other Secretariats responsible for tourism and transportation; agriculture and environment; or ocean, science, and technology also participate in international activities and EU funding. The foreign affairs team includes also the president's adviser on external relations (*assessor do presidente para as relações externas*) and the Azores's representative in Brussels (*conselheiro regional*), who is stationed in the office of the Portuguese Permanent Representation to the European Union. Around fifty people work in the Under-Secretariat and the Directorate of Communities alone.

The region's external priorities on European issues, diaspora (over 1 million people, including second and third generations), and international cooperation are carried out both bilaterally and multilaterally. Under the first approach, the Azores has signed cooperation agreements with the states that host the largest Azorean communities, such as the Brazilian southern states of Rio Grande do Sul and Santa Catarina, or the US states of Massachusetts, California, and Rhode Island, with the purpose of establishing cultural, touristic, and economic exchanges. The Integrated Network for Citizen Support (*Rede Integrada de Apoio ao Cidadão*, RIAC) is a network of centers (most of them located in the archipelago) created and operated by the Government of the Azores that provide administrative support to the population. It is actually interesting to underline that the Azores has even been able to establish RIAC stations in the United States and Canada. The US and Canadian stations are located in Fall River, Massachusetts, and in Toronto—the vital centers of Azorean diaspora in both countries. The importance of the diaspora for Azorean external affairs has been declared openly on several occasions. The Regional Director of Communities of the autonomous government, Paulo Teves, stated in July 2014 that "thousands of Azorean and their descendants are our best ambassadors. As they are strategic partners in culture and economy, they contribute to the international visibility of the region and for the development of all the islands."[1] In fact, the Azores has a compelling policy to support its diaspora, earmarking specific resources in the regional budget for that mission. The government currently co-finances fourteen Azorean Houses (*Casas dos Açores*) located in Brazil, Canada, United States, Uruguay, and mainland Portugal that operate not only as local centers of Azorean culture but may also serve as stepping stones for new business opportunities and political lobbying. In 1997, a World Council of Azorean Houses (*Conselho Mundial das Casas dos Açores*) was established to streamline the Azorean voice globally. The regional government also supports financially institutions that have social programs that cover lower-class Azoreans living in the United States and Canada, provides teaching material to Portuguese-speaking schools abroad, and provides financial assistance to the only Portuguese-speaking school in Bermuda, where there is a large Azorean diaspora.

Bilateral relations are also conducted by the region for geographical and defense reasons. With Cape Verde, an independent archipelago off the coast of Africa, relations are mostly inspired by their common language and history, as well as their location in the Atlantic Ocean. Agreements have been signed, business and trade is increasing in importance, and official presidential visits are frequently organized. But the most challenging bilateral commitment is with the United States and it involves defense. The archipelago hosts the Lajes Air Field, used since the end of World War II by the UN Air Force. Sitting in a strategic location midway between North America and Europe, it accounts for 7–8 percent of the regional GDP (the base is the second largest employer on the Terceira Island). Yet, in December 2012, citing budgetary constraints, the Pentagon announced it was planning a major downsizing in US military operations and personnel at Lajes Air Field. Plans were called for a cut in the workforce of 1,100 US and Portuguese personnel to about half, turning the alarm on in the regional government and putting its foreign policy to test. Without diplomatic ammunition to use, as official bilateral relations are conducted directly between Portugal and the United States, the Azores relied on its own set of arguments— its diaspora—to stall the decision. And it succeeded. In December 2013, the US Congress voted to pass the 2014 National Defense Authorization Act (NDAA), which contained a provision on the Lajes Base allowing it to keep its full capacity until a reevaluation process toward the restructuring of the US military presence in Europe is completed (called the European Infrastructure Consolidation Assessment). Soon after, President Barack Obama signed the annual defense policy bill, which earmarked resources to operate the base in its normal capacity. The legislative process was repeated one year later in the enactment of the 2015 NDAA. According to interviews with the regional government, they believed that they had to act quickly, even if defense is a sensitive sovereign issue, as "the decision would have a significant economic impact over job losses on the island and in the economy of the archipelago."[2] Apparently, there was collaborative work between the archipelago and the central government, but it was amply acknowledged by the Portuguese press that the Azorean government's intervention was instrumental to passing the provision. The regional government called upon their diaspora in the United States (mostly in California, Massachusetts, and Rhode Island) and primarily to the congressmen that represent them "to act on behalf of the Azorean people." Although the European Infrastructure Consolidation Assessment was presented in early 2015 and the initial plan to downsize the Lajes Base was resumed, this episode is paradigmatic for several reasons: it showcases the vital role that could be played by local foreign policies and its positive impact on the population; it makes the case for the importance of encouraging effective collaborative work between paradiplomacy and diplomacy; it provides one of the rare examples of a regional government participating directly in defense issues; and illustrates the power of the diaspora to mold decisions in foreign countries.

Azorean interests are also advanced through participation in multilateral arrangements such as the European Union's Committee of the Regions (founding member and served in 2014 as rapporteur of the European Strategy for Coastal and Maritime Tourism), the Congress of Local and Regional Authorities of the Council of Europe, the Conference of Peripheral Maritime Regions (president in 2014–2016), the Assembly of European Regions (vice-president in 2013–2014 and it headed in 2006–2012 the Eurodyssey mobility program and the European Observatory on Professional Mobility), the Conference of Presidents of Ultra-Peripheral Regions (president in 2011–2012), FOGAR (founding member), the Pact of Islands (founding member), the Network of European Regions Using Space Technologies (NEREUS), the Conference of European Regions with Legislative Power (REGLEG), the Atlantic Area Transnational Cooperation Program, and R20 (founding member and elected in 2013 vice-president for Europe). Although the list is long, the Azores plays a role primarily in the forums that discuss the specificity of peripheral and island regions. Azorean presidents often take part in the gatherings and are very vocal about the distinct needs and opportunities of the European outermost regions, whose status is defined in Article 349 of the Treaty of the European Union. "It is mostly in these forums that we ensure proper returns," said an official in an interview.[3] Its specific geographical status puts it in a special position to negotiate European funds, such as the European Regional Development Fund (ERDF) and Programme d'Options Spécifiques à l'Éloignement et l'Insularité (POSEI).

Despite the activism of the Azores abroad and even if culture and identity play a pivotal role in the makeup of its external role, the Azores is a good case of how a local cultural paradigm (*açorianidade*) can be protected under a centralized country through paradiplomatic means. In a speech held in California in August 2014, where the president of the Azores, Vasco Cordeiro, laid out his vision toward the Azorean Houses, he declared emphatically that the robustness of the Azores's foreign affairs along with the size of its diaspora contribute to the "affirmation and projection of Portugal in the North and South Atlantic."[4] The local officials interviewed were also very assertive in saying that the Azores's external policies are complementary and not conflicting vis-à-vis the central foreign policy of Portugal. "We all contribute to the external participation of our country," stated an official.[5]

Bavaria (Germany)

The Free State of Bavaria is the largest German state by area and one of the richest regions in Europe. Although Bavarians have often emphasized a separate identity and considered themselves as "Bavarians" first, "Germans" second, the foreign policy of the state has stayed away from heralding an independency agenda and has remained perfectly institutionalized within the framework of the German federation and laws.

The foreign affairs of the region are led mostly by two high-ranking administrative bodies: the Bavarian State Chancellery (*Bayerische Staatskanzlei*) with its powerful state minister for European Affairs and International Relations, and the State Ministry of Economic Affairs and Media, Energy and Technology (*Bayerisches Staatsministerium für Wirtschaft und Medien, Energie und Technologie*). The Chancellery is the governor's cabinet and the most influential policymaking body in the administration. As one of the two state ministers in the Chancellery, the minister of European Affairs and International Relations has broad leeway to handle bilateral relations with Bavaria's foreign partners and address EU-related issues. With a staff of approximately sixty people, the minister oversees his/her direct Office (*Büro der Staatsministerin*), the group responsible for international relations (*Gruppe Internationale Beziehungen*) and the group that manages relations with the European Union (*Gruppe Europapolitik*). The Chancellery also runs three key offices abroad, in Brussels (since 1987),[6] Quebec (since 1999), and Prague (since 2014).

With a dozen officials, the State Ministry of Economic Affairs and Media, Energy and Technology has two specific divisions to command the region's foreign trade and FDI policy (Internationalization and Industry; and Investment, Financing, and Structural Policy). Bavaria's economy is highly export-oriented and relies on high-quality manufacturing (cars, machines, and chemistry products). The main trade partners are the European Union, which counts for more than half of trade volume, the United States, and China. The goal of the ministry is hence to cement Bavaria's position in the global economy and to support small and medium-sized companies in developing new sales markets with a variety of services and funding programs. To assist in that goal, Bavaria International was founded in 1996. It is an export-promotion agency for small and medium-sized Bavarian companies, and it markets Bavaria globally as a business location. In addition, the ministry also manages the business promotion agency, Invest in Bavaria, which is in charge of attracting direct investment. Created in 1999, it supports companies from Germany and abroad in setting up or expanding operations in Bavaria. According to official sources, from 1999 until the end of 2013, Invest in Bavaria has successfully supported around 1,150 investment projects throughout Bavaria. As a result, around 36,000 new direct jobs have emerged according to data from companies who have invested in Bavaria.[7] Both agencies employ approximately fifty people.

The Ministry of Economic Affairs, through Invest in Bavaria, also coordinates Bavaria's economic network abroad (*Bayerische Repräsentanzen*), established since the mid-1990s and composed of nearly thirty representations. The network is tasked with opening up markets and encouraging foreign firms to open branches in Munich. These offices are located in traditional European markets but also in emerging locations such as China, Brazil, Japan, India, Russia, Chile, and the United Arab Emirates. These representations can either be attached to local German institutions (e.g., German Chamber of Commerce or Association of German Chambers of Industry and Commerce) and be headed by locally hired staff or, alternatively, have a more autonomous profile and be led by staff dispatched from Munich. The offices in Brazil, Poland, or Russia are examples of the first, whereas the branches in China or India are illustrations of the second. Each has from two to five staff.

In Bavaria's foreign affairs structure an additional entity is worth highlighting. The Bavarian Research Alliance is a private nonprofit organization founded in 2006 and based in Munich, Nuremberg, and Brussels (with approximately fifty employees). Its mission is to encourage international research and technological development activities of researchers from universities and small and medium-sized enterprises in Bavaria (1) to enhance their capability to participate in EU funding programs, (2) to stimulate cross-sectorial cooperation between academia and industry, and (3) to promote Bavaria as a focal region for science and innovation.

Bavaria's foreign activities are guided by the government's "internationalization strategy," first launched in 2010 and regularly updated (generally on a biennial basis), and by other sectorial guidelines. The region has a strong track record both in the bilateral (such as with Quebec) and multilateral fronts, but it is mainly on European-related issues that its leadership has been more tangible. Working together with other European regions, Bavaria was instrumental in pushing the European Council to create the Committee of the Regions at the Maastricht summit of December 1991. Established three years later, the Committee is the assembly of local and regional representatives that provides subnational authorities with a direct voice within the European Union's institutional framework. Bavaria's backstage influence was also vital to ensure that the Treaty of Lisbon, signed in December 2007, would considerably strengthen the principle of subsidiarity by introducing several control mechanisms to monitor its application. Interesting results are also detectable in agriculture. The recent European agricultural policy 2015–20, which secures a sound financial basis for Bavarian farmers, was strongly influenced by the Bavarian government. Other European funding lines are worth mentioning. In 2010 Bavaria brought together the support of several EU member states to successfully propose the establishment of European Union Strategy for the Danube Region with funding from the ERDF. It has also been able to increase the research funds allocated to Bavarian universities and ensure its participation in the Galileo program, Europe's initiative for a state-of-the-art global satellite navigation system. Officials estimate that around 70 percent of the legislation that impacts Bavarian citizens emanates from the European Union, creating a strong direct connection between Brussels and Munich.[8] The European Union is not seen as entirely "foreign" in Bavaria, but rather as another—and highly formalized—layer of the complex federal structure of European governance (Eberle and Prášil 2013). This is why the government looks down at the term "lobbyist" to characterize the role of its representation in Brussels. They stress that the regions are an integral part of the European administrative structure and elucidate that in the areas of exclusive competences of the German *länder*, a *länder* minister accompanies the federal minister to the negotiations in the Council of Ministers in Brussels.

Bavaria also participates in multilateral networks such as the Committee of the Regions, The Climate Group, European GMO-Free Regions Network, the Association of Alpine States (Arge Alp),

International Lake Constance Conference, and the Regional Leaders Summit. These multilateral partnerships have given rise to joint projects, for example, in the fields of research and technology, as well as education and youth work, language, and culture.

Finally, Bavaria is one of the few regional governments that has a development cooperation policy whose goal is "to make a contribution within the scope of its possibilities toward fighting poverty, sustainable and peaceful development throughout the world, and international understanding."[9] Although it has a timid reach and limited resources (€1.2 million in 2014), Bavaria's development assistance has some interesting projects under its belt. For instance, it promotes the technology training of professionals as well as young leaders from countries in Asia, Latin America, and Africa. Topics include renewable energy and energy efficiency, environmental technologies, and management methods for building a strong economy. The program operates with the participation of Bavarian companies and has mobilized dozens of participants from developing and emerging economies. The management of Bavaria's development assistance is shared between the State Ministry of Economic Affairs and the Chancellery.

Buenos Aires (Argentina)

Buenos Aires is the capital and largest city of Argentina, and the second largest metropolitan area in South America, after São Paulo. Its municipal government is also one of the most active internationally on the Latin American continent. In 2015, Buenos Aires ranked first among Latin American cities in the Global Cities Index, which examines how globally engaged cities are. The institutional heart of this policy is the General Secretariat (*Secretaría General*) of the government of the autonomous city of Buenos Aires and its Directorate General for International Relations and Cooperation (under the Under-Secretariat of International and Institutional Relations). Other departments, agencies, and secretariats such as those on economic development, culture, or education also conduct international activities but the core team is centered in the General Secretariat, the mayor's political body. With a staff of close to thirty people directly involved with external relations (it grows to roughly seventy to eighty if we count the whole city government), the Secretariat carries out international policies according to a dual strategy established during the administration of Mayor Mauricio Macri (2007–2015),[10] addressing both geographical and thematic priorities. The first axis directs Buenos Aires to engage with Latin American cities (primarily São Paulo, Mexico City, Medellín, and Asunción); with subnational governments with whom Buenos Aires shares a common historical, institutional, or cultural heritage (e.g., Berlin, Madrid, Miami, Rome, or Paris); or with rising global cities in the Middle East, Russia, or East Asia (e.g., Beijing and Guangzhou). The second axis defines the areas that concentrate most of the external activities and include sustainable development (waste management, energy, transportation, and housing), innovation and entrepreneurship (smart cities), and social inclusion.

This framework has been consistently applied in the city's bilateral and multilateral relations over the last years. In fact, Buenos Aires is one of the cities in the world with the largest portfolio of international agreements. Since the first sister-city agreement signed in 1974 with Seville, the city has signed seventy-eight agreements (as of early 2015). And some of them have paved the way for interesting bilateral initiatives. With Japan, Buenos Aires has carried out since 2011 the Argentinean version of the "Kids ISO 14000" program that develops environmental awareness among children and young people. A cooperation project between the city's Ministry of Education and the Japan International Cooperation Agency (JICA), it enables a few thousand elementary school pupils from Buenos Aires to work with their teachers in creating strategies to incorporate sustainable habits in their homes. On sustainable development, it is worth singling out the "climate partnership" that Buenos Aires (through the *Agencia de Protección Ambiental* and the General Secretariat) established with Berlin (via the Berlin Senate Chancellery and Berlin Energy Agency) in late 2012. Besides the exchange of experts and consultancy provided by German experts on energy efficiency and energy conservation in Buenos Aires's public buildings, the German organization Engagement Global gGmbH—Service für Entwicklungsinitiativen has set up an energy lab for children (*laboratorio de experimentación en materia de energía*) in the capital city. The project is part of the German program "50 Municipal Climate Partnerships by 2015," which aims to strengthen cooperation between German municipalities and municipalities in the Global South in the field of climate change mitigation and adaptation. Finally, programs on social inclusion include, for instance, the Goal for Inclusion (*Gol por la Inclusión*) carried out in 2014 with the US Embassy, which aimed to use football as a tool for the social inclusion of women in poverty-stricken communities (Villa Soldati and Villa 1-11-14 slums). As acknowledged by the city government, the international programs are not large enough to impact millions of people, but despite their limited scope they provide positive results that are tangible and measurable. In addition, they reinforce and complement other city programs that impact larger segments of the population.[11]

The Argentinean capital is also engaged with international networks of cities, including the Union of Ibero-American Capital Cities (*Unión de Ciudades Capitales Iberoamericanas*, UCCI), United Cities and Local Governments (UCLG), C40, Mercocities, the Federation of Latin American Cities, Municipalities and Associations of Local Governments, UNESCO Creative Cities Network, the Ibero-American Center for Strategic Urban Development (*Centro Iberoamericano de Desarrollo Estratégico Urbano*, CIDEU), Local Governments for Sustainability (ICLEI), the International Solar Cities Initiative, World Association of Major Metropolises (Metropolis), World e-Governments Organization of Cities and Local Governments, United Nations Advisory Committee of Local Authorities, and the Network of South American Cities.

The weight that is put on each of them varies, however. UCCI and Mercocities are given strong preference as they enable Buenos Aires's leadership to be recognized by its Latin American peers, "open cooperation windows with other cities in the region" and empower the city to cultivate neighboring relations,[12] as directed by the internal strategy mentioned earlier. But participation in C40 and Metropolis is also much valued by Buenos Aires. This is where the city has access to funding, can increase its global visibility, and advocate for causes that rank high in the city's agenda (such as climate change and social inclusion). Participation permits the mayor to interact with other global leaders and gain additional stature.[13] Buenos Aires has also benefited from the expertise of these two networks. Through its participation in the C40, Buenos Aires was able to access *pro bono* expertise from President Clinton's Climate Initiative (CCI) Cities Program to implement its network of dedicated bus lanes—the first in Argentina. To reinforce its participation in the networks that it gives preference to, Buenos Aires generally takes part in their committees and working groups and takes the lead in the organization of their annual summits (such as the 2015 Metropolis Annual Meeting and the 2015 C40 Latin America Mayors Forum).

Buenos Aires's international promotion strategy also encompasses the organization of large events, such as the 2018 Summer Youth Olympic Games, and the active application for international awards. This latter policy has proved very successful. Only in recent years, Buenos Aires won the 2015 Organization of American States' Inter-American Innovation Award for Effective Public Management, the 2015 Global Entrepreneurship Cities Challenge, the City Climate Leadership Awards 2014 (Solid Waste Management category), the 2013 Sustainable Transport Award (from the Institute for Transport & Development Policy), the 2013 C40 Citizens Choice Award, the 2013 City of the Year GovFresh Award, and the 2013 Ibero-American Digital Cities Award (Open Government category).

California (United States)

California's economic size—the largest regional economy in the world with a population of close to 40 million people—creates large expectations about its international activities. Consequently, although the state has only a mild international portfolio, California's foreign initiatives end up drawing global attention. California's international activities were born in the administration of Gerald "Pat" Brown (1959–1967) who was "the first governor to grasp the importance of international trade and tourism for California's growth" (Lowenthal 2009, 38; Goldsborough, 1993). By the time he left office, the state had offices in London and Tokyo and was about to open a third one in Frankfurt. All were closed a few years later by Governor Ronald Reagan (1967–1975) who, as a conservative liberal, saw no utility in expanding public institutions and spending public money overseas. Reagan's successor was Edmund Gerald "Jerry" Brown Jr. (1975–1983) (Gerald "Pat" Brown's son) who quickly put California back on the international track. He opened the state's first Office of International Trade in 1977 in the new Department of Economic and Business Development (transformed in 1980 into the California Commerce Department, and in 1992 into the Technology, Trade and Commerce Agency) (Lowenthal 2009, 38). The following governors (George Deukmejian, Pete Wilson, and Gray Davis) were less vocal about foreign affairs, but were conscious of the fact that a state the size of California needed to have a government that supported international businesses. Trade offices were opened in Tokyo and London in 1987, in Mexico and Frankfurt in 1989, and in Hong Kong in 1990. If in 1983 the state was spending less than US$500,000 to promote world trade, by 1987 that figure rocketed to US$9 million. In 1999, the state was spending US$16.1 million and had the largest trade and investment program of the fifty US states (Lowenthal 2009, 121). Also emblematically, in 1999, Governor Davis nominated his chief of staff, Michael Flores, to the new post of Secretary of Foreign Affairs. Although the position was highly symbolic, its major duties were of a protocol nature (organizing foreign missions and welcoming foreign dignitaries) and maintaining close contact with diplomatic representatives located in California to ensure closer social, economic, and political ties between the state and its international partners. The 1980s and 1990s were also punctuated by a flurry of sister and other bilateral agreements. Out of the current portfolio of twenty-seven agreements, nineteen were adopted in that period. After decades of work, at the beginning of this millennium, California had twelve trade centers abroad. But then the economy was hit hard by the electricity crisis of 2000–2001 and by speculative bubbles leading to a gubernatorial recall election. Backers of the recall effort cited Governor Davis's alleged lack of leadership combined with California's weakened and hurt economy. Despite this scenario, it was with Governor Arnold Schwarzenegger (2003–2011) that California started to be more aware of its global weight and soft power.

Despite the long international track record, the state has never adopted a formal umbrella plan on foreign affairs and its external activities are more issue-driven or partner-driven. Relations with China, Japan, and Mexico have always played an important role. Currently, two main sectors draw California's interests overseas. The first and foremost is still trade and investment promotion. In 2013 and 2014, Governor "Jerry" Brown (who returned to power in 2011) led two large trade missions to China and Mexico, respectively. In China, in April 2013, Governor Brown signed a landmark agreement with the Ministry of Commerce to bolster economic ties and cooperation between California and China. The first-of-its-kind between a subnational entity and the Ministry of Commerce, it establishes a joint working group that includes California, the Ministry of Commerce, and leaders from six provinces—autonomous regions and municipalities directly under the central government—Jiangsu, Inner Mongolia, Shanghai, Shandong, Guangdong, and Chongqing, representing more than 350 million people. In June of the same year, Brown met with Chinese President Xi Jinping to discussing mutually beneficial economic development opportunities (figure 4.1).[14] In the following year, a trade mission was organized to Mexico. Brown, who was accompanied by approximately ninety business, economic development, investment, and policy leaders, signed a trade and investment agreement with the Ministry of Economy and met with Mexican President Enrique Peña Nieto. These missions are generally planned long in advance and tailored to produce business results, more than diplomatic or cultural achievements. In 2014, California also championed a pioneering agreement with Ontario on impact investment with the goal of co-investing in

FIGURE 4.1 Governor Edmund G. Brown Jr. of California meets President Xi Jinping of the People's Republic of China (2013)

© Joe McHugh, California Highway Patrol

investment infrastructure, knowledge exchange, venture exchange, and joint programming to support industry development.

The second major issue is the environment. In 2013 California made foreign-policy history by becoming the first subnational government to sign an agreement with China's powerful National Development and Reform Commission, which oversees the country's economic growth. Just as significant is the objective: fighting climate change by circumventing deadlocked decision-making in Washington and Beijing. Similar interesting results were achieved with other countries. During Governor Brown's mission to Mexico in July 2014, California signed an agreement with Mexico's Ministry of Environment and Natural Resources to help reduce greenhouse gas emissions and combat climate change. The agreements with Mexico and China came on the heels of similar agreements signed in 2013 with the governments of British Columbia and the states of Oregon and Washington. At the UN Climate Change conference in Paris at the end of 2015 he met with world leaders and touted the state's ambitious efforts to reduce greenhouse gas emissions. Together with Michael Bloomberg, he was regarded as the subnational leader with a stronger stance on climate change.

Given its economic size, California's government tends to be circumspect in the way it conducts its foreign policy and the temperature in Washington is generally measured before taking any action abroad. State officials are generally wary of the idea of showing international prominence because it is believed that the US State Department should not be rivaled in any possible way. When trade missions are organized, the federal Department of Commerce is kept informed and mutual assistance is ensured. But on issues where the federal government has failed to take a more proactive role, such as on climate change, California has been filling up the gaps and voicing their concerns on the global stage.

The state's foreign activities are managed by the External Affairs Office within the Governor's Executive Cabinet (headed by a director) and by the Governor's Office of Business and Economic Development (commonly known as "GO-Biz") that serves as California's single point of contact for economic development and job creation efforts. Within GO-Biz, there is an international affairs and trade development unit (headed by a deputy-director) that has the mission to expand California's international business, which includes boosting international trade through marketing and logistical support. It also functions to attract and support new foreign investment to the state, in conjunction with the California Business Investment Services program. California is the number one US state for attracting FDI. In 2014, the California International Trade and Investment Advisory Council was also established to advise GO-Biz on strategies to expand international trade and investment for California businesses. The first chair was former US ambassador Eleni Kounalakis. Both the External Affairs Office and GO-Biz may interact with other departments—such as tourism or education—on a demand basis. In total, California counts fifteen to twenty staff dedicated to its foreign activities.

California established an Office of Trade and Investment in Shanghai, China (managed by GO-Biz) in April 2013, during Governor Brown's visit to the country. It is a privately funded office staffed and operated by the Bay Area Council. The state's first since 2003, it was made possible in part by the Assembly Bill 2012, which allowed GO-Biz to establish a public–private partnership to create state trade and investment offices. All twelve of California's foreign trade offices and the Technology, Trade and Commerce Agency mentioned earlier were closed in 2003 amidst budget shortfalls, but the Shanghai office is likely to be the first in a set of new openings. As Governor Brown mentioned in 2013: "Our lack of foreign trade offices left us as the only U.S. state without a broad-based international trade and investment program. This wrong will now soon be righted."[15]

The state also participates in international organizations such as the Border Governors Conference, an annual, bi-national meeting between the governors of the four American states and six Mexican states that form the Mexico–US border; the Climate Group, an organization that aims to promote clean technologies and policies, with the aim of expanding clean technology markets and reducing global greenhouse gas emissions; the R20-Regions of Climate Action, a nonprofit organization founded in 2010 by former Governor Schwarzenegger that aims to achieve global environmental and economic goals; the US–China Governors Forum, established in 2011 to serve as a platform of cooperation between subnational leaders of both countries; the Pacific Coast Collaborative, that brings together the leaders of British Columbia, California, Oregon, and Washington to reduce emissions and transition toward renewables; and the Under 2 MoU, an agreement among subnational jurisdictions to limit the increase in global average temperature to below 2 degrees Celsius—the warming threshold at which scientists say there will likely be catastrophic climate disruptions (initiative spearheaded by California and Baden-Württemberg and launched in 2015). The state generally uses these forums to advance the issues that rank high on its domestic agenda, such as climate change or cross-border immigration.

Catalonia (Spain)

Historically, Catalonia has always had an interest in fulfilling its international role due to its geographical position as a gateway to Europe and point of connection with the Mediterranean. Yet, it was only in the mid-1980s that the region started to execute a more palpable foreign policy consistent with its internal objectives. Catalonia established its first office abroad, in Brussels, the very same year Spain joined the European Union (1986). Yet, the foreign affairs of the region have been never so intertwined with its expectations toward more autonomy or statehood as in recent years. In the words of a senior official of the Catalan government, "Our government has the responsibility to give international exposure to Catalonia as a country of prestige and quality, a country which can be trusted, the driving force for Southern Europe," which presupposes also explaining "to European and international actors . . . why Catalan citizens are expressing their will about the 'right to decide.'"[16] Catalonia is one of the strongest examples today in the world of sovereign paradiplomacy, or protodiplomacy.

The Secretariat for Foreign and European Union Affairs (*Secretaria d'Afers Exteriors i de la Unió Europea*) is the body responsible for coordinating and developing Catalan foreign policy. It is divided into three main areas: the Directorate General for Foreign Affairs, the Directorate General for Development Cooperation, and the Directorate General for Multilateral and European Affairs. The Secretariat has therefore a comprehensive portfolio, guided by the mantra that internationalization is an important instrument for the social and economic development of the region. In other words, their international relations personnel are service providers. An important role is also played by the Agency for Business Competitiveness (*Agència per a la Competitivitat de l'empresa*, ACCIÓ), a government-led organization devoted to promote Catalan business. According to official reports, from 1985 (foundation year) to 2015, ACCIÓ has managed 4,961 investment projects that generated €8.1 billion in inward investments and created 40,000 direct jobs.[17] The internal structure is complemented with a presence worldwide consisting of a network of approximately sixty-five offices, including seven delegations representing the government of Catalonia, the "Generalitat" (in France/Switzerland, European Union, Germany, United Kingdom/Ireland, Austria, Italy, and the United States/Canada/Mexico), thirty-four offices of the Agency for Business Competitiveness, four branches of the Institut Ramon Llull, an organization constituted in 2002 in order to "promote Catalan language and culture internationally," and the five offices of the Catalan Institute for the Cultural Companies, a public institution, attached to the Catalan Ministry of Culture that is charged with promoting and fostering the development of the Catalan cultural industry. To promote tourism, the Catalan Tourism Board was created in 2007 (replacing the *Turisme de Catalunya consortium*) and it currently has eleven offices abroad. Finally, the network is also composed of the Catalan Agency for Development Cooperation (*Agència Catalana de Cooperació al Desenvolupament*, ACCD), which is responsible for managing the government of Catalonia's development cooperation, peace building, and humanitarian action policy. ACCD has three offices in Colombia, Morocco, and Mozambique. The growth in representations abroad in recent years is thanks to the Statute of 2006, which incorporated the possibility of establishing political offices abroad and to the presence of more independent-leaning leaders over the last years. It is indicative that four out of five Generalitat's offices abroad (Berlin, London, New York, and Paris) were set up after 2009. By then the region was involved in a heated political debate where the opposition side headed by Arturo Mas put special emphasis on initiating a process, known as the Refoundation of Catalanism (*Refundació del Catalanisme*), to build upon the principles and values of the Catalanist movement in order to spread nationalist feeling in Catalonia. To tap into the opposition's reservoir of support, the Catalan government led by Jordi Pujol decided to sponsor a more active international presence.

The external affairs are carried out under the 2006 Statute of Autonomy (Title V), which recognizes Catalonia's right to conduct foreign relations in the areas corresponding to its powers

(Art. 193). The Statute is the highest law, negotiated between the Catalan and the Spanish governments and approved by the Catalan and the Spanish Parliaments. Besides this, one should also consider Catalonia's External Action and European Union Relations Law, adopted in November 2014. According to a senior official from the Secretariat for Foreign and European Union Affairs, "the main objective of the Law is to strengthen the relationship with the EU institutions, move forward to achieve a coherent external action policy and to foster Catalan interests around the world, strengthening the relations with other governments, international networks and international organisations. The Law considers a key element the promotion and divulgation of the Catalan language and culture."[18]

To pursue this agenda, Catalonia has established a solid network, albeit not very extensive compared with other regions of the same size, of bilateral and multilateral partners. From a bilateral perspective, Catalonia selected a series of states and regions, which, for different reasons, are regarded as priority for external action. The first circle of interest lies within its immediate geopolitical environment: Andorra, France, Portugal, and the Maghreb countries. A second group of priority countries are its main economic partners, such as Germany, the United Kingdom, the United States, Japan, or Finland, with which Catalonia maintains strong economic, commercial, and cultural relationships. A third set of countries include Latin America, a region where Catalan cooperation is very active, above all in Central America and the Caribbean (particularly Guatemala, Nicaragua, and El Salvador). Catalonia has also shown in recent years a novel interest in emerging economies, such as in Brazil, India, or China.

To safe keep these relations, Catalonia has signed MoUs with some of them (e.g., Israel, Massachusetts, Argentina, and Uruguay), adopted country plans with Japan and Morocco, and established bilateral cooperation committees with traditional partners such as Quebec and Flanders. Agreements may be proposed according to geographical proximity and political directives, but in recent years the need to increase exports, promote tourism, and attract FDI has played a very significant role. Culture and identity also carry weight. Back in 2003, Catalonia made history by signing an MoU with UNESCO aimed at developing and strengthening cooperation in the fields of education, science, culture, and communication. The agreement produced more symbolic than concrete results, however, paving the way to the signature of a second agreement in 2013, which provided a more formal framework of cooperation and was "intended to facilitate Catalan institutions' participation in UNESCO-led international meetings, projects and programs of mutual interest in accordance with UNESCO rules and regulations" (First Commitment).

Multilaterally, Catalonia is a member of six networks: the Four Motors of Europe, the Conference of Peripheral Maritime Regions, Regions United/FOGAR, nrg4SD, Working Community of the Pyrenees, and Pyrenees-Mediterranean Euroregion. Historically, the region used to focus its activities in its direct geographical region (Pyrenees and the Mediterranean), but more recently Catalonia has become increasingly involved with global multilateral organizations such as the nrg4SD, which is a founding and active member of its executive committee and served many years as co-chair for the North (there is a co-chair for the Southern Hemisphere).

Chungcheongnam-do (South Korea)

The province of Chungcheongnam-do (aka South Chungcheong and abbreviated Chungnam) is South Korea's second richest province. With a small population of only 2 million, it boasts one of the highest per capita GDPs in the world. It leads South Korea in the field of technology development and commercialization, which in turn attracts start-up businesses and FDI. This strong economic profile is a reflection of South Korea's globalized economy; it was therefore inescapable that the provincial government established its own foreign affairs capabilities, centered on the International Relations and Trade Division. Located in the Economy and Trade Secretariat (also known as Bureau, in English), the division is composed of four smaller units: International Coordination, International Relations,

International Trade, and Overseas Branch Offices. This latter supervises the work of Chungnam's "trade promotion offices" in Los Angeles, Shanghai, and Kumamoto. The largest mission of the division is to support the export of locally produced products, primarily by boosting the international dimension of small and medium-sized companies. In total, around thirty people are involved with foreign affairs (five of them working in the offices abroad).

As matters move further away from Chungnam's trade promotion endeavors, the more ceremonial the province's external relations become, as openly acknowledged by its officials.[19] The bedrock of the province's internationalization policy was the sister agreement signed with Kumamoto (Japan) in January 1983. The process continued in the 1990s and presently Chungnam has another five "sister relations": Hebei (China), Amur (Russia), Wielkopolska (Poland), Misiones (Argentina), and South Australia (Australia), and eighteen "cooperative relations" with mostly Asian provinces (eight of them in China and two each in Russia and Japan). These privileged relations are solidified in endless visits and exchanges of correspondence, but their end-result is not always obvious. An exception to the rule is Chungnam's relations with its neighbors. With Chinese subnational governments, for instance, sister and cooperative agreements are leveraged to help the province to expand exchange and cooperation and, most important, to gain access to new markets. This was visible in Governor Ahn Hee-jung's visit to China in December 2014 to conduct what was coined by the local government as "sales diplomacy." A similar track is followed with Russia. In May 2008, Chungnam issued the first subnational government bonds for FDI promotion in South Korea, paving the way to attract $650 million from the DI Group in Russia. In fact, a strong focus is directed toward neighboring countries—mainly China, Russia, and Japan—that account for the majority of visits and cooperation projects, as they all belong to a similar web of interconnected economic and cultural relations. Farther away from this neighboring ecosystem, international relations tend to cool off and maintaining the "initial drive imposes a great deal of difficulties," as very often relations are nothing more than "an empty shell" restricted to "commemorations and congratulations," as pointed out by local officials.[20] When they actually produce some fruits, cooperation projects have limited ambitions. In 2010, the province signed an agreement with São Paulo state on sports, which paved the way for the Brazilian state to host ten taekwondo and archery experts from South Korea, and for Chungnam to receive Brazilian football and volleyball professionals for a few weeks. After the first round of exchanges, the program stalled mostly due to changes in government and budget reductions. It is an interesting program, but timid in its ambitions.

Other programs have higher goals and resources, though. Chungnam, and a handful of other South Korean regions, embody the few subnational governments in the world that have in place a program like Korea Heart-to-Heart (K2H). An in-service training program created by the Governors' Association of Korea, it invites civil servants from local governments all over the world to spend a six-month or one-year period at a Korean administrative agency. Within the frame of K2H, every year officials from Chungnam's "sister partners" are invited to get immersed in Korean public administration, history, culture, and language. All expenses in the country are covered by the hosting government. Initially established in 2004, it hosted forty foreign officials in the first decade. Other mobility programs have been carried out in alliance with the Local Government Officials Development Institute (LOGODI), attached to the South Korean Ministry of Security and Public Administration. LOGODI offers programs on "Local Administration Development" to foreign officials from the subnational governments with whom South Korean provinces have established bilateral relations. The programs are designed to share South Korea's experiences in the areas of economic development, local administration, local finance, and transparency. Aside from training and mobility, Chungnam has also launched development assistance policies with other regions centered on the donation of emergency vehicles (fire protection and emergency relief). Between 2012 and 2014, twenty of these vehicles were donated to Long An (Vietnam) and Siem Reap (Cambodia).

At the multilateral level, Chungnam has a more targeted perspective and the focus is on the Association of North East Asia Regional Governments (NEAR). Since it was officially founded in 1996, NEAR has facilitated exchange and cooperation projects in various fields ranging from economy and trade to education and culture, or science and technology. With the accession of new members at the 8th General Assembly held in October 2010, NEAR has grown into an organization representing Northeast Asia with over seventy member regional governments from six countries (China, Japan, South Korea, North Korea, Mongolia, and Russia). The largest organization of its kind in Asia, NEAR had its cradle in the North East Asia Regional Convention held in Shimane (Japan) in 1993, which brought together local leaders from China, Japan, South Korea, and Russia. Its headquarters are located in Pohang, South Korea.

According to the provincial government, Chungnam's foreign relations are carried out with the strong support of the South Korean government, which allows for the "unrestricted external activities" of the provinces. Despite the important political backup, South Korean provinces are not immune to human and financial constraints. As local officials recognize, their scope is much shorter than national foreign policy and there are limitations to their ambition.[21]

Flanders (Belgium)

Flanders has been a major player in European trade and international affairs since the Middle Ages, when a number of Flemish towns, such as Bruges and Ghent, served as major trading centers. If the region was the cradle of modern European capitalism in the thirteenth century, presently it is at the forefront of any global discussion on decentralization, subsidiarity, and local power. Flanders is a prime example of "sovereign paradiplomacy" as its foreign affairs are perfectly intertwined with its cyclical claims for independence or more autonomy. Although the region carries a thick legacy of international involvement, modern foreign affairs emerged only out of the Belgium State Reforms, a process initiated in 1970 toward finding constitutional and legal solutions for the tensions among the different segments of the Belgian population, mostly Dutch-speakers of Flanders and French-speakers of Wallonia. The establishment of the Flemish region, with its own government and parliament, dates back to the Second State Reform held in the 1980s. It was only then that Flanders was given leverage to engage internationally with autonomy.

Symbolically, its first international agreement was signed with a region that had similar political ambitions: Quebec. In 1989, they adopted a general cooperation agreement in the areas of the economy, science, technology, education, culture, society, and the environment.[22] The agreement was renewed in 2002 and 2013. A standing joint cooperation committee created in 1986 meets every two years to decide which projects will be backed by the two governments. Flanders (and other subnational governments in Belgium) pursues its foreign policy only in the areas of its competencies, using its full power to conclude treaties (*ius tractandi*), including negotiation, conclusion, and ratification, under the principle *in foro interno, in foro externo*. As new State Reforms were being adopted and Flanders expanded its authority over additional areas (e.g., tourism in 1980; education and trade in 1988–1989; and agriculture, fisheries, and development cooperation in 2001), its foreign affairs portfolio grew. Hence, Belgian communities and regions have exclusive authority over the international aspects of their areas of competence, including the conclusion of international treaties. Between 1993 and 2008, Flanders concluded thirty-three of these so-called exclusive treaties (twenty-seven bilateral and six multilateral) (Criekemans 2010c, 48). At present, Flanders is a partner in more than six hundred treaties and other agreements. The treaties are very diverse in terms of theme and impact. They vary from cooperation agreements with organizations such as UNESCO, to treaties with the Netherlands with regard to the oversight of the river Scheldt, to agreements with the state of São Paulo on port management.

Apart from its bilateral relations with dozens of countries, Flanders has also established contacts with international organizations. UNESCO and Flanders signed their first cooperation agreement in 1998. It is one of the rare agreements concluded between UNESCO and a substate entity. From 1999, in the framework of the cooperation agreement, Flanders decided to create two funds-in-trust in order to provide a specific financial support to UNESCO's projects and programs: the Flanders UNESCO Science Trust Fund to support scientific programs and the General Flemish Trust Fund to cover UNESCO's other fields of competence. The Belgian region is also a member of a handful of different multilateral networks such as The Climate Group, nrg4SD, Association of Cities and Regions for Recycling and Sustainable Resource Management (ACR +), REGLEG, Committee of the Regions, Conference of European Regional Legislative Assemblies, Peri Urban Regions Platform Europe (PURPLE), Network of European Regions for a Sustainable and Competitive Tourism, European Chemical Regions Network (ECRN), Districts of Creativity (DC) Network, European Regions Research and Innovation Network (ERRIN), and Vanguard Initiative for New Growth by Smart Specialization. Yet, despite the ample set of forums it belongs to, it participates more actively only in the ones that deal directly with European Union or sustainability issues, as they are closer to its domestic priorities.

In the wake of the third state reform (1989), Flanders also embraced competencies regarding export promotion and the attraction of foreign investment and know-how. This is carried out through Flanders Investment & Trade (FIT),[23] an externally autonomous agency with its own Board of Directors that provides extensive services to Flemish enterprises in their international outreach. The FIT network abroad is the largest for a subnational government on economic issues and includes more than ninety "economic representatives" that spread all over the world,[24] with the overwhelming majority stationed in Belgium embassies and consulates. Flanders accounts for 82 percent of Belgium's exports and its most important customers are Germany, France, the Netherlands, and the United Kingdom. In 2014 the region' exports reached a record level of €293.5 billion. Even if Flanders still faces some obstacles to export growth, such as the regime for exports to countries within the European Union, FIT has been a very successful agency.

Tourism promotion is also an important pillar in the international strategy of Flanders, as the sector contributes significantly to the province's economy. Since the second state reform of 1980, tourism is a competence of the regions, allowing Flanders to explore autonomously its tourist potential. In 2012, Belgium received a record 6.2 million international visitors, of whom 48 percent (3.0 million) visited Flanders, 13 percent (0.8 million) Wallonia, and 39 percent (2.4 million) the city of Brussels (OECD 2014). The executive organization for tourism administration lays with Tourism Flanders-Brussels and the Flemish Department of Foreign Affairs (Tourism Enterprise and Strategic Goods Division), which manage a network of representatives in fourteen countries, mostly in North America, Asia, and Europe.[25] They not only identify and capitalize on specific opportunities in new markets (e.g., Asia and Latin America) but also financially support projects and programs to enhance the tourism potential of Flanders regions by working with private and public actors. Most initiatives revolve around the Flemish Art Cities: Brussels, Bruges, Ghent, Antwerp, Mechelen, and Leuven.

Another key pillar in Flanders's foreign affairs structure is its development cooperation policy in foreign countries. Initiated in the early 1990s, it has the mission to contribute to eliminating extreme poverty and hunger, generalizing access to basic education, combating gender disparity, increasing the fight against the most important poverty diseases, guaranteeing ecological sustainability, and developing a global partnership for development. The development policy was conducted by the Flanders International Cooperation Agency (FICA) from 2006 to 2014, and it is currently pursued by the Department of Foreign Affairs.[26] In 2013, the development cooperation budget totaled €57 million,[27] the largest part of which was used to support projects in southern Africa (South Africa, Malawi, and Mozambique).

Flemish institutional capacity on external affairs is very ample. The Flemish Department of Foreign Affairs, a full-fledged ministry of foreign affairs, led by a secretary-general, acts as the coordinating body of all bilateral and multilateral foreign actions. The structure includes also three networks of representatives abroad. Besides the FIT and Tourism networks, mentioned earlier, a third network of "Representatives of the Government of Flanders" is directly managed by the Flemish Department of Foreign Affairs and it currently comprehends eleven representatives—in The Hague, Paris, London, Berlin, Warsaw, Vienna, Madrid, New York, Pretoria, Geneva (multilateral), and Brussels (European Union).[28] The overall structure includes, finally, the Policy Research Centre for Foreign Affairs (Leuven Centre for Global Governance Studies) that works as the Flemish government think tank on foreign affairs.

The density of its foreign relations is correlated with the number of staff, the largest for a subnational government. By December 2013, Flanders Investment & Trade had 356 people (195 abroad), the Department of Foreign Affairs had 148 (29 abroad), Tourism Flanders-Brussels had 193 (47 abroad), the Flanders Foreign Affairs Council had four, and Flanders International Cooperation Agency had 29 (6 abroad). The last of these was later reintegrated in the Department of Foreign Affairs after FICA's dissolution in 2014.[29]

Flanders's considerable experience and unquestionable strengths in foreign affairs put the region on top of paradiplomatic practices worldwide. As pointed out by a former Minister-President of Flanders, given that Flanders and all the other Belgian regional governments have the (quasi) sovereignty to enter into foreign relations, including full treaty-making power in their areas of jurisdiction, "one can ... hardly speak of the existence of sub-state diplomacy," or infra-state foreign relations (Den Brande 2010, 200). The depth and width of its foreign policy demands the development of regular strategies and visions to guide its actions. These include Flanders in Action ("Vlaanderen in Actie") a social and economic action program for the future of Flanders, which was established by the Flemish government in July 2006; Pact 2020, a mission statement adopted in 2009, which defines a range of policy goals for 2020 for the Flanders region; the Policy Notes tabled in Parliament by the secretary-general for foreign affairs; and the Coalition Agreements of its successive governments. In the latest Agreement (2014–2019), Flanders makes its foreign affairs case strongly: "In this globalised world it is essential that we comprehensively defend our interests and resolutely employ our assets at the international level. Therefore, Flanders has the ambition to stand tall and self-assured in the world in economic as well as broad political terms."

Guangzhou (China)

Guangzhou (formerly Canton) is the capital and largest city of Guangdong province in South China. With a population of more than 16 million, it is one of the five national-level central cities in China and holds sub-provincial administrative status. Located on the northern edge of the Pearl River Delta, adjacent to the South Sea, Hong Kong, and Macao, Guangzhou is the transportation and communication hub and trading port of South China, best known as the Southern Gateway of China. Given its economic assets, Guangzhou started to develop its external affairs in the late 1970s. They are currently coordinated by the Foreign Affairs Office of the People's Government of Guangzhou Municipality. The first purpose of the Foreign Affairs Office is to conduct foreign relations with sister cities. This type of partnership raises some eyebrows in European countries due to its frequent aimlessness, but it is regarded highly in Chinese (and, more widely, Asian) political culture.

The first Guangzhou international agreement was signed with Fukuoka in May 1979 by Yang Shangkun, Director General of the Guangzhou Revolution Committee, and Shindou Kazuma, Mayor of Fukuoka. Although the agreement had a strong symbolic weight, and it is still lauded as a landmark in Guangzhou's foreign policy, outcomes are only strong on the ceremonial front. The first collaboration initiative, still in 1979, was sending two Chinese pandas to an exhibition held in Fukuoka and, in the following decades, cooperation was centered on formal visits and "fraternal discussions." Since then, Guangzhou has signed an additional thirty-five sister-cities agreements, making it one of the Chinese cities with the largest portfolio of international accords. Gradually, however, these agreements are gaining more content and creativity. Whereas it signed ephemeral sister agreements with Los Angeles in 1981 and Auckland in 1989, in November 2014 Guangzhou mayor Jianhua Chen, LA mayor Eric Garcetti, and Auckland mayor Len Brown signed a major economic agreement that established a Tripartite Economic Alliance to promote cooperation among the cities in trade, entertainment, tourism, and innovation. The three work to develop future trade missions and expand the business opportunities in each of the cities. The agreement, the first global threefold city agreement of its kind, set a new standard for how modern cities engage and collaborate.

The Foreign Affairs Office also manages Guangzhou multilateral relations within the frame of the UCLG and Metropolis. When compared to other cities of the same size, Guangzhou participates in a fairly small number of city networks, but the quality and intensity of its contribution is comparatively higher. During the mandates of Mayors Wan Qingliang (2010–2011) and Chen Jianhua (since 2011), Guangzhou sought to be regarded as a global leader in urban innovation. And the city's most successful policy toward that end was the establishment, together with UCLG and Metropolis, of the biennial Guangzhou International Award for Urban Innovation, which rewards innovations to improve the socioeconomic environments in cities and regions. The award quickly reached international recognition. Right in its first edition in 2012, submissions arrived from 153 cities and regions around the world (177 cities in the second edition). In addition to this, Guangzhou was elected co-president of UCLG and co-president of Metropolis and it is the host city of Metropolis' Asia Pacific Regional Office. Even more relevantly, it has explored how best to tap the expertise generated by the Guangzhou Award. The city developed in 2013 an interactive database containing all submissions to the award,[30] which constitutes an important reservoir of urban best practices. It also established the Guangzhou Institute for Urban Innovation as a network of partner institutions that meets to share views and to discuss ways forward for mainstreaming lessons learned from urban innovation. Moreover, in 2014 it championed the proposal for setting up a UCLG Community on Urban Innovation to enhance the international exchange and cooperation in urban innovation. Finally, the city organizes the biennial Guangzhou International Conference on Urban Innovation (a large global gathering of subnational officials), which, in 2014, was held together with the biennial China International Friendship Cities Conference that celebrates Chinese sister-cities tradition.

Aside from the Foreign Affairs Office, other bodies and institutions are also involved with Guangzhou's international relations, such as the Bureau of Foreign Trade and Economic Cooperation, which is in charge of the foreign trade; the Tourism Administration, responsible for tourist promotion; and the Overseas Chinese Affairs Office, which is tasked to liaise with overseas Chinese residing abroad or returning to China. In total, as of late 2014, Guangzhou counts approximately 150 people working with foreign affairs. To provide internal coordination, the municipality established a "Leading Group on Foreign Affairs Policies" composed of different heads of municipal departments who are mandated to draw annual plans and priorities on foreign affairs.

The Guangzhou municipality is also strongly engaged in marketing the city as a global commercial hub. The Chinese Import & Export Commodities Fair has been held biannually in Guangzhou since 1957, and the city boasts the Guangzhou Industrial Zone, which hosts automobile assembly, biotechnology, and heavy industries. The Guangzhou Free Trade Zone also promotes international trade, logistics, processing industry, and computer software. Its GDP, the third largest at the city level in China (after Shanghai and Beijing), reached US$270 billion in 2015 and local authorities have set a US$425 billion target for 2020. In 2014 its import and export trade reached US$119 billion, increasing by 1.5 percent over the previous year. Its international profile is also seen in the fairly large number of foreign consulates (44) and Fortune 500 companies (228) (2014 data).

History plays at its advantage. As a 2,200-plus-year commercial city, Guangzhou has been the maritime trade center since the Qin and Han Dynasties, and it was the only foreign trade port city in the Ming and Qing Dynasties. Guangzhou was the starting point of the ancient "Maritime Silk Road" and was recognized as one of the important ports in the ancient world. In modern times, and despite (or because of) its growing international weight, challenges lay ahead. According to Zhou Jian, the Foreign Affairs Office's Deputy Director, the main objective is to obtain practical results out of its international relations, either through sister cities (bilateral cooperation) or international organizations (multilateral cooperation).[31] Modern paradiplomacy should be guided more by results than symbolism and serve as an instrument that brings concrete benefits at the local level.

Île-de-France (France)

Île-de-France (IDF) is the wealthiest and most populated of the twenty-two regions of France, and it boasts the largest subnational GDP in Europe. IDF's international policy is legally rooted in the principle of decentralized cooperation (*coopération décentralisée*), which regulates the relations that French local authorities maintain with foreign local authorities and is enshrined in a handful of national laws (see Chapter 1). But the region has also outlined its foreign affairs pledges in several policy documents, such as the International Policy Report of 2010, which places four priorities at the heart of IDF's foreign policy: decentralized cooperation, solidarity with the peoples and territories affected by disasters or conflicts, promotion of its expertise internationally, and regional activities to create a bridge between its international actions and territorial policies in IDF. Although the report has been guiding all international activities of the region ever since it was produced, IDF has also designed supplementary reports and policies toward Europe (2007) and the Mediterranean (2012).

A substantial part of IDF's commitments abroad are related to its participation in multilateral networks. The French region is the subnational government that participates in the most international arrangements with subnational authorities (eighteen in total). These include the Assembly of European Regions, the Council of European Municipalities and Regions of Europe via its French section (*Association française du Conseil des Communes et Régions d'Europe*, AFCCRE), Airport Regions Conference, ACR +, Assembly of European Fruit and Vegetable Growing and Horticultural Regions, European Federation of Agencies and Regions for Energy and the Environment, European Forum for Urban Security via its French section (*Forum Français pour la Sécurité Urbaine*, FFSU), PURPLE, Network of European Metropolitan Regions and Areas, ERRIN, EU-Network of GMO-Free Regions, POLIS network (urban transport), UCLG, Metropolis, Global Fund for Cities Development, International Association of Francophone Regions, The Climate Group, and R20. According to the IDF government, several phenomena contribute to the multiplication of international networks globally, such as "the rise of local authorities as opposed to states and intergovernmental organizations, the decline in resources mobilized by states and intergovernmental organizations in times of economic crisis, as well as the growing awareness of the link between local and global issues (such as in the fight against climate change or urban innovation) and their growing importance on public policy agendas throughout the world."[32] The local level is increasingly called upon to co-finance and provide political legitimacy thanks to its proximity to citizens.

At the bilateral level, IDF's policies are guided by economic opportunities, European directives, or cultural Francophone ties. The latter are explored mostly with subnational governments in the Southern Hemisphere, such as Antananarivo (Madagascar), Nouakchott (Mauritania), Dakar (Senegal), Hanoi (Vietnam), or Kayes (Mali). Public transportation projects in Hanoi have, since 2002, helped to strengthen local capacity for planning and management. The construction of pilot projects (such as the interchange stations of Cau Giay and Long Bien, the bus depot of Thuy Khuê, and the bus lanes of Yen Phu and Hoan Quôc Viet) have had a significant impact on the quality of public transportation in Hanoi. Since 2004, IDF has also supported the healthcare and economic empowerment of people living with HIV in Nouakchott. According to the French region, local authorities have a distinct role to play in development assistance. "A region is not a sovereign state and it is not a humanitarian NGO either. Its added-value as a local authority lies in its ability to share its expertise in specific areas—such as institutional support, support for the implementation of public policies, support for decentralization and urban management for instance—as well as in its ability to support the work of civil society actors engaged in the field."[33]

Although with some subnational governments, cooperation is somehow uneven and based on development assistance, IDF also deploys an array of other international policies that mirror more sustainable and balanced relations. In June 2013, it launched a public market to enable local small and medium-sized enterprises to reach out to areas with high economic potential, such as São Paulo, Beijing, Santiago, or Quebec City. The initiative aims to promote economic and technological cooperation by providing specific support to companies in their external outreach efforts. In Chile, a project was carried out for innovative start-ups and clusters (Systematic in the fields of systems and ICT, and Cap Digital in the field of innovative economy) in partnership with INRIA Chile, a Santiago-based center of excellence set up by the French Institute for Research in Computer Science and Automation (*Institut National de Recherche en Informatique et en Automatique*, INRIA). IDF also launched a mobility program targeting unemployed and/or unqualified youth from the metropolitan region of Paris. Since 2002, the "Mobil'Asie" program has sent to Hanoi twenty young jobseekers for professional training for a period of six months, so that they increase their employability when they return home. In 2015, similar programs started in Beijing, São Paulo, and Santiago. Other bilateral programs are also noteworthy. With São Paulo state, IDF signed an agreement in December 2014 establishing the "2014 Île-de-France and São Paulo Year for Sustainable Urban Development." The program aimed to ensure that the two regions were aligned in the area of urban development, which includes topics such as transport, infrastructure, sanitation and depollution of rivers, and the environment, among others. Launched by São Paulo Governor Geraldo Alckmin and IDF's President Jean-Paul Huchon, in the presence of French President François Hollande, it led to the implementation of approximately ten initiatives.

To handle the external portfolio, IDF has a Vice-President of European and International Affairs in charge of the International and European Affairs Directorate. In total, over thirty staff members are directly involved with international relations, including the local representatives in São Paulo, Haiti, Hanoi, and Antananarivo. In the opinion of Roberto Romero, then Vice-President in charge of International and European Affairs, the critical challenges ahead for local authorities in the field of international policy are connected to the funding of international cooperation in times of economic downturn, and to the search for more efficient, coordinated, and result-oriented policies. The international voice of local authorities is a pragmatic one—one that is close to the concerns of the people in terms of urban management, the environment, water and sanitation, and public transportation. "Paradiplomacy is foreign policy with a local touch."[34]

Lombardy (Italy)

Lombardy (capital Milan) is the most populous region in Italy and one of the richest in Europe. With nearly 10 million inhabitants and accounting for 20 percent of the total GDP of the country, the region is the industrial heart of Italy. In the course of its history, the city-states located in Lombardy have had a very strong international presence and Lombardy may be regarded as one of the cradles of city diplomacy. But the entrance of the region onto the global stage in modern times was made through the Four Motors of Europe, a network established in 1988 by Baden-Württemberg, Catalonia, Lombardy, and Rhône-Alpes, with the aim of becoming actively involved in the process of European integration. Lombardy was not the proponent of such an initiative, but it went along loyally. Yet, the region had to wait until the 2001 reform of the national constitution to start playing a more convincing role internationally. The changes in the legal landscape reasserted the principle of subsidiarity and recognized the region's right to conduct its international relations. In some ways, 2001 could be regarded as the official starting point of Lombardy's foreign affairs.[35]

Presently, the regional government acts through a complicated network of different layers of power to conduct its international affairs. The first layer right below the region's president has a strong political nature and includes the Minister of Housing, Expo 2015, and Internationalization of Enterprises (*Assessore alla Casa, Housing sociale, Expo 2015, and Internazionalizzazione delle imprese*), the Under-Secretary on the Implementation of the Program, National Institutional Relations and International Relations (*Sottosegretario all'Attuazione del programma, ai rapporti istituzionali nazionali e alle relazioni internazionali*), and the Under-Secretary that handles relations within the European Strategy for the Alpine Region (EUSALP) and the Four Motors of Europe (*Sottosegretario ai rapporti con il Consiglio regionale, alla Macroregione alpina [EUSALP], ai quattro motori per l'Europa e alla programmazione negoziata*). All three represent a fraction of the foreign affairs menu and all report directly to the president. Even so, the institutional heart rests with the Directorate of International Relations and Expo 2015 (*Direzione Rapporti internazionali e raccordo Expo*) and its Unit on International Relations (*Struttura Relazioni internazionali*). With a staff of approximately twenty people, it is responsible for the institutional international relations with bilateral partners and multilateral networks and the carrying out of development cooperation projects. It also supports Expo 2015 S.p.A (the entity responsible for the organization and management of the Expo Milano 2015) in its international activities, including maintaining contacts with the International Exhibitions Bureau (*Bureau International des Expositions*, BIE). With a strong operational and technical nature, the Directorate reports to the president through the Secretary General (*Segretario Generale*), the president's chief of staff.

The governance apparatus also includes the region's office in Brussels (*Regione Lombardia Delegazione di Bruxelles*), which represents the region vis-à-vis the European institutions and negotiates structural funds; and the Ministry for Productive Activities, Research and Innovation (*Attività produttive, Ricerca e Innovazione*), which handles the programs on international trade and FDI. It is directly responsible for Invest in Lombardy, a service agency promoted by

Unioncamere Lombardia, the Lombardy Chambers of Commerce network and Promos—the Special Agency of the Milan Chamber of Commerce. Invest in Lombardy is structured as a regional network that works closely with business communities and helps address their needs. It also draws from Promos's ten offices abroad (the first opened in Moscow in 1994).

The Italian region has signed more than 80 bilateral agreements with foreign partners, and Milan houses the consulates of over 110 countries (the second largest concentration of consular corps in the world, after New York), but the region's multilateral policies have drawn more attention than its government-to-government relations. Lombardy is a member of a large number of multilateral networks, such as the Four Motors for Europe, Association of Alpine States (Arge Alp), EUSALP, Vanguard Initiative for New Growth by Smart Specialization, DC Network, ECRN, NEREUS, European Regions and Municipalities Partnership for Hydrogen and Fuel Cells, Association of European Regions for Origin Products, European Association of Elected Representatives from Mountain Regions, Art Nouveau Network, Air Quality Initiative of Regions, and The Climate Group. In addition, Lombardy championed the creation of the World Regions Forum, a network of close to twenty regional powerhouses aimed at discussing a variety of challenges faced by subnational governments—from healthcare to environmental sustainability. Successful summits were organized in 2009 and 2011 but after Lombardy's president Roberto Formigoni's stepped down in 2013, ending a cycle of almost twenty years in power, the Forum faded gradually into its final dissolution. Budget cuts, change in political reasoning, and questionable results laid the network to rest.

But with other multilateral schemes Lombardy did a better job. Although the government does not have a specific budget tagged for participating in multilateral networks,[36] Lombardy is strongly involved with the Four Motors of Europe and the Vanguard Initiative through which projects on trade and R&D have emanated. But the best illustration of multilateral involvement is the creation of EUSALP, which aims at ensuring mutually beneficial interaction between the mountain regions and the surrounding lowlands and urban areas. Lombardy was one of the initiators of the project together with the seven Alpine countries (Italy, Austria, Switzerland, Germany, Slovenia, Liechtenstein, and France) and six other substates (Bavaria, Rhône-Alpes, Tyrol, PACA, Piedmont, Aosta, Venetia, Friuli-Venezia Giulia, Trentino-Alto Adige, and Grisons) and has been working since 2011 for its success. The Alpine region is one of the largest economic and productive regions in Europe, housing 70 million people to live and work, as well as an attractive tourist destination for millions of guests every year. EUSALP includes forty-eight regions. Lombardy coordinates Italian regions and champions the themes of competitiveness and innovation which make up one of the three pillars of the strategy (the others are environmentally friendly mobility and sustainable management of energy, natural, and cultural resources). Although EUSALP is composed of both national and subnational states, it builds on the experiences of the already existing national macro-regional strategies: the European Strategy for the Danube Region and the European Strategy for the Baltic Sea Region.

Finally, Lombardy was naturally very involved with Expo 2015 in Milan. Besides being directly engaged with the candidacy to the BIE and advocating on its behalf through bilateral and multilateral contacts, the regional government co-organized the "World Expo Tour," a massive effort to promote the Expo abroad, foster bilateral cooperation and present investment opportunities in Lombardy. In 2014 and 2015, close to thirty tours were organized to destinations in Asia, Europe, and the Americas.[37]

Massachusetts (United States)

With a GDP of US$474 billion (ahead of Austria and the United Arab Emirates) in 2015 and with the highest concentration of educational institutions in the United States, Massachusetts is a natural candidate for the global spotlight. The cradle of Massachusetts's external policy became intertwined with Governor Michael Dukakis's return to power in 1983. As the new mantra in Beacon Hill's State

House was to achieve economic development, the state put together new measures to increase its exports and attract FDI. Only a few years after the normalization of US relations with the People's Republic of China, Massachusetts reached out to China's richest province, Guangdong, to sign an MoU on economic cooperation. That was November 1983 and it was the first international agreement signed by Massachusetts. One year later, Dukakis established the Massachusetts Office of International Trade and Investment (MOITI) within the Executive Office of Economic Affairs with the express objectives of assisting Massachusetts companies in expanding their sales in overseas markets and encouraging foreign investors to choose Massachusetts as an investment location. MOITI replaced the ineffective Massachusetts Foreign Business Council that had been established in August 1979 by Governor Edward King (1979–1983). In the 1980s, the United Kingdom, Germany, Japan, Canada, and China were the principal target countries of the state's foreign policy. Trade missions to Japan (Nagoya, Tokyo, Kyoto, and Osaka) and China (Guangdong) were organized in 1985. In 1988, after spending nearly US$2 million in public resources, MOITI claimed to be responsible for a total of US$35 million in contracts for the export of Massachusetts products.

If we fast-forward to current times, the state's foreign affairs strategy has not changed much. But it has changed a bit. MOITI still assists Massachusetts companies in growing internationally, but during Governor Deval Patrick's administration (2007–2014), MOITI gained the additional mandate to serve as the diplomatic arm of the state government. It maintains relationships with the consular corps (around sixty countries are represented in Boston) and Massachusetts-based foreign economic development agencies, and implements agreements with other countries and regions. Although it counts only five officials (divided by geographical regions), it serves as an extension of the governor's office on foreign affairs and protocol. The second major difference is that Massachusetts no longer has representations abroad. In different points in time, MOITI managed overseas trade offices (Jerusalem, Berlin, Mexico City, São Paulo, and Guangzhou), but in 2010, due to a budget shortfall but also due to some questions over their effectiveness and deliverables, the last offices were dismantled and MOITI was put under the jurisdiction of the Executive Office of Housing and Economic Development, dropping its quasi-public agency status and becoming a state agency.

In practical terms, MOITI makes use of the traditional arsenal of an investment agency, including organizing trade missions, signing international agreements, and ensuring that the governor meets with world leading figures. During his mandate, Governor Patrick met with various heads of state or government, including the Prime Minister of Japan Shinzo Abe (December 2013), British Prime Minister David Cameron (March 2011), Israeli Prime Minister Benjamin Netanyahu (March 2011), Irish Prime Minister Enda Kenny (May 2013), the President of Peru Ollanta Humala (June 2013), Kenyan Prime Minister Raila Odinga (April 2011), Armenian Prime Minister Tigran Sargsyan (December 2012), and the President of Brazil Dilma Rousseff (April 2012), leveraging Massachusetts's presence in the global marketplace. As Governor Patrick mentioned in an address at the Montreal Council on Foreign Relations: "Massachusetts is home to a globally recognized creative economy and talent pool. . . . In order to maintain our competitive edge, we must strengthen our global relationships and show the world everything Massachusetts has to offer."[38]

Even if it is relatively common for US states to set up trade missions, Massachusetts stood out vis-à-vis other subnational governments, with ten high-profile missions to fifteen countries during Governor Patrick's two mandates: China (December 2007), United Kingdom and Israel (March 2011), Brazil and Chile (December 2011), Colombia (February 2013), Ireland (May 2013), Canada (October 2013), Japan, Hong Kong, and Singapore (December 2013), Panama and Mexico (March 2014), Israel and United Arab Emirates (May–June 2014), and Denmark, United Kingdom, and France (September 2014). Although the local press has often looked down on these international trips,[39] the state government has been able to associate each mission with announcements of new agreements and new businesses into Massachusetts. Unlike Patrick,

Governor Charles Baker (2015–to the present) took a much lower profile. To signal the difference from his predecessor, no international trade mission was organized and no major reception to an international political leader was held in his first year in office.

In total, Massachusetts signed thirty-one agreements between 1983 and 2015, mostly with European and Asian countries on economic, industrial, technological, and commercial cooperation. Even if "it is quite common for most of the accords to become dormant," according to a MOITI official,[40] the state's bilateral relations still produced some noteworthy results. The highlight of Governor's Patrick first mandate was the opening of the Massachusetts Technology Center at the Shanghai Zhangjiang Hi-Tech Park, encouraging innovation and collaboration between businesses in Massachusetts and China. The center was open to any business in Massachusetts for exhibiting and marketing products to Chinese companies, but it was closed in 2010 due to the budget shortfall. During his second mandate, one of the most successful programs was the Massachusetts–Israel Innovation Partnership (MIIP), which derives from an MoU signed in March 2011 with the goal of promoting greater collaboration among companies in both Israel and Massachusetts. MIIP is implemented by the Israeli Industry Center for R&D, on behalf of the Office of the Chief Scientist in the Israel Ministry of Economy and by the Massachusetts Clean Energy Center. MIIP established a grant program to stimulate the development of new products for commercialization into global markets.

At the multilateral level, the track record is less perceptible. Massachusetts is a member of the Council of State Governments–Eastern Regional Conference, which aims to facilitate the exchange of ideas among state policymakers, business leaders, and the academic community in eighteen US and Canadian states. It also participates in the New England Governors and Eastern Canadian Premiers (NEGECP) Annual Conference, an organization established in 1973 to advance the interests of the six states (Connecticut, Maine, Massachusetts, New Hampshire, Rhode Island, and Vermont) and five provinces (New Brunswick, Newfoundland and Labrador, Nova Scotia, Prince Edward Island,

and Quebec) located in America's northeast region. But the state has a limited engagement with these groups due to budget downfalls and skepticism over the added-value of the networks.[41] For a state of its economic size, Massachusetts is poorly connected to global governmental networks and participates only residually in global discussions that affect subnational governments.

Massachusetts also possesses a dense portfolio of public and quasi-public agencies that have a role to play in international affairs, such as the Massachusetts Export Center, the Massachusetts Office of Travel and Tourism, the Massachusetts Global Student and Alumni Network, Massachusetts Port Authority (Massport), the Massachusetts Life Sciences Center, the Massachusetts Clean Energy Center, the Massachusetts Development Finance Agency (MassDevelopment), the Massachusetts Convention Center Authority, the Massachusetts Alliance for Economic Development, and the Massachusetts Technology Collaborative. This latter agency published in 2010 the report "An International Strategy for Massachusetts," with multiple recommendations to promote economic development and job creation statewide through international activities, but only a handful of them were actually implemented. The guiding mandate of the foreign affairs team stems primarily from the domestic priorities set out by the governor's office, which focuses on infrastructure, education, and innovation. The foreign affairs mandate is therefore a natural spillover from the domestic strategy.

Medellín (Colombia)

Medellín is the second largest city in Colombia and the capital of the northern department of Antioquia. With more than 6 million people and accounting for 15 percent of Colombia's GDP, Medellín is also the top exporting region of the country. This provided a fertile ground for Medellín to become the most active Latin American city internationally. Back in 2002, the International Cooperation Agency of Medellín (*Agencia para la Cooperación Internacional,*

ACI) was established as a result of a partnership between different public entities. It incorporated the mayor's office, the metropolitan area of the Aburrá Valley, and different private companies to enhance the participation of the city in the international scenario. It was the country's first municipal international cooperation management agency.

But despite the initial expectations, ACI had a weak start and was guided by trial and error. Initially, ACI was dedicated to managing the receipt of international resources without much fine tuning or guidance. It was only when the city hall implemented a development plan (2008–2011) called "Medellín is Generous and Competitive" (*Medellín es Solidaria y Competitiva*) that the parameters to start, effectively, the process of internationalization of the city were set. Interestingly, although the plan laid out a strategy to mitigate poverty, it contended that this overall goal could only be achieved with an international perspective. The fifth out of the six strategies of the program was in fact called "City with regional and global projection." Consequently, ACI was given better conditions and a budget to operate internationally.

As a consequence of consultancy work carried out by the United Nations for Industrial Development Organization on ACI's future opportunities, in 2006 the agency gained an additional purpose— to attract FDI to the city—and its name was changed to Agency for Cooperation and Investment of Medellín. Business results soon followed. Between 2006 and 2014, it attracted US$1.3 billion in FDI (on average US$144 million/year). In 2010, ACI got Hewlett Packard to set up a global service center in Medellín that created 1,000 direct jobs. According to an action plan drafted that year, ACI's specific objectives and strategies were divided into: cooperation, investment, outreach, communications, and administration. With a strong institutional capacity, results have been noteworthy. According to ACI senior officials,[42] between 2009 and 2014, it welcomed 630 foreign delegations and participated in more than 70 international events. In the same period, the agency managed the reception of US$66.2 million in technical and financial resources from international cooperation through the Medellín mayor's office. These resources were used to support the implementation of strategic projects in the areas of education, gender, civic culture, social urbanism, entrepreneurship, and security. If we consider the fact that Medellín is a city that was segregated from the world for generations, the figures are not far from remarkable.

When the city started to be treated by the international press and international organizations as a role model in urban transformation, ACI also turned into the main interlocutor to promote Medellín transformation and its best practices. At the height of Colombia's drug wars in the 1990s, Medellín was one of the most violent cities in the world. But over the last decade, the city has worked hard to recover from years of violence, not only with law-enforcement initiatives but by making a series of innovative public investments—such as urban gondolas and a hillside escalator, designed to integrate the city's low-income residents and communities with its wealthier commercial center. The transformation process is also at the heart of Ruta N, the city's innovation agency. Funded through a private/public partnership model, it focuses on driving the city's knowledge economy, clustered around specific industry sectors (health, energy, and ICT). Its strategy includes plans to turn Medellín into the most innovative city in Latin America by 2023. In parallel, Medellín is engaging in the protracted Colombian peace process. According to officials, the city will pursue effective programs on reconciliation, as a significant part of the demobilized guerrilla members will likely settle down in Medellín and Antioquia.[43]

These achievements have been acknowledged by the international community. In 2010 alone Medellín received four major international awards by organizations such as UN-Habitat and the World Health Organization-Pan American Health Organization. In 2011, it won another three. In 2013 it was nominated Innovative City of the Year by Citi and the *Wall Street Journal*, beating out finalists New York City and Tel Aviv and in 2016 it won the prestigious Lee Kuan Yew World City Prize. As the city became a laboratory of creative public policies, ACI joined forces with the IDB and UN-Habitat in 2012 to produce a book that systemized the Medellín model in ten significant practices.

Medellín's external actions are conducted both bilaterally and multilaterally. The city has strong relations with several Latin American cities (e.g., Buenos Aires, Panama City, and Mexico City) and with a handful of municipalities in Spain, especially Barcelona. The fact that Medellín and Barcelona have transformed themselves from industrial to knowledge/technology cities, are the second largest cities in their countries, and have credible foreign policies makes them "the strongest allies," in the words of a senior ACI official.[44] The partnership started up in 1998 with the adoption of the cultural project Know Your City (Conoces Tu Ciudad). In 2013, the thrust of the cooperation was Barcelona's support to the revitalization of downtown Medellín using as model the renovation of the El Raval neighborhood in Barcelona. Medellín and Antioquia's relations with Spain are also cultivated through the program Spain and its Regions Exchanging Knowledge with Antioquia (España y sus Regiones Intercambian Conocimiento con Antioquia), which was established in 2006 to bring together different public, private, and academic entities from Spain and Antioquia to engage in "inter-institutional exchanges." In more recent times, the Colombian city has also reached out to Scandinavian and Dutch partners.

Medellín is also a member of several multilateral networks, including ICLEI, Metropolis, Mercocities, CIDEU, International Association of Educating Cities, and the Cities for Mobility network. It is noteworthy that the city was invited to join Mercocities, a network of Mercosur cities when Colombia is not a part of the regional organization. According to a senior ACI official, that occurred "because Medellín has become a role model in Latin America that other cities try to emulate."[45]

Indeed, Medellín has not only been a Latin American leader in executing foreign policies at the city level but also in laying out doctrine. In 2005, ACI launched the International Decentralized Cooperation Manual (updated regularly). This pedagogical tool guides local governments and foreign organizations on the essentials of paradiplomacy by presenting the main concepts, the legal framework in Colombia for cooperative endeavors, case studies, and a comprehensive directory of cooperating entities in the world.

And in 2013 it launched the Medellín's International Cooperation Public Policy, a set of principles and targets that guide the internationalization of the city. It is also designed to facilitate communication between local and international players, from a technical and political perspective and to encourage novel partnerships. It was first mandated by the International Cooperation network of Antioquia, comprising about thirty organizations—including Antioquia's NGO Federation, the University of Antioquia, Comfenalco Comfama, Instituto para el Desarrollo de Antioquia, the Government of Antioquia, Medellín Mayor's Office, and the ACI. This network is another good example of how different public entities can join forces to present a coherent vision of a local government abroad. In fact, integrating internationalization into the development plans of its partners, especially the mayor's office and other metropolitan officials has been the key ingredient in ACI's success (Bañales 2011). As of early 2015, ACI had a staff of about fifty people.

New South Wales (Australia)

During British rule, Australian provinces were entitled to have representatives in the United Kingdom, the so-called agent-generals. New South Wales (NSW) appointed its first agent-general in London in 1864,[46] and it has maintained a representative in the British capital ever since, either through the Agent-General's Office (1864–1932), the New South Wales Government Office (1932–1999), Destination NSW London office (since 1999), or the NSW Department of Industry representative (since 2015). The gradual mutation of its presence abroad is an indicator of the crescive importance it places on tourism, trade, and investment as a means to attain economic development. NSW boasts the largest subnational economy in Australia; in 2014, NSW's GDP was valued at US$385 billion, representing 31 percent of Australia's total. With Sydney as its capital, the state is home to 44 percent of Australia's finance and insurance industry.

With these economic credentials, the state's foreign affairs have naturally been built on the promotion of trade and investment. In 2013–2014, exports of NSW goods and services generated over US$44 billion in revenues, representing 18.1 percent of Australia's trade.[47] In the administrations of Premier Nathan Rees (2008–2009) and Kristina Keneally (2009–2011), NSW went to great lengths to develop a modern foreign policy, which included opening or re-opening offices in Guangzhou and Shanghai (2009), Mumbai (2009), and Abu Dhabi (2009). Her successor, Barry O'Farrell (2011–2014), took the same route and opened offices in San Francisco (2012) and Tokyo (2013). These are typically two to three person offices headed up by senior local managers with regional market knowledge. The offices provide a contact point for foreign companies who want to do business in Sydney and NSW. The office staff also works with NSW companies looking for commercial opportunities abroad.

NSW efforts in trade and foreign affairs are managed by the Department of Industry, Skills and Regional Development (known as the NSW Department of Industry), which replaced in 2015 the Department of Trade and Investment, Regional Infrastructure and Services (DTIRIS, known as NSW Trade & Investment), a structure established in 2011 by Premier O'Farrell. It unites key NSW government economic development agencies, offices, and authorities to drive regional economic growth and increase the competitiveness of doing business in the state. According to the annual report: "In 2013–2014, NSW secured $3.2 billion [US$2.4] in business investment through 143 investment projects in NSW and $515 million [US$377] in 140 export wins. Over the next three years this activity will generate 5,700 jobs" (NSW Trade & Investment 2014, 2).

The narrowing down on economic issues also sets the stage for the Australian region to organize frequent trade and investment missions. During Premier O'Farrell's term, premier-led missions were organized to India (2011 and 2012), India and Singapore (2013), Japan and the Philippines (2014), Lebanon and United Arab Emirates (2012), and China (2011, 2012, 2013, and 2014) to raise awareness of New South Wales as a business partner and investment destination. When his successor Mike Baird took office in mid-2014, the overlap between trade and foreign policy became even more conspicuous. His first international trade missions targeted the three NSW major export destinations: Japan and South Korea (May 2015) and China (November 2015). Showing alignment with federal trade policies, the missions were also a strategy to take advantage of bilateral agreements signed between the Australian government with those countries in the same period (the Japan Australia Economic Partnership Agreement, the Korea-Australia Free Trade agreement and the Australia-China free trade agreement came into effect in January 2015, December 2014, and December 2015, respectively).

To provide guidance to its international efforts, the NSW adopted in April 2013 its International Engagement Strategy "to position the State to attract more international investment, facilitate exports, create jobs and grow the economy." Designed by a high-level group which was tasked to review NSW's external affairs, the strategy identified new and priority markets, suggested means to pursue them, and recommended the NSW government to double its offices overseas, adding Britain, South Korea, Singapore, Malaysia, and Indonesia. The strategy was quickly implemented and NSW trade representatives were stationed in these countries in 2014 and 2015 (co-located with the Australian Trade Commission). In addition, in the same period NSW launched a Japan Strategy, a China Strategy, and an India Strategy outlining how the government plans to strengthen and grow its economic ties with these three countries.

To pursue its economic interests, NSW also adopts sister-state agreements. The first was signed in 1979 with Guangdong—the first of its kind between an Australian state and a Chinese province. Unlike most agreements of this kind, NSW and Guangdong were able to steer it to produce some substance. Since 1990 a Joint Economic Meeting is held annually, generally attended at the highest level (governor/premier) and supported by leading businesses and research institutions, with the aim of pursuing economic advantages. In the frame of the sister-state agreement, the governor of Guangdong, Zhu Xiaodan, visited NSW in September 2014, and together with Premier Mike Baird they announced other cultural and educational partnerships including the establishment of a Young Leaders Exchange Program and Collaborative Education Programs. Xiaodan also made history by becoming the first Chinese leader to address the NSW Parliament.

Other similar agreements were adopted with Tokyo Metropolis (1984), North Rhine-Westphalia (1989), Seoul (1991), Jakarta (1994), California (1997), and Maharashtra. The latest, with India's leading industrial and finance state, was adopted in November 2012, during Premier O'Farrell's mission to India. The agreement aims to build increasing trade and investment in areas including financial services, energy, minerals and mining, agribusiness, urban infrastructure, and environmental protection. However, despite the fact that these agreements were signed with pomp and were expected to herald new developments, they fell short and produced poor results when compared to the Guangdong partnership.

International protocol also plays a part in the game. NSW and Sydney in particular, host hundreds of inbound delegations from all over the world each year. Even though only a small number of these delegations have direct interest or relevance to the economic export and investment agenda of the NSW, there is a need to receive them properly. This is carried out by the Protocol and Special Events unit in the Department of Premier and Cabinet. It provides management and coordination services for NSW officials for special events, official visits, honors and awards, and community programs.

Despite the fact that NSW external affairs are strongly clustered on trade and investment, tourism is an additional important piece of the international puzzle. Destination NSW, a government agency, was established in 2011 to support the growth of tourism and events, both from Australia and overseas. By marketing NSW as a premier tourism destination and securing major sporting and cultural events, it wishes to achieve the NSW government's goal of doubling expenditure within the state's visitor economy by 2020. To attend to its most important market, in 2012 it presented a China Tourism Strategy to guide business development and consumer marketing activity between 2012 and 2020. Destination NSW has three offices in China (Chengdu, Shanghai, and Hong Kong), along with Auckland, London, Los Angeles, Tokyo, Mumbai, Singapore, and Seoul.

New York City (United States)

As the most populous city in the United States and the most globalized city in the world, expectations are always rocket high for New York City's capacity to develop its international affairs and to serve as a global player. New York City performance history, however, undulates between true global leadership and bashfulness. Historically, the city's interaction with foreign partners was carried out through the Sister City Program, a post–World War II citizen diplomacy organization that connected American and foreign cities through MoUs that articulated cultural and commercial bonds in general terms. The first of these agreements was signed with Tokyo in 1960 (see chapter 1), during the administration of Mayor Robert Wagner (1954–1965), and was followed by Beijing (1980), Madrid and Cairo (1982), Santo Domingo (1983), Rome and Budapest (1992), Jerusalem (1993), London (2001), and Johannesburg (2003). Although several of these agreements have their anniversaries celebrated on a regular basis and have set the stage for cultural exchanges, they underpin a relationship marked more by protocol rather than productivity.

To sustain these initial steps, New York started to develop its own institutional capacities. In 1962, at the suggestion of US Ambassador Adlai Stevenson, Mayor Wagner established the position of the New York City Commissioner for the UN to act as liaison between the diplomatic community and local residents, businesses, and government. Four years later, Mayor John Lindsay (1966–1973) expanded the Commissioner's role into a full-fledged Commission for the United Nation. In 1970, the Commission gained additional competencies when the Consular Corps Committee was transferred from the Department of Public Events to the Commission, thereby establishing the Commission for the United Nations and the Consular Corps. In 1997, the City's protocol office, which had various names dating back to 1913, merged with the Commission for the United Nations and Consular Corps. But the final model was only reached in 2012 when Mayor Michael Bloomberg (2002–2013) changed the name from the Commission for the United Nations, Consular Corps, and Protocol to the Mayor's Office for International Affairs.

The Office's primary mission has remained intact throughout. New York is host to the UN Headquarters and has the largest diplomatic corps in the world (115 consulates). A visible part of the Office's job is handling incoming visits of foreign dignitaries with municipal agencies and articulating operational issues such as diplomatic parking, compliance with health and safety codes, and improved security at the United Nations. This is what may be called the reactive dimension of New York's foreign affairs.

The second dimension is more proactive. During Mayor Bloomberg's administration, efforts were made to turn the city into a global power. The first step was to question the relevance of the sister agreements signed since the 1960s. The model ended up being considered old-fashioned and in 2003 a new version was presented. New York started organizing annual Global Partners Summits, each devoted to a specific theme, to bring together foreign mayors and other city officials to discuss common challenges and best practices. The organization was restructured and renamed New York City Global Partners, Inc. in 2006 with the aim of expanding New York's interaction with world cities while maintaining its historic ten sister-city relationships. The organization continues its membership in Sister Cities International but no longer enters into new sister-city agreements.

More than one hundred cities are presently part of this network. NYC Global Partners produced and hosted twelve international summits during Bloomberg's administration and the results have been positive. According to an official report:

> Most summits resulted in the creation of professional networks. By providing in-person shared experiences, the summits facilitated the creation of long-term online relationships. Best

practice reports were produced, and some comprehensive articles were published—for example, on workforce development, and on public health and climate change. In other cases, City agencies expanded their relationships with particular foreign cities. (City of New York 2013, 18)

NYC Global Partners was a solid step in the right direction, but Bloomberg's global leadership only solidified when in 2010 he was elected to chair the C40 Cities Climate Leadership Group, reinforcing the role of New York as a global power city. C40 is a network of the world's megacities taking action to reduce greenhouse gas emissions. It works with participating cities to address climate risks and impacts locally and globally. The C40 was created in 2005 by former Mayor of London Ken Livingstone, and forged a partnership in 2006 with the Cities Program of CCI to reduce carbon emissions and increase energy efficiency in large cities across the world.

While it cemented its global network of partners, New York did not overlook its bearing as a financial and economic center. More Fortune 500 financial services companies are headquartered in New York than in any other US city, and 18 of the top 20 foreign-owned banks have their US headquarters in the city. In 1992, Mayor David Dinkins (1990–1993) established the Division for International Business in the Commission's portfolio to assist foreign companies in opening or expanding operations in the five New York boroughs. According to *fDi* magazine, in 2012 New York City attracted 1.08 percent of global FDI, and in the same year the total number of FDI projects in New York increased by 10.4 percent from the previous year. It was named the top city in *fDi* magazine's rankings of "The American Cities of the Future 2013/14." In 2007, New York launched PlaNYC, a comprehensive effort to address the city's long-term challenges that put economic competitiveness in tune with priority decision-making.

Much of the activism shown by New York for over a decade was dependent on the personal style and drive of Mayor Bloomberg. During his term, he was unquestionably the mayor worldwide who received (or was received by) the highest number of heads of state and government, including Israeli Prime Minister Benjamin Netanyahu (2012), President Higgins of Ireland (2012), British Prime Ministers Gordon Brown and David Cameron (2008 and 2010, respectively), and South Korean President Roh Moo-Hyun (2003), among several others. After stepping down in 2013, he was nominated UN special envoy for cities and climate change, advocating that cities should take a stand against climate change; and he maintained his focus on city management through Bloomberg Philanthropies. During the administration of Bill de Blasio (elected in 2013), New York's foreign affairs fell back into its original mission: to host the diplomatic community and organize meetings with foreign authorities. NYC Global Partners international summits were discontinued in 2013.

Ontario (Canada)

Ontario is the most populous and the richest of the ten Canadian provinces, besides being home to the nation's capital city, Ottawa, and the nation's most populous city, Toronto. One of the most multicultural cities in the world, about 43 percent of Toronto's population was born outside of Canada. Aside from Quebec, which has long harbored ambitions for international prominence, Ontario is the Canadian province with the best track record in foreign affairs. The region has a dense international history. It opened its first office abroad, in London, in 1918, and after the war it established a presence in Chicago (1953), New York (1956), and Los Angeles and Cleveland (1967). The province also opened offices in Europe and Asia, including Milan (1963), Stockholm (1968), Brussels, Vienna, and Tokyo (1969), Frankfurt (1970), and Mexico City (1973) (Kukucha 2009). In October 1944, Ontario made some efforts to establish an office in Paris immediately after the liberation of the city, but the Canadian government was not enthusiastic and the idea was abandoned (Dyment 2001).

Presently, Ontario's international engagement is primarily tuned with its domestic agenda, which includes economic growth and job creation. This agenda is carried out mostly through the promotion of trade and foreign investment. According to Ontario officials, "the province's exports account for approximately 25 percent of the province's GDP and the Conference Board of Canada notes that every $100 million increase in exports creates 1,000 new jobs."[48] To showcase its pedigree as the economic and financial capital of Canada, Ontario has also gone a long way to build its brand as an ideal trading partner and investment destination, boasting a highly educated and diverse workforce. From 2005 to 2013, premier-led trade missions visited China, Hong Kong, India, Pakistan, Israel, and the West Bank resulting in over $1.6 billion in agreements between organizations and businesses. In 2012–13, the Ministry of Economic Development, Trade and Employment helped more than 550 companies participate in outbound trade missions. It came therefore as a natural step to present, in September 2013, Ontario's Going Global strategy to help expand the province's presence in global markets, grow the economy, and create jobs. The plan is predicated upon four pillars: diversification of markets, increase in exports, branding, and streamlining of resources.

To support the ambitious strategy, the province's workforce and institutional capacity is comparatively robust, with three pillars directly related to international relations. The first is the Office of International Relations and Protocol (OIRP), within the Ministry of Intergovernmental Affairs (Cabinet Office). It is responsible for government-to-government relations—including official visits from heads of state and government and other senior officials—and relations with the consular corps in Toronto (over one hundred countries are represented in the city making it, along with New York, Milan, and São Paulo, one of the largest in the world) and the diplomatic corps in Ottawa. It also serves as a secretariat for the premier, the lieutenant-governor, the speaker, and ministers across the provincial government to support their international interactions and events with policy advice and protocol services. It organizes on average over two hundred visits and meetings every year with foreign dignitaries. OIRP also works with the Canadian Department of Foreign Affairs, Trade and Development (DFATD) and other provincial ministries to provide information and advice to the Premier's Office and makes a strong contribution to the premiers' international missions. Its protocol side is mainly operational, while the international relations specialists focus mainly on policy.

The second pillar is the International Trade Branch of the Ministry of Citizenship, Immigration and International Trade, which is responsible for helping Ontario companies export into foreign markets. The team manages Ontario's Going Global strategy and the business program for premiers' and ministers missions abroad. The branch is also responsible for the province's International Trade Development Representatives (ITDRs) who are consultants contracted to provide in-market assistance to Ontario exporters in Mexico, Brazil, Chile, the United Arab Emirates, and Southeast Asia. In 2012 alone, they helped more than 1,200 companies develop their exporting skills and identify new market opportunities for their goods and services. From 2011 to 2014, the Trade Branch (then attached to the previously called Ministry of Economic Development, Trade and Employment[49]) organized and led over 180 trade missions, including six led by the premier.

The third pillar is the International Representation Branch within the same Ministry of Citizenship, Immigration and International Trade, which is responsible for overseeing the province's International Marketing Centers (IMC). Co-located in a Canadian embassy, high commission, or consulate, they are headed by a senior economic officer with diplomatic status and supported by one or two locally engaged staff. They are responsible for Ontario's broad economic mandate including helping the province's companies export their goods and services, attract FDI into Ontario and facilitate research and commercialization partnerships. Presently IMCs are located in New York, San Francisco, Mexico City, São Paulo, London, Paris, Munich, Beijing, Shanghai, Chongqing, New Delhi (with a satellite office in Mumbai), and Tokyo. The International Representation branch is also tasked to supervise the International Investment Development Representatives (IIDRs), which are contracted consultants whose priority is to identify FDI opportunities for Ontario. Consultants are located in the United States, United Kingdom, France, Germany, China, India, Japan, and South Korea. Ontario's large foreign network—comprised of IMCs, ITDRs, and IIDRs—could raise some questions related to co-ordination and streamlining. Interviews, however, showed that in markets in which there is an IMC and either an ITDR or IIDR, there is sufficient collaboration between the different offices on trade and investment files.[50] Brazil, where there is an IMC and ITDR, is a good example.

The workforce in the three pillars amounts to over fifty people. Although they represent the institutional core of Ontario's foreign affairs, several other ministries have program areas related to international relations, such as the Ministry of Economic Development, Employment and Infrastructure; the Ministry of Research and Innovation; the Ministry of Tourism, Culture and Sport; and the Ministry of Training, Colleges and Universities. If we count the overall structure, the staff involved with foreign affairs is much larger.

As the heart of Ontario's international strategy is related to investment and trade, the province has participated only very timidly in multilateral networks. It is only an associate member of the Council of Great Lakes Governors and of the Great Lakes Commission—organizations that lead regional efforts to protect the environment and accelerate the Great Lakes region's economy—and leaves it up to the Canadian government to represent Ontario's interests in international fora.[51] Compared to Alberta and Quebec, Ontario tends to work much closer to the federal government. Bilateral engagements are much stronger, however. According to the OIRP, which negotiates and manages Ontario's international agreements, the province has signed approximately 270 memoranda, of which about half are still active. Two of the most paradigmatic and long-standing arrangements are with Jiangsu (since 1985) and Baden-Württemberg (since 1987). An Ontario–Jiangsu Business Council was established in 2005, as a direct result of an Ontario premier's trade mission to China, to help create jobs in the two provinces by deepening collaboration in the areas of trade and investment, science and technology, education, tourism, agriculture, and environmental protection. The Council's working plans are updated regularly and meetings are held routinely. Several other agreements on education, environment, and tourism have been signed between Ontario and Jiangsu over the years.

Ontario's official relationship with Baden-Württemberg, one of Germany's most industrialized states, dates back to the mid-1980s, when a commercial MoU between the two jurisdictions was signed. This partnership was strengthened after an interregional conference was hosted in 1990 in Toronto by the premier of the day. At that conference, Ontario and Baden-Württemberg entered into a multisector partnership agreement focusing on commercial development, scientific research, the commercialization of new technologies, human resources and skills development via academic exchanges, and the promotion of culture. In 2006 and 2012, new agreements were signed with the intent of further expanding the close relationship that has existed for many years. The most notable offshoot of this cooperation has been in the area of education and student mobility. From 1987 to 2014, partnership programs between twelve universities in Ontario and nine universities in Baden-Württemberg supported the exchange of more than 2,000 Canadian and German students and academics. The exchange has become a model for other countries.

Ontario has also been very efficient in adopting partnerships with countries that boast a promising R&D market. These include the Ontario–China Research and Innovation Fund, the Ontario–India Research Collaboration Fund, and the Ontario–Israel Collaboration Program. The programs launch annual calls for proposals to support research and product development in areas such as bio-economy and clean technologies, digital media and information and communication technologies, or pharmaceutical research and manufacturing. According to Ontario's officials, it is generally accepted through the government that for the province to remain competitive, it has to be able to create international partnerships with foreign partners that help meet its economic growth goals.[52]

Quebec (Canada)

Quebec is probably the most robust example of a subnational foreign player worldwide. Already in the nineteenth century, at the very beginning of the Canadian federal regime, the Quebec government, by virtue of its general powers, took steps to be represented abroad and to send experts on technical missions (Blondeau 2001). While the Canadian state bureaucracy was still being formed, Quebec dispatched immigration agents to the United Kingdom and the United States (New England) in 1871, appointing an "official representative of the Government of Quebec for all negotiations concerning the attributions of the province" in Paris in 1882 and stationing an agent-general in London in 1911 and in Brussels in 1915. Although these local representations were closed in the 1930s during the Great Depression, an office opened in New York in 1940 with the mission of boosting trade and tourism.

Despite these embryonic steps and although some discussions were held at the end of the Maurice Duplessis government (1944–1959) to establish an official representation in France, Quebec's international relations only really took off during the 1960s, as a reaction "to internal as well as external stimuli which largely resulted from unpredictable and therefore uncontrollable events" (Lubin 2003–2004, 24). One of these events was the visit of Premier Jean Lesage (1960–1966) to France and the establishment of a Maison du Quebec in Paris in 1961 (at the call of the French president). This happened well before the creation of the Quebec Ministry of Intergovernmental Affairs in 1967 (precursor of the present *Ministère des Relations Internationales*), and long before Quebec's first comprehensive enunciation of its international policy in 1984. These initiatives were carried out within the larger context of the so-called Quiet Revolution, a period of intense change in the region characterized by the effective secularization of society, the creation of a welfare state (*état-providence*), and realignment of politics into federalist and sovereignist factions. This period brought about the rapid modernization of Quebec society and Quebec's economy.

Although it is not a consensual view, some authors even argue that, in a real sense, the champion of Quebec's modern foreign affairs was French president Charles De Gaulle (1959–1969) who in 1961 accorded the delegate-general of Quebec in Paris the status and diplomatic privileges of an ambassador conforming to French protocol. And in 1967, during a controversial visit to Canada, De Gaulle openly supported Quebec's demands: "Vive le Quebec Libre." France's tacit support of Francophonie worldwide had the collateral effect of boosting Quebec's international presence (Lubin 2003–2004, 24). It was also in this period that Quebec adopted its first international agreement, with France.[53] In fact, this agreement consisted of only an exchange of letters in early 1964 between the minister of Youth of Quebec, Gérin-Lajoie, and the president of the Association for the Organization of Courses for Technicians in France (*Association pour l'Organisation des Stages de Techniciens en France*), Marcel Demonque, but it set the stage for an exchange of professionals between Quebec and France "to achieve technical, scientific and economic progress."[54] After De Gaulle, other French presidents continued to support Quebec, and it was because of French intervention that Quebec was able to become a full member in the international Summit of the Francophonie (Bursens and Deforche 2010, 165).

It was also in the 1960s that the "Gérin-Lajoie doctrine" was first presented. The theory, which then-Liberal Education Minister Paul Gérin-Lajoie first developed in a PhD thesis in the 1950s and then expressed in a speech in Montreal in April 1965 before the consular corps, states that Quebec has exclusive jurisdiction abroad in areas like health and education ("*le prolongement externe des compétences internes du Quebec*" [The external extension of Quebec's internal competences]). The doctrine, which was formulated to justify the signing of international agreements without Ottawa's supervision, is considered as the official foundation of Quebec's international policy. In the 1970s, "sovereign paradiplomacy" gained more relevance. Rene Levesque's Parti Quebecois (PQ) separatist government used foreign policy as a means of generating support for a proposed referendum on Quebec independence. Specifically, the PQ sought diplomatic immunity for its foreign representatives, made statements on human rights issues (such as South African apartheid), and considered an independent defense policy for a sovereign Quebec (Kukucha 2009).

Over the last fifty years, Quebec's presence in the world has oscillated between protodiplomacy and paradiplomacy, depending on what political party sits in power in Quebec City and on the political culture of the moment (McHugh 2015). But the province consistently remains one of the most proactive foreign players at the subnational level. Today, Quebec has over twenty-five delegations, offices, and local representatives in eighteen countries (see chapter 2). It maintains bilateral relations with thirty-five federated states and regions of the world, mainly in Western Europe and North America and has concluded more than eight hundred agreements (around three hundred are active) with about eighty countries and federated states in many areas of activity. Among these, particularly strong relations are held with the United States (trade and energy), Bavaria (trade and education), and France (language and culture). In fact, in the corridors of power in Quebec City, France is universally called "the privileged partner."[55] The provincial government has also been a participating member of the International Organization of La Francophonie (OIF) since its inception in 1970. Quebec is one of the OIF's five major donors and is considered one of its most active members. The OIF is the only multilateral government organization in which Quebec is a full-fledged member. At UNESCO Quebec also plays an important role, but it is carried out through Canada's official mission to the organization. The province is not a full-member (see chapter 2).

Quebec's foreign affairs are also advanced through participation in fourteen international groups of federated states and regions with a global or regional scope. These include: The Council of Atlantic Premiers, NEGECP, Council of Great Lakes Governors, Great Lakes Commission, Southeastern United States–Canadian Provinces Alliance, Northern Forum, REGLEG, Assembly of European Regions, Western Climate Initiative, Regional Greenhouse Gas Initiative, nrg4SD, The Climate Group, Regional Leaders Summit, and World Regions Forum. The selection of networks and the degree of involvement generally reflect a triple objective: either to cultivate good neighborly and cross-border relations with Arctic and US provinces to deal with issues of common concern (energy, water pollution, and environmental concerns), to cultivate the historical links with Europe, or to shape global agendas on sustainable development and climate change. After Île-de-France, Quebec is the subnational government that participates in the most multilateral networks.

In May 2015, it also joined the Carbon Pricing Leadership Coalition, an initiative of the World Bank that brings together leaders from government, business, and civil society with the goal of implementing effective carbon pricing policies.

On another front, in recent years, Quebec has placed considerable emphasis on international development initiatives. Specifically, the province has developed an international solidarity program that targets social issues in francophone developing countries in Africa, the Caribbean, and Latin America. Instead of designing its development policy as aid delivery, Quebec generally partners up with the private sector or nongovernmental groups that are members of the Association Québécoise des Organismes de Coopération Internationale. One solidarity initiative is Quebec without Borders, which was created in 1995 to sponsor the participation of Quebec citizens, between the ages of eighteen and thirty-nine, in international development projects (Kukucha 2009). For the year 2014–2015, the program received US$1.6 million from the Ministry of International Relations budget. Since 1997, Quebec has provided financial support for more than five hundred international development projects. The team responsible for this portfolio—International Solidarity mandate within the Department of Multilateral Affairs—has a transversal competence and articulates its actions across a wide range of internal bodies and departments. With one of the largest foreign affairs infrastructure at subnational levels, Quebec's government has also invested considerable efforts in bringing its external policy to a more systematic and result-oriented level, by adopting a variety of guiding directives. This includes not only its International Policy ("Working in Concert") (see chapter 2), which permeates all foreign activities, but also the Ministry's quadrennial strategic plans, strategies toward specific countries (e.g., Quebec Government's Strategy in Regard to the United States), action plans, and annual management reports. As of December 2014, the Ministry of International Relations and Francophonie has 529 positions: 223 in its network of representations abroad and 306 in Quebec. In addition, other staff are working in sectorial ministries (Tourism, Culture, Economy, and Exportation) and organizations that are internationally active and participate in the promotion of Quebec's interests abroad.

Quebec's Ministry of International Relations and Francophonie is the first subnational ministry of foreign affairs worldwide. It was established by the government of Daniel Johnson (1966–1968) in 1967 as the Ministry of Intergovernmental Affairs (*Ministère des Affaires intergouvernementales*), replacing and expanding on an earlier Ministry of Federal-Provincial Relations (*Ministère des Affaires fédérales-provinciales*).

São Paulo (state) (Brazil)

With a GDP of close to US$800 billion and a population of 43 million, the state of São Paulo consistently ranks in the G20 of the world's largest economies. The state's GDP is larger than Colombia, Chile, Uruguay, and Paraguay's combined economies. Appositely regarded as the economic, financial, and industrial lighthouse of Latin America, part of the economic success is explained by its historical openness to the world. Since the late nineteenth century, São Paulo has received close to 3 million immigrants mostly from Europe (Italy, Germany, Portugal, and Spain), Asia (Japan), and the Middle East (Syria and Lebanon) contributing instrumentally to the economic development of the state and to its social mix. The state is also regional home to most Fortune 500 companies and therefore has a competitive economy that is open to international markets. Its international status is also mirrored in the size of the consular corps. With over ninety countries represented, it is the fourth largest in the world, after New York, Milan, and Toronto.

Immigration was what originally compelled the state government to enter into the arena of foreign affairs. The first international agreement was signed in September 1907 with an emigration company on behalf of Japan (*Companhia de Emigração e
Colonização do Império do Japão*). This paved the way for the first
wave of Japanese emigrants (in 1908) (figure 1.1). It was one of
the first international agreements signed by a subnational state
worldwide. But when the need for foreign migrants abated, so did
the external affairs conducted by the state government. The resur-
gence occurred only in the 1970s when the first sister agreements
started to be signed: Mie (1973), Gunma (1980), Tokushima
(1984), Toyama (1985), and Tokyo (1990). They were all with
Japanese subnational governments, which reflects the weight
of the cultural link between São Paulo and Japan. They were all
proposed by the Japanese diaspora living in the Brazilian state,
and they all had a strong ceremonial and symbolic tone and led to
meager practical results.

The government created its first agency for international activities in March 1991, in the form of the Office for Foreign Affairs
(*Assessoria Especial de Assuntos Internacionais*). It enjoyed the same
status as a cabinet-level department, under the governorship of
Luiz Antônio Fleury Filho. The Office for Foreign Affairs aimed
to "advise the Governor on external contacts for financial, commercial, cultural, scientific, technical and technological cooperation with foreign private entities, international organizations and
specialized agencies of foreign governments" (Decree No. 33129).
The Office for Foreign Affairs was also composed of two committees: the Management and External Financing Committee and the
Business Relations Committee. In November of that same year,
the São Paulo State System for International Promotion was also
established with the purpose of stimulating São Paulo's economic
participation on the international stage. The system, composed of a
Board, Advisory Board, Executive Secretariat, and São Paulo Offices
of Trade Promotion Abroad, should have worked primarily with the
agencies and offices abroad of the Bank of the State of São Paulo S/
A (Decree No. 34253).

This ambitious structure never really took off and the Office for Foreign Affairs, along with its associated bodies, was closed down in 1996. The incoming governor Mário Covas (1995–2001) believed that the government had to direct its energies solely to domestic efforts and the Office's accumulated results were not sufficiently strong to convince him otherwise. Covas's sudden death in 2001 put in power his deputy, Geraldo Alckmin, who, approaching the end of his mandate in 2005, decided to re-establish the Office of Foreign Affairs, but with a limited mandate and only devoted to ceremonial issues. It was designed to organize the incoming visits of foreign dignitaries and the governor's trips abroad. During the administration of José Serra (2007–2010), the office preserved its circumscribed nature. International cooperation was virtually non-existent and the office was primarily prepared to deal with incoming visits (approximately thirty a year on average). Another point of interest was the fact that Brazilian diplomats were seconded to head the office, giving it an accessory nature vis-à-vis the federal Ministry of Foreign Affairs. Whereas worldwide the tendency was to provide subnational governments with native capacities on foreign affairs, until 2010 the philosophy that guided political authorities in São Paulo was that foreign affairs was an issue to be dealt with primarily by Brazil's federal government, not state governments. International actions were therefore mostly reactive, experimental, or context-specific.

In January 2011, Geraldo Alckmin was elected back into power, a fresh foreign affairs team took office and a new model for the external affairs of São Paulo was presented. This model had two major goals: "firstly, to make São Paulo state a global player acknowledged by its peers; and secondly, to ensure that international actions have a direct impact on its population. Such fields as health, transport, public safety, and education must be managed with an overseas arm to attract resources and study best practices" (São Paulo Government 2014, 5). Its diplomacy was meant to be "grounded, pragmatic and targeted" (São Paulo Government 2014, 5). São Paulo obeys the principle *in foro interno foro externo*, in other words, the government may act overseas in those fields in which it enjoys internal competencies.

To fulfill these goals, the government worked in three fronts (the three "i's," as it called them). The first was "Institutionalization" and it meant the adoption of legal and organizational instruments and the identification of human and budgetary resources to enable the state's international relations policy to be executed with long-term goals. In this light, the government adopted its first foreign affairs plan in April 2012: São Paulo in the World—International Relations Plan 2011–14 (*São Paulo no Mundo—Plano de Relações Internacionais 2011–2014*), established in law (Decree 57,932). It allowed for three general objectives, sixteen sectorial priorities, and fifty-four specific goals. To ensure internal cohesion and transparency, it also established its first diplomatic registry to sum up all the activities held or scheduled with hundreds of foreign partners. With the expansion in staff and competencies, the Office of Foreign Affairs was also remodeled internally, training and capacity-building programs were followed, and the Boston Consulting Group was called upon to ensure that each international cooperation project had tools to enable risk analysis, execution, and monitoring.

The second pillar was "Internationalization" and it aimed at adopting an increasing number of international cooperation programs and projects, and organizing missions overseas, in order to raise São Paulo's level of participation in, and recognition on, the international stage. From 2011 to October 2014, São Paulo hosted 1,595 foreign delegations (including twenty-two heads of state and government), a number similar to Brazil's federal government and much higher than most Latin American countries (figure 4.2). It signed 234 agreements, mostly on infrastructure, research and innovation, culture, education, and health that are associated with a portfolio of close to 150 cooperation programs, projects, and actions. It organized 104 events, including summits, conferences, and presentations, and carried out 230 missions abroad, mostly to take part in international gatherings, advance cooperation programs, or present the economic opportunities in the state. It established relations with 116 countries and formalized bilateral and direct relations with four of them (United States, Canada, France, and United Kingdom) (see chapter 2) (Tavares 2013).

FIGURE 4.2 Governor Geraldo Alckmin of São Paulo's state receives President François Hollande of France (2013)

© State government of São Paulo

Several projects reflect this renovated activism. International exchange programs allowed thousands of state-school pupils to travel free-of-charge to the United States, New Zealand, Britain, Spain, Chile, Argentina, and France to enhance their knowledge of a foreign language. The pursuit of innovative safety solutions led the state to import the intelligent monitoring system used by the New York Police Department. Designed by Microsoft and now being used outside New York for the first time, the software system integrates the state's thousands of surveillance cameras and databases (such as the 190 hotline), helping law enforcement officers on the street and in their investigations, and helping plan police actions. In another international program, São Paulo took, from 2011 to 2014, $3.8 billion in loans from credit agencies—IDB, World Bank, JICA, Development Bank of Latin America (*Corporacion Andina de Fomento*, CAF), and French Development Agency (*Agence Française de Développement*, AFD—to invest primarily in infrastructure.

Finally, the third pillar is related to "Information" and aims at disseminating information about São Paulo overseas, using a number of communication tools. During that period, the state adopted its first international portal, produced multilingual marketing publications, and engaged more actively in social media. From 2011 to 2014, São Paulo won thirteen international awards. It topped the list of "South American States of the Future (2014/2015)" in *fDi*, a magazine published by the Financial Times Group; it won a World Bank's regional contest on Initiatives to Promote Gender Equality in Latin America and the Caribbean (in 2014); and Line 4 of São Paulo's subway was voted Best Latin American and Caribbean Public Private Partnership (PPP) by the World Bank. In addition, Access São Paulo, the state government's digital inclusion program, won the 14th "Access to Knowledge" Prize awarded annually by the Bill & Melinda Gates Foundation and Geraldo Alckmin won the 2012 edition of the prestigious South Australian International Climate Change Leadership Award.

Although São Paulo foreign affairs are conducted primarily bilaterally, the state participates in ten multilateral networks: CIDEU, ICLEI, Mercocities, Metropolis, nrg4SD, FOGAR, R20, Regional Leaders Summit, The Climate Group, and the World Regions Forum. The intensity of São Paulo's participation varies widely though, and it is only active in the networks that deal with urban development and sustainability. It was nrg4SD's vice-president for Latin America and the Caribbean who led a Metropolis initiative on PPPs and metropolitan development.

São Paulo's foreign affairs are conducted by a network of several government agencies and entities—state secretariats, corporations, autarkies, and public foundations—and with approximately 120 officials. At the core lies the Office of Foreign Affairs, within the Governor's Cabinet, that is accountable for the general supervision of all foreign activities. The Office of Foreign Affairs also macro-manages the foreign activities of all state secretaries. They are, in fact, the executors and financial backers of the government's international cooperation. With growing demand, several secretariats created their own international bureaus in order to drive their cooperation with overseas partners. In this network, two additional entities play a vital role. The first is São Paulo's Investment and Competitiveness Promotion Agency (*Agência Paulista de Promoção de Investimentos e Competitividade*)—Invest São Paulo, which leads the strategy to attract incoming investment. From January 2011 to October 2014, eighty-two companies announced investment in the state supported by Invest São Paulo, creating 38,747 direct jobs and US$9 billion in investment. There is also the Foundation to Support Research in the State of São Paulo (*Fundação de Amparo à Pesquisa do Estado de São Paulo*, FAPESP), a public scientific advancement body that has pursued a robust strategy to globalize São Paulo's scientific activities. From 2011 to October 2014, FAPESP signed eighty international cooperation agreements with institutions in sixteen countries, thus expanding its global presence in scientific research.

Sydney (Australia)

Sydney is the most populous city in Australia and Oceania and one of the most multicultural cities in the world, with over 180 nations represented.[56] With strengths in finance, manufacturing, and tourism, its economy (US$284 billion in 2015) is the size of Denmark or Colombia and represents 23 percent of Australia's gross domestic product. Despite the fact that it is presently one of the most globalized cities on the planet, up until the mid-1970s, Sydney remained relatively isolated culturally from its Asian neighbors. Australia's relative cultural isolation extended economically, with relatively high tariff protection barriers to support its strong manufacturing base. Even so, it was in this context that Sydney took its first, even if humble, step internationally, through the establishment in 1968 of its first sister-city partnership, with San Francisco. It aimed to "stimulate the already existing friendship between two Pacific port cities and to strengthen civic, cultural, business, trade, tourism, and sporting ties." Over the years, the relationship has not always been active, but in 1977 cooperation between gay activists in both cities led the way to the first Sydney Gay Mardi Gras the following year.

With Australia's opening up in the 1980s, other city partnerships followed suit, with Nagoya (1980), Wellington (1983), Portsmouth (1984), Guangzhou (1986), and Florence (1993). The decade was a period of generalized excitement over sister city agreements and most mayors acted primarily out of impulse, rather than reason. The vast majority of Sydney's agreements were indeed adopted in that period, but in 1985 the city distinguished itself by becoming one of the first in the world to have its municipal government adopt clear Guidelines for Sister City Relationships. These were confirmed in 1992 and still guide city hall's decisions on the matter. The document establishes criteria for entering into any further relationship with other cities, such as: (1) that there exists significant historical, cultural, social, or geographic similarities between Sydney and the prospective city; (2) that the prospective city is, or is moving toward, being governed in a democratic fashion; (3) that the prospective city has, or is moving toward, a reasonable human rights record; (4) that the establishment of the proposed relationship will benefit specific strategic, national, and/or regional interests; (5) that there exists significant community support for the proposed relationship; and (6) that there is funding available for the relationship. It is interesting to note that the adoption of such a judicious roadmap on sister agreements led inevitably to their shrinkage. The latest of these agreements was signed as far back as in the early 1990s. Sydney may also be one of the first, and one of the very few, cities in the world to establish democratic and human rights guidelines for its external action. But implementation fell short and poor human rights in China did not hold Sydney back from signing the agreement with Guangzhou. As an official stated, it was considered appropriate by the then Council to move forward as it was believed that China unquestionably would develop increasingly important relationships with Australia in the coming decades and this fact had already been recognized by the NSW state government.[57]

Sydney also has friendship city relationships with four cities around the world: Paris (1998), Athens and Berlin (2000), Dublin (2002), and Wuhan (2015), but involvement is not as high as a sister-city relationship, and there was no need to establish guidelines for these more timid contacts.

With the turn of the millennium, the municipality's foreign affairs gained a more pragmatic and less ceremonial nature and its primary objective became to project Sydney globally as a modern, competitive, and lively city. In 2007 it presented Sustainable Sydney 2030, an integrated municipal plan that addresses the environment, society, culture, and economy. Although it is fairly common for large cities to develop similar plans, Sydney 2030 has some features that set it apart, not only because it was a truly inclusive program (12,000 people were directly consulted) but because it gained an imperative status, turning out to be the cornerstone of everything that city hall does. The 2030 vision focuses on ten strategic directions and the first one is "A Globally Competitive and Innovative City." Each direction includes different objectives and future actions, such as fostering economic collaboration and knowledge exchange with other national and global cities. Putting Sydney on the global map and solidifying its foreign affairs was then elevated to a major governmental aim. In 2013, a ten-year Economic Development Strategy was put forward with the intention of strengthening the city economy and supporting business. The plan concluded that Sydney's economic development presupposes maintaining strong linkages with international markets, increasing its interdependence on regional and global economies.

Both the 2030 vision and the Economic Development Strategy give emphasis to the mission of turning Sydney into an education destination—one that can provide not only educational quality but also a colorful lifestyle. Presently, over 35,000 international students study in the city and the municipality has gone a long way in providing an adequate structure to assist them. In 2013 it launched the International Student Leadership and Ambassador program. On an annual basis, forty international students go through six months of training to be able to serve as representatives of the international student community. The sense of belonging and attachment that flourishes within the student community plays an important role in growing and strengthening the city's global connections. Sydney is the world's most popular city to study in, according to the AT Kearney 2014 Global Cities index.

Beyond the large strategies and visions, the city government carries out smaller, but equally effective programs to vindicate the idea of Sydney as a global hub. For instance, it provides a range of public talks ("City Talks") that aim "to inspire, challenge and stimulate creative thinking in Sydney." The keynote addresses are made by major international thought leaders and industry experts (previous speakers include Joseph E. Stiglitz, Tim Berners-Lee, Cate Blanchett, and Ken Livingstone) who present ideas on significant issues at the global, national, and city level.

Sydney's external relations emanate directly from its 2030 vision and additional sectorial strategies and therefore it is the municipal office responsible for long-term planning (the Research, Strategy & Corporate Planning division) that also plays a part in conducting Sydney's foreign affairs. Presently, its Economic Strategy unit has been mandated to design an International Action Plan, as specified in the Economic Development Strategy, to be endorsed by the city council by 2016. Alongside initiatives on long-term planning, the city operates a Protocol unit for the overall management and delivery of the visits of international government officials (approximately one hundred delegations a year), and calls on other operational units to negotiate international agreements, depending on the topic at stake. All agreements must align with the city's Sustainable Sydney 2030 vision and be formally adopted by the municipal government (composed of ten councilors).

Besides working to realize its long-term goals, the municipality also explores ways in which it can build on its strong cultural connection with countries in Asia to strengthen economic ties and promote trade and investment. China is an important part of the equation. Each year, over 350,000 visitors from China visit Sydney (expected to grow to over 600,000 by 2021) and the Asian country's trade with the Sydney area is estimated at around $10 billion a year. Sydney manages and hosts the largest Chinese New Year festival outside Asia and people of Chinese ancestry make up nearly 10 percent of the city's population and over half of all Australians born in

China live in Sydney. Symbolically, the city launched its new Global Sydney marketing campaign at the 2014 China International Fair for Trade in Services in Beijing to showcase the opportunities that could be afforded by a closer relation. In May 2014, Sydney's Mayor Clover Moore joined a business delegation to China (Shenzhen, Guangzhou, Xi'an, Beijing, and Wuhan) and met with the mayors of each city. Another beacon of the close bilateral link is the annual Sydney China Business Forum, which brings together Chinese state-owned and nongovernment-owned agencies with Australian businesses and government agencies. The event is organized by the University of Sydney and hosted by the city of Sydney.

At the multilateral level, Australia's largest city is engaged with several global networks, such as The Climate Group, UCLG, 100 Resilient Cities network, and more emphatically C40. Besides being a founding member, in 2014–2015, it co-chaired (with Tokyo) the C40 Private Sector Buildings Energy Efficiency Network, spearheading the establishment of a work plan on energy efficiency.

Sydney is considered an alpha + world city, according to Loughborough University's globalization and world cities research network, which measures the connectivity of cities in terms of position and influence. Sydney is ranked in the top 10 most connected cities alongside New York, London, Tokyo, Paris, and Hong Kong. Its initiatives on sustainable development have also been acknowledged by the international community. The city's Renewable Energy Master Plan 2030 was awarded the European Solar prize in 2014 for excellence and innovation.

Tokyo (Japan)

Tokyo Metropolitan is one of the forty-seven prefectures (regions) of Japan and the most populous metropolitan area in the world, with 38 million people. It was formed in 1943 out of the merger of the former Tokyo Prefecture and the city of Tokyo. Due to Tokyo's sheer importance to Japan, almost hosting the same number of people and GDP as South Korea, the governor of the metropolis has often enjoyed disproportionate influence vis-à-vis other governors (Shen 2014). It is only natural, therefore, that Tokyo boasts the strongest foreign affairs credentials for a subnational government in Japan.

Tokyo's international relations emerged in February 1960, when it signed its first sister agreement (姉妹都) with New York. In 2010, both cities celebrated the 50th anniversary of their special bond by hosting a panel exhibition in Tokyo introducing the history of exchange between the two cities with a chronological display of photographs, received gifts, and special events. Since 1960, the two cities have developed common cooperation programs including baseball tournaments, staff exchange, student and teacher's mobility, and cultural events. In more recent times, collaboration is grounded on the exchange of best practices on urban and metropolitan management. Besides New York, Tokyo has adopted similar agreement with Beijing (1979), Paris (1982), New South Wales (1984), Seoul (1988), Jakarta (1989), São Paulo state (1990), Cairo (1990), Moscow (1991), Berlin (1994), Rome (1996), and London (2015). Most of them went dormant over time.

Under the leadership of Governor Shintaro Ishihara (1999–2012), Tokyo's foreign affairs were somehow dichotomist. If often the focus was put on cordial relations between cities ("ceremonial paradiplomacy") and on fraternal cooperation, Ishihara also used foreign affairs to embody a resurgent Japanese nationalism and to distract attention away from his tired administration. He advocated a hawkish stance on Japan's relations with China and North Korea, calling for pre-emptive strikes on Beijing and Pyongyang. On one occasion, the governor used an interview with the London *Times* to call for a Falklands-style war with China to settle the disputed status of an uninhabitable group of islands claimed by Tokyo as falling under its jurisdiction. In 2012, he also used a speech in the United States to make further claims on the disputed Senkaku Islands in the East China Sea, later culminating in an ultimatum designed to provoke the national government into a spat with China over their ownership and control (Stevens 2012).

His successor, Naoki Inose (2012–2013), resigned following a political funds-related scandal, but Tokyo's foreign affairs gained a new dimension with the election of Governor Yōichi Masuzoe in 2014. Making international city diplomacy a focus of his administration, he has shown support for the idea that subnational entities can cooperate without having to consider political issues that cause friction between national governments.[58] Subnational diplomacy started thus to be used to defrost or bypass Japan's foreign bilateral agenda. Soon after assuming office, Masuzoe promised to strengthen Tokyo's links with the cities of Beijing and Seoul to help improve relations between Japan and its two closest neighbors. Those relations have been in a deep freeze over territorial disputes and differing views of wartime history, with continued tension preventing Prime Minister Shinzo Abe from holding formal bilateral summits with the leaders of China and South Korea. In April 2014, Masuzoe symbolically visited China and declared tacitly that "I think it would be good if our city-to-city diplomacy could lead to an improvement in relations between Japan and China."[59] Despite some 355 twinning arrangements between Japanese and Chinese cities, there has been little contact between mayors of the two countries during the past twenty years.

In July of the same year, Masuzoe visited Seoul against a background of strained relations between the two countries to meet President Park Geun-hye and the mayor of Seoul, Park Won-soon. On the occasion, he declared that "as with Japan–China relations, Japan–South Korea relations are strained. I hope this interaction will help improve ties, even if only slightly."[60] While Tokyo has had a sister "friendship" with Seoul since the late 1980s, Masuzoe's official invitation to visit the South Korean capital was the first for a Tokyo governor since 1996. If this trend persists, Tokyo could become a hub to present an alternative diplomatic agenda that represents populist demands, or even a check and balance against the diplomatic bureaucrats in the central government (Shen 2014). In his first years in office, he also visited Moscow, London, Berlin, and Paris to promote the Japanese capital in Europe's leading cities as well as garner knowledge on smart cities and Olympic legacy. And regularly receives visits from world leaders such as then London Mayor Boris Johnson (they signed a friendship agreement) or British

Prince William. Masuzoe's foreign policy also carries a business dimension. He has promoted the development of Tokyo as an international business hub using the special zone program, which eases regulations "to draw out the potential of the private sector to the maximum," in his own words.[61] And in 2015 he championed the listing of dollar-denominated bonds on Tokyo Stock Exchange's professional-oriented Tokyo Pro-bond Market, capitalizing on the city's high creditworthiness to attract more money from abroad. In late 2014, Tokyo launched Creating the Future: The Long-Term Vision for Tokyo with 360 policy targets and a three-year execution plan. To restore Tokyo's position as a global financial center and to make Tokyo a global hub were at the core of the new vision.

At the multilateral level, Tokyo is strongly involved with the Asian Network of Major Cities 21, an international network of Asian capitals and major cities headquartered in Tokyo. For a region that shares roughly 40 percent of the world's GDP and approximately 60 percent of the current population, the need for Asia to carve its own influence in the world, even at the subnational level, is ever growing. It was Tokyo's Governor Shintaro Ishihara who first proposed the establishment of an Asian-centric network of member cities to undertake joint projects for the collective prosperity of Asia.

With other multilateral organizations, Tokyo's involvement is primarily centered on the issue of sustainability. It is the only city government to have participated in the International Carbon Action Partnership since 2009 and is also a member of the ICLEI, an association of local governments committed to sustainable development. Tokyo has also shown strong support for the C40 network (joined in 2006) and in 2008 it organized the C40 Tokyo Conference on Climate Change in Tokyo, with the participation of 1,400 people from thirty-two cities.

Tokyo Metropolitan's foreign affairs are dealt with by the International Affairs Division, located in the Governor's Cabinet. With a staff of approximately forty people, the International Affairs Division oversees the full spectrum of Tokyo's bilateral and multilateral relations. In addition, during Yoichi Masuzoe's administration the post of Special Advisor to the Governor on International Affairs was also created. But the institutional setup is larger as it includes international relations experts operating in most of Tokyo's departments on issues such as tourism promotion, disaster management, infrastructure, and education. Tokyo also counts a small but effective network abroad that includes representatives working at the Japanese Embassies in Jakarta and Hanoi and at the New York, London, and Singapore offices of the Council of Local Authorities for International Relations.

Western Cape (South Africa)

In the African context, paradiplomacy is still young and only in South Africa does it deserve a public eye. The Western Cape province is arguably the subnational government (along with Gauteng) that holds the best track record, acting as a role model within the developing world. In 1995, right after the first democratic elections of 1994 in South Africa, the Western Cape established its first body to deal with international relations—the Directorate of International Relations in the Premier's Department—with the goal of promoting the province in the international arena. Still active today, it is not only responsible for providing protocol services to the premier and the cabinet and for coordinating the logistical arrangements of official missions abroad, it also promotes the province strategically abroad and handles international cooperation agreements.

Over the years, the international relations component has become more strategic, dealing with issues beyond protocol. The International Relations Directorate is currently under the Chief Directorate for International Relations and Priority Programs (established in 2012), which is itself accountable to the Strategic Programs Branch of the Premier's Department.[62] The institutional arrangement has another novelty. In September 2010, Premier Helen Zille announced that then Minister for Sports, Arts and Culture, Ivan Meyer, would be given the additional responsibility of Minister for International Relations. It was the first time in South Africa that a provincial minister also held the international relations portfolio. In 2014, Zille was re-elected and Meyer was given the Minister of Finance post, keeping his duties in international relations. In practical terms, the position is more political and symbolic than operational, as he does not directly supervise the work conducted by the Directorate of International Relations. But the minister has the duty of directly assisting the premier in her external role and, according to protocol, is the second in line. In total, about ten people are directly involved with international relations in the provincial government. The strategic agent of the province for Destination Marketing, Investment and Trade Promotion Agency for the Western Cape is Wesgro, which has operated since 1982 for the promotion of investment into the Western Cape economy.

At the bilateral level, the Western Cape has agreements signed with roughly twenty subnational states (e.g., São Paulo state, Bavaria, Burgundy, Upper Austria, and Shandong) but only one-third of the twenty are actually active and producing concrete results. The first agreements were signed in 1995 with Florida, Upper Austria, and Bavaria, and it is mainly with the latter that the Western Cape has engaged in a more solid cooperation. Since the Joint Communiqué signed in 1995, another six agreements were adopted including an Action Plan in 2011, paving the way for the design of cooperation projects on education, environment, and regional and rural economic development. According to the South African Constitution, provinces are not responsible for foreign affairs, but they are able to establish cooperation agreements with provinces and regions around the world in order to promote trade and inward investment, as well as tourism. The Western Cape provincial government uses such agreements to develop the Western Cape economy through bilateral trade and foreign investment and to contribute to the socioeconomic development of the region.

Thanks to its relatively strong and globally integrated economy, which leaves it with a high global visibility, the Western Cape has been able to complement its bilateral partnerships with participation in transnational networks of subnational governments, namely the Regional Leaders Summit, a strategic alliance of seven international regions founded in 1999 to promote cooperative multidimensional exchanges between the regions. It provides a forum for the exchange of best practices in areas of mutual interest. The Western Cape successfully hosted the Fifth Summit in Cape Town in 2010, which included the participation of Governor Jiang Daming from Shandong, and Minister-President Horst Seehofer of Bavaria, among other representatives from the other members. The province is also a member of nrg4SD and The Climate Group. It is a signatory to the latter, but has never been a formal member, whereas it was an active member of the nrg4SD from 2004 to 2008; but it withdrew in 2010 owing to budget and capacity constraints, according to a senior official from the premier's office.[63] Back in 2005, provincial Minister of Environmental Affairs and Development Tasneem Essop was elected as the international co-chair of the network and as the vice-chair for the Africa region. She shared the chairmanship with the Basque Government's Sabin Intxaurraga, Minister of Land Planning and the Environment. However, later provincial environment ministers prioritized the local over the international sphere and the participation of the Western Cape in multilateral environmental forums of subnational governments was less of a priority.

In an attempt to focus on international involvement, in 2013 the provincial cabinet adopted its first International Relations Strategy, with clear-cut objectives:

> This strategy seeks to harness ownership of the development agenda for the WCG [Western Cape Government] and its partners while aligning donor funding to provincial policies and priorities. The strategy also aims to harmonize donor and South African government financial and policy processes to ensure efficiency and effectiveness. The economic diplomacy approach advocated by the national Department of International Relations and Cooperation is central to this strategy. (Western Cape Government 2013, 10)

Before the strategy was adopted, many departments were engaged weakly and were unable to maximize opportunities or adequately respond to global issues that affected the province. This hampered policy design and policy implementation. As stated by the premier, "Even though IR [International Relations] is still largely the domain of nation-states, regional governments are playing an increasingly critical role. The WCG must keep pace with this trend and ensure that we form effective partnerships with key global actors" (Western Cape Government 2013, 1).

The Western Cape Government has also provided strong support for the organization of large events in Cape Town as a means to promote the province and its capital city abroad. Besides the FIFA World Cup in 2010, which received strong human and political support from the provincial government, Cape Town was awarded the World Design Capital distinction in 2014. Managed by the International Council of Societies of Industrial Design, it is a city promotion project that recognizes and awards accomplishments made by cities around the world in the field of design.

According to Nganje, paradiplomacy in South Africa is to a large extent devoid of any political undertones, as is the case with the foreign relations of most subnational governments in the developed world. A good example of this is the Western Cape province. Despite the fact that it has been governed by a national opposition party (the Democratic Alliance) since 2009, international relations are defined within the framework of the national foreign policy and are sometimes conducted in close collaboration with the national government's departments and agencies (Nganje 2014). A senior member of the Premier's Department has underscored that: "Helen Zille is a very loyal South African. She is intensely proud of the democracy which has been built in South Africa since 1994. While she is fiercely critical of the ruling party at national level, she is proudly South African." According to the same source, the central government is believed to have recognized the benefit of an independent voice as an indicator of the maturity of South Africa's democracy.[64]

5

Challenges Ahead

Homework

In the state of Mexico, we believe that by opening ourselves to the world, we can achieve more and better results, because the states and towns are the engines of prosperity and economic development.
— ERUVIEL AVILA, *governor of the state of Mexico, Mexico*

By sidelining subnational states and politics, we dramatically undermine our ability to understand and thus participate meaningfully and effectively in the ongoing global processes of change in the spatial organization of the state system and the global political economy. Indeed, throughout the book it became clear that the ability of central governments to find adequate solutions for many major problems is in decline. This incapacity stems partly from the growing importance of new intermestic issues that are not completely within a nation-state's jurisdiction (e.g., environmental pollution, terrorism, currency crises, and AIDS) and partly from the fact that older domestic issues are increasingly linked with international components (e.g., health, education, transportation) (Cohn and Smith 1996). Our world is indeed interdependent. The environmental, social, and economic challenges that regional governments face are often global in scope and require collaborative solutions involving governments, businesses, and organizations around the world. The success of policymaking therefore depends on the ability to create and maintain positive relations with individuals, governments, business associations, community groups, and academic institutions abroad. Public policies by subnational governments are not simply domestic or foreign as they are undertaken both within and outside the demarcated territories.

But despite the fact that paradiplomacy is a major global trend and cities and states will increasingly occupy larger economic and political spaces, there are still some challenges ahead.

Better Policies and More Resources

Given the fact that more than twenty subnational governments have fairly resilient foreign policy structures and resources, it would be far-fetched to say that there is no institutional capacity at the substate levels. In fact, there is. But the majority of subnational governments still have fragile paradiplomacy structures which can take several forms. In some cases, the state is itself weak or fragmented, or there is excessive dependence on personality-dependent governance and charismatic leadership with no efforts for rationalization and institutionalization of governance. In these cases, the contract between government and the governed—imperfect in rich countries—is often altogether absent in poor countries. Subnational diplomacy, if it actually exists, is conducted with precariousness. Some African or Latin American substates come to mind.

There are also examples of diplomatic structures that face fragility within a vaster context of institutional and governmental stability and maturity. Given that paradiplomacy is a fairly new phenomenon, subnational diplomacy bodies compete, from a non-advantageous perspective, with more traditional departments over resources and political oxygen and thus often lack the financial and personnel resources to properly implement major initiatives. This is an issue of major concern. In 1985 the European Charter of Local Self-Government of the Council of Europe asserted that "local authorities' financial resources shall be commensurate with the responsibilities provided for by the constitution and the law" (Art. 9(2)). In the United States, for instance, virtually every governor's office and state executive bureaucracy has offices and personnel devoted wholly or partially to international affairs, primarily economic affairs and to foreign policymaking. But international affairs still constitutes a very small portion of state and local budgets and only a tiny sector of state and local bureaucracies (Kincaid 1999, 119). The exception here, besides the protodiplomacy states of Quebec, Flanders, and Catalonia, are Japan's subnational governments, whose budget comes from the national government through the Local Allocation Tax mechanism; allocations from the budgets of the Ministry of Foreign Affairs (MOFA), JICA, and Japan Bank for International Cooperation (JBIC), and from subnational governments' own budgets.

In some cities and states, the lack of resources has not deterred local leaders from embarking on foreign trips that have no clearly defined objectives. The use of paradiplomacy to promote personal goals partly accounts for the predominance of so-called study tours in the international relations toolkit of provinces and municipalities. These occur at the expense of equally beneficial activities such as capacity-building and people-to-people exchanges (Nganje 2014). As paradiplomacy is a rather recent phenomenon and subject to a great deal of experimentalism, there have been issues on the costs and benefits of these initiatives. Some cities and regions have come to realize that a great deal of what they do is of questionable value. There is therefore a need to streamline internal policies and ensure better articulation between domestic objectives and external actions. Several officials interviewed reported that although their governments had been conducting foreign affairs for over a generation now, they were still lagging behind in terms of capable policy design and implementation.

This goes side-by-side with the issue of training. As we saw earlier, paradiplomats are still poorly trained, have no specific career track, and only a few universities and policymaking research institutes provide any training on the topic. The challenges and tools available to subnational diplomats are much different from the ones used by traditional diplomats and therefore training would need to be customized. Classical International Relations or International Business university degrees do not necessarily equip foreign affairs team in cities and states. National diplomats also have to be better trained on the issue of paradiplomacy. Traditional diplomatic preparation tends to be theoretical in orientation and less application- and management-focused, but in today's dynamic and crisis-prone international arena, where new complex problems emerge in sometimes rapid succession and where alliances form, shift, and dissolve quickly, much of the pre-programmed and predominantly history-oriented learning and curricula of traditional diplomatic training no longer ensures acquisition of new competencies to fit the demands of contemporary diplomacy. Diplomatic schools and institutions have not been perceived as responding to these new challenges and work requirements in a timely and apt manner. Therefore, we ought to invest in training. That includes (1) training on paradiplomacy to traditional diplomats, (2) foreign affairs training to local governmental staff, and (3) more and better university training.

In other countries, subnational units may have signaled their intention to adopt foreign initiatives, but they have to count on the support and the intermediary role of national governments. The governor of Baghdad, Ali al-Tamimi, for instance, expressed the wish in 2014 to link with other subnational governments to attract investments for infrastructure and sanitation, but the international contacts were led mostly by Iraq's diplomatic network rather than by the city itself. This is also related to the issue of diplomatic communication, which, in the case of subnational partners, needs to be made more agile. Given the absence of tested diplomatic channels and the adoption of transversal communication norms, subnational governments sometimes improvise in their communication, follow less secure communication channels, or rely on the embassies of their countries to link them up with foreign partners. When the latter occurs, letters might take up to three months to reach their destination. Subnational governments, even the ones with robust foreign policies and resources, often use the national embassies and consulates-generals to arrange for meetings with foreign leaders. The intermediary role of a diplomatic representative provides, it is often believed, more legitimacy to the request.

Paradiplomacy may also be abducted by hardcore political behavior or political vanity. There have been situations of political interference causing poor service delivery as the level of institutional fragility may affect the extent of opportunistic political behavior. As foreign affairs are believed to have an aura of glamor and cosmopolitanism, subnational politicians may play this card to shape their image as global statesmen and women. Individual agendas and not collective needs may be the guiding principle. In 2015, when the then mayor of London Boris Johnson decided to visit Iraq to meet British troops helping to train local fighters involved in the war against Islamic State, he argued that his presence in Kurdistan was pertinent as the region was going through considerable economic growth and social development and London had a role to play "as an active ally in this." But the opposition was right to point out that the mayor was meddling with defense issues to leverage his national "leadership ambitions."[1] The conduct of paradiplomacy is also embedded in a specific political and party milieu that is not immune to the directions that this larger environment may take. If the same party rules in the federal and local governments, then local authorities may have more opportunities to expand their foreign affairs, since local officials would face fewer hurdles in pursuing their own activities because of similar political agendas, as well as personal and party links with the federal government, and thus could be included in government visits abroad, in negotiating teams, or in the national representation in international organizations (Schiavon 2010, 91). Changes of government are another way for politics to step in and shake up paradiplomacy. New leaders carry fresh visions and priorities, which are translated in variations in budgets and political will. Although North Rhine-Westphalia was one of the strongest contributors to the nrg4SD, the 2005 election promoted a shift in power between the Social Democratic Party (SPD) and the Christian Democratic Union leading the *länd* to suspend its membership. The new leadership looked at nrg4SD policies on climate change as too associated with SPD (Happaerts et al. 2010). In Alberta, the opposite occurred. It was the election of Peter Lougheed of the Progressive Conservative Party in 1971 that encouraged "the emergence of the strong interest of the province to international relations" (Kuznetsov 2015, 133). A ministry with competencies on foreign affairs was established in 1972.

In the end, success boils down to having better policies and resources. The most well-intended and well-thought-out policies may not have an impact if they are not implemented properly. Unfortunately, the gap between intention and implementation can be quite wide. The weaker the structure, the more vulnerable it becomes to internal and external forces. Research on the US political landscape has shown that governors

> with greater institutional and personal powers are more likely to take part in foreign policy. It makes sense from the perspective of federalism and state politics literature that governors with greater institutional controls—such as appointment power, tenure potential, and veto power—could have a greater role in shaping their U.S. state's international programs and strategies to deal with international forces and problems. More institutional powers also means that governors have increased party control and can attempt to gain support for new initiatives, perhaps through paradiplomacy. (McMillan 2008, 241)

Coordination with National Foreign Policy

Paradiplomacy is frequently controversial, not because of its material scope or its supposedly undesirable legal consequences for the affected states, but to the extent that it appears as symbolically relevant—significant expressions of certain values that seem to question precisely those other values that sustain the centralization of international relations (Cornago 2010, 30).

Despite this, full coordination between national and local governments on foreign affairs is more the exception than the rule. In the 1980s, Ivo Duchacek stated that the reason for the absence of coordination is mainly because of the "lack of awareness." The reason for this is that "national policymakers and administrators often do not know what is actually going on in the borderlands or in other subnational networks abroad" (1984, 24). Another reason for the lack of coordination is that national administrators see subnational arrangements as only being marginally important. While assessing paradiplomacy in France, Manuel Duran underscores that each region is entitled to engage in external relations, without having to coordinate with higher or lower-level local authorities, causing "a lot of asymmetries, divergences and overlapping policies" (2011, 345).

Although this lack of coordination does not generally produce incidents, in some cases, cooperation between national and subnational entities is not only a matter of institutional cordiality or electoral convenience, but it is directed at the core of policymaking itself. Taking the environment or international trade as examples, it is clear that regions are at the foundation of these policies with considerable jurisdictional overlap between central and regional levels of government. The implications of this are that the effectiveness or otherwise of international environmental or trade agreements can, at least in part, be explained by attitudes and policies at the local level (Hocking 1999, 27). Not surprisingly, US governors were especially active in supporting President Clinton's efforts to obtain congressional approval of NAFTA in 1993 and the Uruguay Round of the GATT in 1994. Forty governors publicly supported NAFTA and about an equal number supported GATT (Kincaid 1999, 124). In security issues, full coordination is also of paramount importance. For instance in 2009, the United Kingdom regarded President Obama's direct negotiations—without British Foreign Office consent—with Bermuda's government (a British Overseas Territory) over the release of four Guantanamo Bay detainees as humiliating (Cornago 2010, 32).

Federal and local governments may also dispute visions on specific foreign affairs issues. Cases are rare, but do exist. In 1998 representatives from the republics of Bashkortostan, Dagestan, Yakutia, Tatarstan, Tuva, Khakassia, and Chuvashia attended a conference in Istanbul that recognized the Turkish Republic of North Cyprus, with the consequent irritation of Moscow (Cornago 2000, 3). In the 1970s, Idaho sponsored trade missions to Libya when the country was at odds with the US government. In the 1980s, at the height of the conflict between the Reagan and Sandinista administrations, American cities moved to establish sister-city relations with municipalities in Nicaragua to clearly oppose Washington foreign policy. In Japan, MOFA at times opposed Hokkaido Prefecture's contacts with nearby Sakhalin in Russia, claiming these contacts worked against the national interest (Jain 2005, 66). In 2012, the Tokyo governor's attempt to purchase the Diaoyutai/Senkaku Islands (archipelago at the center of a long-running territorial dispute between Japan and China) from their private owners also sparked new rounds of crisis (Shen 2014). There are other examples. In 1985, the British Parliament passed legislation targeting California specifically over the state's so-called unitary tax on transnational corporate revenues, whereas in 1998 the governments of both the European Union and Japan requested and were granted a dispute resolution panel with the United States over a Massachusetts law that effectively banned state and local government purchases from corporations doing business in Myanmar (Paul 2005, 2–3).

Another issue that has been faced by subnational governments is related to the Dalai Lama's international traveling. As local politics are more immune to national diplomatic straitjackets, it is often the case that cities and states are welcoming to the idea of hosting events with the participation of the Dalai Lama—to the dismay of Chinese authorities. Central governments aligned with Beijing often have to intervene to put out the fire or to pull the reins in. As an example of this, the 2014 World Summit of Nobel Peace Laureates planned for October 2014 in Cape Town was suspended because the South African government withheld a visa for the Dalai Lama, whom Cape Town had invited. Another example comes from Brazil, which officially only recognizes the Dalai Lama's religious power, and not his political authority. In September 2011, although the São Paulo state government follows Brazil's official position, then vice-governor Guilherme Afif took part in an event in São Paulo's capital (in his personal capacity) to honor the Dalai Lama. This sparked a stream of protests by the Chinese embassy directed toward both the state and the federal governments.

Cities may also get caught up in national foreign policy disputes—often involuntarily. In mid-2015, Amsterdam Mayor Eberhard Van der Laan announced the intention to tighten connections between his city and Tel Aviv through a sister-city agreement, but his plans came under a firestorm of criticism from local left-wing parties and pro-Palestinian activists, forcing him to abandon the agreement. By the end of the year the twinning agreement was modified to include also Ramallah paving the way to its approval, but the tiresome diplomatic zigzagging took away the initial bilateral impetus and ultimately demonstrated that cities are not immune to global chess games.

Despite the need for better synergies, some obstacles still lay ahead. In interviews with national government employees, Duchacek found seven reasons for national opposition toward subnational diplomacy. First, it is "opposition in principle"—in other words, they oppose the fact that central power is being diluted. Second, there is fear of anything new, the fact that it is a break in the normal and established routine. Third, there is a fear of a more "complex and complicated pattern." If managing diplomatic relations is difficult enough when confined to only sovereign nations, bringing subnational officials into the mix risks exacerbating policy gridlock rather than easing it. Fourth, there is a fear of what the consequences might be of the "relative inexperience, diplomatic gullibility, and lack of negotiating skills" (1984, 21) of the local and subnational personnel. Fifth, there is a fear that the effectiveness of the national operations will be compromised and that other nation-states could exploit this fact to use a "back entrance into a nation-state" (1984, 21). The sixth reason is a fear of "subnational egocentrism," which means that it could be detrimental to some of the other "federal components" and could lead to possible tension between these components. Lastly, there is a fear of a "secessionist potential in some subnational initiatives" (1984, 22).

In the 1990s, Duchacek summarized the issue stating that "in our era, in which nations have not yet adapted to the international presence of non-central governments, their forms of diplomacy necessarily raise questions of diplomatic protocol, leading to potential tensions with the diplomatic and consular representatives of a central government abroad, as well as a problem of compliance with foreign laws concerning non-diplomatic foreign agents" (1990, 26).

He adds that "subnational contacts with foreign centers of political power may become vehicles for various forms of trans-sovereign meddling ... [and] too many subnational initiatives abroad may lead to chaotic fragmentation of foreign policy and cause a national to speak with stridently conflicting voices on the international scene" (Duchacek 1990, 28).

To overcome these psychological blocks and possible disconnects, some coordinative models could be adopted. The first and the most common one is a high-level channel of consultation where coordination and information sharing have been established between the "top echelons" of both the national and the subnational (Duchacek 1984, 27). Although not always successful, this was the strategy established in South Africa. The Consultative Forum of International Relations (CFIR) was created by the Department of International Relations and Cooperation (DIRCO) as a way for the three spheres of government to have a forum for "regular coordination and strategic planning" about the international programs of the country. In principle, the CFIR meets twice a year under the auspices of DIRCO and is charged primarily with facilitating information sharing, foreign policy guidance, planning and coordinating international visits, as well as conveying necessary feedback on key foreign policy issues (Nganje 2014). According to a senior official from the Western Cape province, participation is very "useful" because provinces receive confidential and detailed briefings on particularly sensitive issues of South Africa's diplomacy or on major global political challenges. Guests may also be invited to hold presentations on international trends. And best practices are discussed among the provinces and metropolitan areas represented.[2] Up to ten members take part in the meetings.

Another interesting example comes from Mexico. In 2013 the Foreign Ministry and the National Conference of Governors organized a seminar on Mexico's foreign policy and the international agenda of local governments. The goal of the seminar was to strengthen the international activities of the state and local governments. The event was attended by representatives from state and local governments who were given an overview of the foundations and priorities of Mexico's foreign policy and of best practices in the international activities of local governments. One of the goals was to encourage the governments to coordinate with the Foreign Ministry, under the terms of the Treaties Act, to sign interagency agreements and to shape their international agendas. In his speech, foreign secretary José Antonio Meade said the Foreign Ministry believes in the importance of federal diplomacy for the development of the states and municipalities. "One of the priorities of the Foreign Ministry is to be an ally of the local actors," he said.[3]

Another way of ensuring this coordinative measure would be to include, for instance, one or more subnational representatives in "delegations and negotiating teams abroad" (Duchacek 1984, 27) or to establish "inter-administrative links" such as "liaison offices in the ministries of external affairs" (Duchacek 1984, 27) or having local foreign policy being administrated by national diplomats. This latter case is tricky and may lead paradiplomacy to be molded against federal policies.

Internal and Global Acknowledgment

Paradiplomacy has not yet entered the mainstream political agenda. Despite the growing robustness of the phenomenon, scholars, policymakers, media, and people are not generally aware of the multiple foreign activities carried out by subnational governments. This is visible first within academic circles. Simon Curtis points out that "the relative lack of engagement with the rich literature on global cities is a significant lacuna for the International Relations community, which seems to have discounted the city as an important object of analysis after its long centuries of subjugation to the state" (2011, 1945). But it is most evident in the policy sphere. The words of Duchacek, one of the pioneers of scholarship on paradiplomacy, were as accurate back in the 1990s as they are today: "International activities undertaken by democratic non-central governments have already become facts of international life, however much their effects may be minimized as marginal and purely technical by some, or described as portents of diplomatic chaos by others" (Duchacek 1990, 28).

Indeed, foreign policymakers are likely to regard subnational diplomacy as, at best, a distraction, and at worst a threat to their prerogatives and prestige (Moore 2013). In Japan, a country that boasts intense paradiplomatic activities by its local government, some academic studies are available, but most accounts have appeared in semi-official publications or from practitioners such as governors, mayors, and local officials (Jain 2005, 4). According to a senior official from Medellín foreign affairs body, although the city is often regarded as a role model in international relations practice, it is still difficult "to get people in the country to understand the value of international cooperation when we are not simply recipients of international development assistance."[4] In the 1980s, when more than eight hundred American cities passed nuclear-freeze resolutions, some critics dismissed these as trivial measures that had little influence on US nuclear policy despite their intention to incite policy change. Globally, when there is some knowledge on the subject, it is generally equated with a strategy for statehood, and some provinces in Canada, Spain, and Belgium came promptly to mind. Voters also have little understanding of the need for state and local international competence. In the United States, for instance, many still believe that the country is an attractive target for foreign investors in any event and therefore the need for most states to pursue foreign investment may be alleviated.

Subnational foreign affairs officials also face challenges in their own backyard. Their work may sometimes be looked down on by officials from their very governments, who do not promptly detect the connection between foreign policy and better public services. As local authorities generally give stronger emphasis to issues such as education, healthcare, or transportation, it may be difficult for paradiplomats to find internal sources of political oxygen to thrive. Several officials interviewed alluded to their frustration of being looked at as an appendix within their own governments when they believe their work provides a fundamental tool to assist other ministries and departments to deliver more efficient services and achieve better results.

It is therefore necessary for the leading subnational governments to better articulate their voice in national and international forums and press for more political space as subnational diplomacy is emerging as a force to be reckoned with. In an era of shrinking budgets for foreign ministries and proliferating challenges, subnational diplomacy can play a valuable part on the global stage. Rather than being seen as an antidote to gridlock in national capitals, subnational diplomacy should be viewed as an integral part of foreign relations in the interdependent twenty-first century.

Notes

Chapter 1

1. The first time the term was used was in an article published by Duchacek in 1984, appearing only once and right in the abstract: "In recent decades, complex interdependence as well as domestic issues have encouraged many constituent governments of larger national polities to assert an international competence of their own, primarily in matters touching upon their respective jurisdictions, such as trade promotion, foreign investment, employment and rights of foreign workers, environmental and energy issues, and tourism. Two forms of the resulting *paradiplomacy* are identified: transborder regional regimes (dominantly based on informal consociational processes) and "global micro-diplomacy" which bring constituent governments, including those of major cities, into direct contact with foreign national and constituent governments" (Duchacek 1984, 5; italics added).

2. In March 1857 Hugh Childers was elected Victoria's first agent-general in London. Yet, one of the first letters he received on arriving in England was the notification of change of government and the cancellation of his appointment. He continued in the office until the end of 1857 but remained Victoria's informal representative in England until 1862, when he was again appointed officially.

3. Hector Fabre was dispatched by Quebec to Paris but was requested by the federal government to represent all of Canada. He and his successor, Philippe Roy, continued to represent both Quebec and Canada in France until 1912 when the federal government asked Roy to resign his Quebec position to avoid conflicts of interest.

4. For instance, the Commissariat Général aux Relations Internationales of the French-speaking community and the Direction des Relations Internationales of the Wallonia region were established in 1982 and 1981, respectively. Later, they were merged into the new Wallonia-Brussels International, a full-fledged agency with a broad portfolio.

5. Former Canadian Ambassador to the United States Allan Gotlieb has articulated this traditional view over the years. See, for instance, "Only One Voice Speaks for Canada," *The Globe and Mail*, October 5, 2005.

6. "Kerry, on Eve of Arctic Summit, Calls for Citizen Pressure on Climate Change," *Washington Post*, April 23, 2015.

7. http://eacea.ec.europa.eu/citizenship/programme/action1_measure1_en.php.

8. Xu Jingxi, "The 2014 China International Friendship Cities Conference Closes in Guangzhou," *China Daily*, November 30, 2014, http://www.chinadaily.com.cn/china/2014-11/30/content_18998329.htm.

9. Cited in "As Borders Blur, Cities Mull 'Foreign Policies,'" *Chicago Tribune*, May 26, 2015).

10. "Local Government External Action," http://www.diplomatie.gouv.fr/fr/sites/cooperation_decentralisee/en/#/.

11. The "Atlas: Le Panorama mondial des projets" can be found at: http://www.diplomatie.gouv.fr/cncd.

12. http://saladeprensa.sre.gob.mx/index.php/comunicados/2865-257.

13. In May 2014, the Office of the Secretary's Special Representative for Global Intergovernmental Affairs was incorporated into the Bureau of Public Affairs under the leadership of Deputy Assistant Secretary David A. Duckenfield. Links between the State Department and local governments are now handled by the Office of Intergovernmental Affairs, within the Bureau of Public Affairs.

14. Shannon Tiezzi, "Tokyo Governor Yoichi Masuzoe Visits Beijing," *The Diplomat*, April 26, 2014, http://thediplomat.com/2014/04/tokyo-governor-yoichi-masuzoe-visits-beijing/.

15. Ibid.

16. "Address by Chinese President Xi Jinping at the China–US Governors' Forum," September 24, 2015, http://www.chinadaily.com.cn/world/2015xivisitus/2015-09/24/content_21966923.htm.

17. http://www.uncsd2012.org/content/documents/814UNCSD%20 REPORT%20final%20revs.pdf.

Chapter 2

1. The State Reforms is a process initiated in 1970 toward finding constitutional and legal solutions for the tensions among the different segments of the Belgian population. So far, sixth rounds of reforms have been concluded (the latest one in 2011).

2. In September 2013, the Flemish government concluded that the landscape of Advisory Bodies, which needed to be consulted for mandatory advice, was overcrowded and that they were slowing down the government's decision-making process. A number of Advisory Councils were to be merged and a few to be dissolved, such as Flemish Foreign Affairs Council.

3. As of December 31, 2013, the Flanders governments counted with 730 people, of which 275 were abroad.

4. As of April 2015, the three core international structures of the Wallonia government had 772 employees: Wallonia-Brussels International (325 people), Walloon Export and Foreign Investment Agency (409 people), and Association for the Promotion of Education and Training Abroad (38 people).

5. As of December 2014, the Ministère des Relations internationales et de la Francophonie had 529 positions: 223 in its network of representations abroad and 306 in Quebec. In late 2015, Premier Philippe Couillard announced deep staff cuts.

6. It includes the staff of Invest São Paulo and the international relations advisers at the different Secretariats. With a new mandate starting in 2015, the number of people involved with foreign affairs decreased substantially due to budget cuts and the adoption of new priorities.

7. http://www.industry.nsw.gov.au/__data/assets/pdf_file/0017/54512/ rel_stoner_20130413_in_eng_strategy.pdf.

8. The current version of the state's strategic concept, called "WOV 2021," is publicly accessible on the state's website at http://www.land-oberoesterreich.gv.at/cps/rde/xchg/ooe/hs.xsl/85110_DEU_HTML.htm.

9. The current working plan, called "Arbeitsübereinkommen 2009–2015," is publicly accessible at https://www.ooevp.at/fileadmin/ ooevp/dateien/2016/OOE_weiter_entwickeln_OOE-Plan.pdf.

10. "Bavaria–Quebec Cooperation," http://www.baviere-quebec.org/office/byqc/index.php.en.

Chapter 3

1. Interview with a senior official of Wallonia-Brussels International held on March 19, 2015.

2. Karel De Gucht, "Strengthening the EU–Canada Ties," December 9, 2010, http://trade.ec.europa.eu/doclib/docs/2010/december/tradoc_147099.pdf.

3. http://www.salon.com/2015/06/22/a_state_by_state_look_at_governors_trade_trips_abroad/.

4. "The Declaration of Rio de Janeiro by Federated States and Regional Governments Committed to a New Paradigm for Sustainable Development and Poverty Eradication," http://rio20.net/en/propuestas/federated-states-and-regional-governments-committed-to-a-new-paradigm-for-sustainable-development-and-poverty-eradication.

5. UN Framework Convention on Climate Change, "Adoption of the Paris Agreement," December 12, 2015, http://unfccc.int/resource/docs/2015/cop21/eng/l09r01.pdf.

6. UN Framework Convention on Climate Change, "Climate Action Now: Summary for Policymakers 2015," http://climateaction2020.unfccc.int/spm/introduction/.

7. "Maharashtra Tourism Diwali at Times Square to be Held on September 20th, 2014," May 23, 2014, http://indiapulse.sulekha.com/local-pulse/maharashtra-tourism-diwali-at-times-square-to-be-held-on-september-20th-2014_post_6428.

8. The Scottish Government, "Arts & Culture," http://www.scotland.gov.uk/topics/artsculturesport/arts.

9. Pew Charitable Trusts, "State and Local Government Spending on Health Care Slowed in 2013," February 9, 2015, http://www.pewtrusts.org/en/research-and-analysis/analysis/2015/02/09/state-and-local-government-spending-on-health-care-slowed-in-2013.

10. "Rio de Janeiro City Receives US$1 Billion for Growth, Education and Health," July 1, 2010, http://web.worldbank.org/WBSITE/EXTERNAL/NEWS/0,,contentMDK:22636897~menuPK:51062077~pagePK:34370~piPK:34424~theSitePK:4607,00.html.

Chapter 4

1. "Paulo Teves destaca importância da posição geoestratégica para a afirmação dos Açores no mundo," July 8, 2014, http://www.azores.gov.pt/Portal/pt/entidades/pgra-ssrpre-drcomunidades/noticias/Paulo+Teves+destaca+import%C3%A2ncia+da+posi%C3%A7%C3%A3o+geoestrat%C3%A9gica+para+a+afirma%C3%A7%C3%A3o+dos+A%C3%A7ores+no+mundo.htm.

2. Interview with a senior official of the Under-Secretariat for External Affairs conducted on December 23, 2014.

3. Interview with a senior official of the Under-Secretariat for External Affairs conducted on December 23, 2014.

4. "Intervenção do Presidente do Governo," August 29, 2014, http://www.azores.gov.pt/GaCS/Noticias/2014/Agosto/Interven%C3%A7%C3%A3o+do+Presidente+do+Governo.htm.

5. Interview with a senior official of the Under-Secretariat for External Affairs conducted on December 23, 2014.

6. The Representation was created in December 1987 as Information Office of the Free State of Bavaria. In the course of the Maastricht-Treaty of 1992 and the establishment of the Committee of the Regions in 1994, the office became the Representation of the Free State of Bavaria to the European Union. Its weight is reflected in the fact that it represents a specific division of the State Chancellery (Vertretung des Freistaates Bayern bei der EU).

7. http://www.invest-in-bavaria.in/content/15-years-invest-bavaria.

8. Interview with senior official from State Chancellery conducted on January 5, 2015.

9. "Development Policy," http://www.stmwi.bayern.de/en/internationalisation/development-policy/?contrast=0.

10. The new dynamic international policy of Buenos Aires is generally credited to Mayor Mauricio Macri. Before he took office, Buenos Aires had only a handful of officials involved with foreign affairs, and it was in Macri's administration that the Undersecretariat of International and Institutional Relations was established.

11. Interview with senior official from the Directorate General of International Relations and Cooperation conducted on December 22, 2014.

12. Interview with senior official from the Directorate General of International Relations and Cooperation conducted on December 22, 2014.

13. Although uncommon by international protocol standards, the Buenos Aires mayor has met with several other global leaders, apart from city mayors, including with heads of state and government. In July 2014 he received Chinese President Xi Jinping in Buenos Aires and in November 2014 he was received in Asunción by Paraguayan President Horacio Cartes.

14. They met again privately on the side of the Third US–China Governors Forum, held in Seattle in September 2015.

15. "Governor, Speaker Join Bay Area Council to Reopen State's Trade Offices,"

http://www.bayareacouncil.org/china/governor-speaker-join-bay-area-council-to-reopen-states-trade-offices/.

16. Interview conducted on December 2, 2014.

17. "Invest in Catalonia Annual Report 2014," http://www.catalonia.com/en/binaris/150429_MemoriasINVEST_2014_FINAL_tcm213-213317.pdf.

18. Interview conducted on December 2, 2014.

19. Interview conducted on December 10, 2014.

20. Interview conducted on December 10, 2014.

21. Interview conducted on December 10, 2014.

22. Quebec held general elections in 1989 and the incumbent Quebec Liberal Party, led by Robert Bourassa, won re-election. He had a deep network of contacts in Flanders and saw it as a model for the Quebec-within-Canada.

23. The predecessor of Flanders Investment & Trade (Flemish Foreign Trade Board) was established in the early 1990s.

24. The full list can be accessed at http://www.flanderstrade.com/site/internetEN.nsf/ContactUsHome?openform.

25. The full list can be accessed at http://www.meetinflanders.com/en/about-us/how-can-we-help/.

26. In September 2013, the Flemish government concluded that its administration was fragmented in too many departments and agencies—and its global overhead cost too high. Therefore, it was decided that

247

a number of departments or agencies with subcritical mass should be merged or sourced into bigger ones. FICA, as one of the smallest agencies, was part of this decision. Its merger with the Department of Foreign Affairs came into effect on April 1, 2014.

27. "The Flemish ODA Report 2014," http://www.vlaanderen.be/int/sites/iv.devlh.vlaanderen.be.int/files/documenten/Flemish%20ODA%20report%202014_ENG_site.pdf.

28. The full list can be accessed at http://www.vlaanderen.be/int/en/search-flemish-representative.

29. Interview with a senior official from the Flemish Department of Foreign Affairs conducted on January 24, 2015.

30. "Urban Innovation Database," http://www.urban-innovations.org.

31. Interview conducted on October 21, 2014.

32. Interview with a senior official of the International and European Affairs Directorate conducted on December 19, 2014.

33. Interview with a senior official of the International and European Affairs Directorate conducted on December 19, 2014.

34. Interview conducted on December 19, 2014.

35. Interview with senior official of the Directorate of International Relations and Expo 2015 conducted on February 9, 2015.

36. Interview with senior official of the Directorate of International Relations and Expo 2015 conducted on February 9, 2015.

37. Amsterdam, Barcelona, Berlin, Bern, Bilbao, Brussels, Bucharest, Dubai, Dublin, Geneva, Istanbul, London, Los Angeles, Miami, Montreal, Moscow, Mumbai, New York, Paris (twice), Prague, Shanghai, Tel Aviv, Tokyo, Warsaw, Vienna, and Washington.

38. http://archives.lib.state.ma.us/bitstream/handle/2452/206233/ocn795183245-2013-10-11d.pdf?sequence=1.

39. The *Boston Globe*, for instance, has written that "it's easy to highlight examples of deals that fizzled and difficult to point to clear game-changers for the Massachusetts economy." See "Deval Patrick's Overseas Trips Yielded Mixed Results," *Boston Globe*, July 8, 2015.

40. Interview on December 16, 2014.

41. Interview with a MOITI senior official conducted on December 16, 2014.

42. Interview with ACI official conducted on December 10, 2014.

43. Interview with ACI official conducted on December 10, 2014.

44. Interview with ACI official conducted on December 10, 2014.

45. Interview with ACI official conducted on December 10, 2014.

46. On November 10, 1864, William Colburn Mayne (1808–1902) became the first agent-general for New South Wales in London, and in 1867 he also acted as head of the New South Wales commission for the Paris Exhibition and spent some time in France. He retained his office as agent-general until 1871 when he was granted a colonial pension.

47. Report by the Australian government online at https://dfat.gov.au/trade/resources/Documents/nsw.pdf.

48. Interview with an Ontario senior foreign affairs official conducted on December 22, 2014.

49. The International Trade Branch moved from the Ministry of Economic Development, Employment and Infrastructure to the Ministry of Citizenship, Immigration and International Trade after the 2014 general election when new ministers were named and the ministries renamed (prior to the election these two ministries were called the Ministry of Economic Development, Trade and Employment and the Ministry Citizenship and Immigration).

50. Interview with an Ontario senior official in IMC conducted on December 26, 2014.

51. Interview with an Ontario senior foreign affairs official conducted on December 22, 2014.

52. Interview with an Ontario senior foreign affairs official conducted on December 22, 2014.

53. In 1935 the Quebec government signed an international agreement with Great Britain. However, the documents were exchanged through an agent at the federal level, in Ottawa. Therefore, the negotiations are not considered to have been conducted directly between the two governments even if Ottawa only played the role of go-between to relay the information.

54. Online at http://www.mrif.gouv.qc.ca/content/documents/fr/ententes/1964-01.pdf.

55. Interview with senior official from Quebec government conducted on January 15, 2015.

56. Half of the city of Sydney's population was born overseas and more than one-third of Sydney residents speak a second language at home.

57. Interview with a senior official from the Sydney Council conducted on January 15, 2015.

58. Interview with member of the International Affairs Division of the Tokyo Metropolitan conducted on October 30, 2014.

59. Shannon Tiezzi, "Tokyo Governor Yoichi Masuzoe Visits Beijing," *The Diplomat*, April 26, 2014, http://thediplomat.com/2014/04/tokyo-governor-yoichi-masuzoe-visits-beijing/.

60. Alexander Martin, "Tokyo Governor Seeks Better Ties with Seoul," *Wall Street Journal*, July 23, 2014, http://blogs.wsj.com/japanrealtime/2014/07/23/tokyo-governor-seeks-better-ties-with-seoul/.

61. Speech held at Chatham House in October 2014, http://www.chathamhouse.org/sites/files/chathamhouse/field/field_document/20141031Tokyo.pdf.

62. Other pillars of the Strategic Programs branch include "Policy and Strategy" and "Strategic Communications."

63. Interview conducted on December 7, 2014.

64. Interview conducted on December 7, 2014.

Chapter 5

1. "Boris Johnson Visits Kurdistan Region of Iraq," BBC News, January 23, 2015, http://www.bbc.com/news/uk-england-london-30942714.

2. Interview conducted on December 9, 2014.

3. Speech online at http://saladeprensa.sre.gob.mx/index.php/en/discursos/2866-023doctor-eruviel-avila-villegas-gobernador-del-estado-de-mexico-y-presidente-de-la-comision-de-asuntos-internacionales-de-la-conferencia-nacional-de-gobernadores-embajador-alfonso-de-maria-y-campos-director-general-de-instituto-matias-romero-senore.

4. Interview conducted on December 10, 2014.

References

Acuto, Michele. 2013. "City Leadership in Global Governance." *Global Governance* 19: 481–498.

Acuto, Michele, and Parag Khanna. 2013. "Nations Are No Longer Driving Globalization—Cities Are." Quartz, May 3. http://qz.com/80657/the-return-of-the-city-state/.

Aguirre, Iñaki. 1999. "Making Sense of Paradiplomacy? An Intertextual Inquiry about a Concept in Search of a Definition." In *Paradiplomacy in Action: The Foreign Relations of Subnational Governments*, edited by Francisco Aldecoa and Michael Keating, 185–209. London and Portland: Frank Cass.

Albina, Elena. 2010. "The External Relations of Tatarstan: In Pursuit of Sovereignty, or Playing the Sub-Nationalist Card?" In *Regional Sub-State Diplomacy Today*, edited by David Criekemans, 99–124. Leiden: Martinus Nijhoff.

Aldecoa, Francisco, and Michael Keating, eds. 1999. *Paradiplomacy in Action: The Foreign Relations of Subnational Governments*. London and Portland: Frank Cass.

Alexander, Colin. 2014. "Sub-state Public Diplomacy in Africa: The Case of the Scottish Government's Engagement with Malawi." *Place Branding and Public Diplomacy* 10: 70–86.

Amen, Mark, Noah J. Toly, Patricia L. McCarney, and Klaus Segbers. 2011. "Introduction." In *Cities and Global Governance: New Sites for International Relations*, edited by Mark Amen, Noah J. Toly, Patricia L. McCarney, and Klaus Segbers, 1–12. Farnham: Ashgate.

Antholis, William J. 2013a. *Inside Out, India and China: Local Politics Go Global*. Washington, DC: Brookings Institution Press.

Antholis, William J. 2013b. "New Players on the World Stage: Chinese Provinces and Indian States." October 22. http://www.brookings. edu/research/essays/2013/new-players-on-the-world-stage#.

Murgadas, Enric Argullol i, and Clara Velasco Rico. 2011. "Introduction." In *Institutions and Powers in Decentralized Countries*, edited by Enric Argullol i Murgadas and Clara Velasco Rico, XXX–XXX. Barcelona: Collecció Institut d'Estudis Autonòmics.

Bachtler, J., F. Wishlade, and D. Yuill. 2003. "Regional Policies after 2006: Complementarity or Conflict?" *Regional and Industrial Policy Research Paper*, 51.

Balthazar, Louis. 1999. "The Quebec Experience: Success or Failure?" In *Paradiplomacy in Action: The Foreign Relations of Subnational Governments*, edited by Francisco Aldecoa and Michael Keating, 153–169. London and Portland: Frank Cass.

Bañales, Jon Garcia. 2011. "Agency of Cooperation and Investment of Medellín and the Metropolitan Area—ACI." In *Medellín Laboratory: An Exhibit of Ten Ongoing Practices*, edited by ACI, IDB, UN-Habitat, Alcaldía de Medellín, 180–195. Medellín: Mesa Editores.

Barros, Marinana Andrade e. 2010. "Outlooks for the Legal Framing of Paradiplomacy: The Case of Brazil." *Federal Governance* 7, no. 3: 39–49.

Beauregard, Robert. 1995. "Theorizing the Global-Local Connection." In *World Cities in a World-System*, edited by Paul L. Knox and Peter J. Taylor, XXX–XXX. Cambridge: Cambridge University Press.

Blank, Yishai. 2006. "Localism in the New Global Legal Order." *Harvard International Law Journal* 47, no. 1: 263–281.

Blase, Julie. 2003. "Has Globalization Changed U.S. Federalism? The Increasing Role of U.S. State in Foreign Affairs: Texas-Mexico Relations." PhD dissertation, University of Texas at Austin. http://www.lib.utexas.edu/etd/d/2003/blasejm039/blasejm039.pdf.

Blatter, Joachim, Matthias Kreutzer, Michaela Rentl, and Jan Thiele. 2008. "The Foreign Relations of European Regions: Competences and Strategies." *West European Politics* 31, no. 3: 464–490.

Blondeau, Jean Marc. 2001. "Quebec Experience in Global Relations." Paper presented at the conference Foreign Relations of Constituent Units, Winnipeg, Manitoba. http://www.forumfed.org/libdocs/ForRelCU01/924-FRCU0105-ca-blondeau.pdf.

Boisier, S. 1991. "La Gestión de las Regiones en el Nuevo Orden Internacional: Cuasiestados y Cuasiempresas." *Revista Paraguaya de Sociología* 28, no. 2: 7–38.

Boisier, S. 1992. *El Difícil Arte de Hacer Región: Las Regiones como Actores Territoriales del Nuevo Orden Internacional*. Cusco: Centro de Estudios Territoriales Bartolomé de las Casas.

Botella, Miquel. 1995. "The Keys to Success of the Barcelona Games." In *The Keys to Success: The Social, Sporting, Economic, and Communication Impact of Barcelona'92*, edited by Miquel de Moragas and Miquel Botella, 18–42. Barcelona: Centre d'Estudis Olímpics i de l'Esport.

Bouteligier, Sofie. 2013. *Cities, Networks, and Global Environmental Governance: Space of Innovation, Places of Leadership*. New York and London: Routledge.

Bouteligier, Sofie. 2014. "A Networked Urban World: Empowering Cities to Tackle Environmental Challenges." In *The Power of Cities in International Relations*, edited by Simon Curtis, 57–68. New York and London: Routledge.

Bradshaw, M. J. 1998. "Going Global: The Political Economy of Oil and Gas Development Offshore of Sakhalin." *Cambridge Review of International Affairs* 12, no. 1: 147–176.

Bursens, Peter, and Jana Deforche. 2010. "Going Beyond Paradiplomacy? Adding Historical Institutionalism to Account for Regional Foreign Policy Competences." In *Regional Sub-State Diplomacy Today*, edited by David Criekemans, 151–172. Leiden: Martinus Nijhoff.

Cabeza, Marta Graciela. 2006. "Las Capacidades Internacionales de Los Entes Subnacionales en Argentina y en Italia." *América Latina Hoy* 44: 135–151.

Campbell, Tim. 2012. *Beyond Smart Cities: How Cities Network, Learn and Innovate*. New York: Earthscan.

Carbajales, Juan José, and Claudia Gasol. 2008. "La Gestión Internacional de las Provincias en el Marco del Sistema Federal Argentino y a la Luz de Sus Propias Constituciones." In *Las Provincias Argentinas en el Escenario Internacional*, edited by Eduardo Iglesias, Valeria Iglesias, and Graciela Zubelzú, 47–82. Buenos Aires: CARI-UNDP.

Cashman, Richard, and Anthony Hughes, eds. 1999. *Staging the Games: the Event and its Impact*. Sydney: University of New South Wales Press.

Cassey, Andrew J. 2014. "The Location of US States' Overseas Offices." *Review of International Economics* 22, no. 2: 310–325.

City of New York. 2013. "Managing the Local and the Global: Diplomacy in New York City." http://globalcities.org/2013_nyc_ia_agency_report.pdf.

Cohn, Theodore H., and Patrick J. Smith. 1996. "Subnational Governments as International Players: Constituent Diplomacy in British Columbia and the Pacific Northwest." *BC Studies* 110: 25–59.

Trevisan, Miryam Colacrai de and Graciela Zubelzú de Bacigalupo. 1998. "El Creciente Protagonismo Externo de las Provincias Argentinas." In *La Política Exterior Argentina 1994–1997*, edited by Alfredo Bruno Bologna et al., 319–332. Rosario: CERIR.

Cornago, Noé. 1999. "Diplomacy and Paradiplomacy in the Redefinition of International Security: Dimensions of Conflict and Co-operation." In *Paradiplomacy in Action: The Foreign Relations of Subnational Governments*, edited by Francisco Aldecoa and Michael Keating, 40–57. London and Portland: Frank Cass.

Cornago, Noé. 2000. "Exploring the Global Dimensions of Paradiplomacy: Functional and Normative Dynamics in the Global Spreading of Subnational Involvement in International Affairs." Paper presented at the Forum of Federations, Workshop on Constituent Units in International Affairs, Hanover, Germany. http://www.academia.edu/2286276/Exploring_the_Global_ Dimensions_of_Paradiplomacy_Functional_and_Normative_ Dynamics_in_the_Global_Spreading_of_Subnational_ Involvement_in_International_Affairs.

Cornago, Noé. 2010. "On the Normalization of Sub-State Diplomacy." In *Regional Sub-State Diplomacy Today*, edited by David Criekemans, 11–36. Leiden: Martinus Nijhoff Publishers.

Crescenzi, Riccardo, Carlo Pietrobelli, and Roberta Rabellotti. 2013. "Innovation Drivers, Value Chains and the Geography of Multinational Corporations in Europe." *Journal of Economic Geography* 14: 1053–1086.

Criekemans, David. 2010a. "Introduction." In *Regional Sub-State Diplomacy Today*, edited by David Criekemans, 1–10. Leiden: Martinus Nijhoff.

Criekemans, David. 2010b. "Regional Sub-State Diplomacy from a Comparative Perspective: Quebec, Scotland, Bavaria, Catalonia, Wallonia and Flanders." *The Hague Journal of Diplomacy* 5: 37–64.

Criekemans, David. 2010c. "Regional Sub-State Diplomacy from a Comparative Perspective: Quebec, Scotland, Bavaria, Catalonia, Wallonia and Flanders." In *Regional Sub-State Diplomacy Today*, edited by David Criekemans, 37–64. Leiden: Martinus Nijhoff.

Curtis, Simon. 2011. "Global Cities and the Transformation of the International System." *Review of International Studies* 37: 1923–1947.

Curtis, Simon. 2014. "The Meaning of Global Cities: Rethinking the Relationship between Cities, States, and International Order." In *The Power of Cities in International Relations*, edited by Simon Curtis, 16–31. New York and London: Routledge.

Daillier, Patrick, and Alain Pellet. 2002. *Droit International Public*. Paris: L.G.D.J.

Den Brande, Luc Van. 2010. "A Practitioner's Perspective." In *Regional Sub-State Diplomacy Today*, edited by David Criekemans, 199–210. Leiden: Martinus Nijhoff.

d'Hooghe, Ingrid. 2013. "China's Public Diplomacy Shifts Focus: From Building Hardware to Improving Software." China Policy Institute Blog. https://blogs.nottingham.ac.uk/chinapolicyinstitute/2013/10/24/chinas-public-diplomacy-shifts-focus-from-building-hardware-to-improving-software/.

Dobbs, Richard, Sven Smit, Jaana Remes, James Manyika, Charles Roxburgh, and Alejandra Restrepo. 2011. *Urban World: Mapping the Economic Power of Cities*. Report by the McKinsey Global Institute.

Duchacek, Ivo D. 1984. "The International Dimension of Subnational Self-Government." *Publius* 14, no. 4: 5–31.

Duchacek, Ivo D. 1986a. "International Competence of Subnational Governments: Borderlines and Beyond." In *Across Boundaries: Transborder Interaction in Comparative Perspective*, edited by Oscar J. Martinez, 11–28. El Paso: Texas Western Press.

Duchacek, Ivo D. 1986b. *The Territorial Dimensions of Politics: Within, among, and across Nations*. Boulder, CO, and London: Westview Press.

Duchacek, Ivo D. 1990. "Perforated Sovereignties: Towards a Typology of New Actors in International Relations." In *Federalism and International Relations: The Role of Subnational Units*, edited by Hans J. Michelmann and Panayotis Soldatos, 1–33. Oxford: Clarendon Press.

Duchacek, I., D. Latouche, and G. Stevenson. 1988. *Perforated Sovereignties and International Relations: Trans-Sovereign Contacts of Subnational Governments*. New York and London: Greenwood.

Duran, Manuel. 2011. "French Regions as Diplomatic Actors: The Case of Provence-Alpes-Cote d'Azur." *French Politics* 9, no. 4: 339–363.

Dyment, D. 2001. "The Ontario Government as an International Actor." *Regional & Federal Studies* 11, no. 1: 55–79.

Eberle, Jakub, and Jan Prášil. 2013. "Zahraniční aktivity Bavorska na bilaterální, regionální a evropské úrovni" [Bavaria's external relations on a bilateral, regional and European level]. Unpublished report for the Czech Ministry of Foreign Affairs.

Erk, Jan. 2004. "Austria: A Federation without Federalism." *Publius* 34: 1–20.

European Commission. 2014. "Town Twinning, Education, Audiovisual and Culture Executive Agency." http://eacea.ec.europa.eu/citizenship/programme/action1_measure1_en.php.

Falleti, Tulia G. 2010. *Decentralization and Subnational Politics in Latin America*. Cambridge: Cambridge University Press.

Felli, Gilbert. 2002. "El Model Organitzatiu Dels Jocs Després de Barcelona '92." In *Barcelona: L'herència Dels Jocs (1992–2002)*, edited by Miquel de Moragas and Miquel Botella, 65–76. Barcelona: Centre d'Estudis Olímpics-UAB, Ajuntament de Barcelona, Editorial Planeta.

Glaeser, Edward L. 2011. *Triumph of the City: How Our Greatest Invention Makes Us Richer, Smarter, Greener, Healthier and Happier*. New York: Penguin Press.

Goldsborough, James O. 1993. "California's Foreign Policy." *Foreign Affairs* 72, no. 2: 88–96.

Goldsmith, Mike. 2012. "Cities in Intergovernmental Systems." In *The Oxford Handbook of Urban Politics*, edited by Peter John, Karen Mossberger, and Susan E. Clarke, 133–151. London and Oxford: Oxford University Press.

Happaerts S., K. Van den Brande, and H. Bruyninckx. 2010. "Governance for Sustainable Development at the Inter-subnational Level: The Case of the Network of Regional Governments for Sustainable Development (nrg4SD)." *Regional & Federal Studies* 20, no. 1: 127–149.

Hauslohner, P. 1981. "Prefects as Senators: Soviet Regional Politicians Look to Foreign Policy." *World Politics* 33, no. 1: 197–232.

Hocking, Brian. 1993. *Localizing Foreign Policy: Non-Central Governments and Multilayered Diplomacy*. London and New York: Macmillan and St. Martin's Press.

Hocking, Brian. 1997. "Regionalism: An International Relations Perspective." In *The Political Economy of Regionalism*, edited by M. Keating and J. Loughlin, 90–111. London: Belhaven.

Hocking, Brian. 1999. "Patrolling the 'Frontier': Globalization, Localization and the 'Actorness' of Non-Central Governments." In *Paradiplomacy in Action: The Foreign Relations of Subnational*

Governments, edited by Francisco Aldecoa and Michael Keating, 17–39. London and Portland: Frank Cass.

Hooghe, L., and G. Marks. 2001. *Multi-Level Governance and European Integration*. New York and Oxford: Rowman & Littlefield Publishers.

Hormats, Robert. 2013. "Metro Diplomacy." *Diplomatic Courier* (November/December edition).

Hsiung, J. C. 1995. "China's Omni-Directional Diplomacy." *Asian Survey* 35, no. 6: 573–586.

Huijgh, Ellen. 2010. "The Public Diplomacy of Federated Entities: Examining the Quebec Model." In *Regional Sub-State Diplomacy Today*, edited by David Criekemans, 125–150. Leiden: Martinus Nijhoff Publishers.

Jain, Purnendra. 2005. *Japan's Subnational Governments in International Affairs*. London and New York: Routledge.

Keating, Michael. 1999. "Regions and International Affairs: Motives, Opportunities and Strategies." In *Paradiplomacy in Action: The Foreign Relations of Subnational Governments*, edited by Francisco Aldecoa and Michael Keating, 1–16. London and Portland: Frank Cass.

Kehoe, Timothy J., and Kim J. Ruhl. 2004. "The North American Free Trade Agreement after Ten Years: Its Impact on Minnesota and a Comparison with Wisconsin." *Center for Urban and Regional Affairs Reporter* 34, no. 4: 1–10.

Kenneth, Christopher, and Miquel de Moragas. 2006. "Barcelona 1992: Evaluating the Olympic Legacy." In *National Identity and Global Sports Events*, edited by Alan Tomlinson and Christopher Young, 177–219. New York: State University of New York Press.

Kincaid, John. 1999. "The International Competence of US States and their Local Governments." In *Paradiplomacy in Action: The Foreign Relations of Subnational Governments*, edited by Francisco Aldecoa and Michael Keating, 111–133. London and Portland: Frank Cass.

Kukucha, Christopher J. 2009. "Dismembering Canada? Stephen Harper and the Foreign Relations of Canadian Provinces." *Review of Constitutional Studies* 14, no. 1: 28–35.

Kuznetsov, Alexander S. 2015. *Theory and Practice of Paradiplomacy: Subnational Governments in International Affairs*. London and New York: Routledge.

La Palombara J. 1994. "International Firms and National Governments: Some Dilemmas." *Washington Quarterly* 17, no. 2: 89–99.

Lachapelle, Guy, and Stéphane Paquin, eds. 2005. *Mastering Globalization: New Sub-States' Governance and Strategies*. London: Routledge.

Lagendijk, A. 2011. "Regional Innovation Policy between Theory and Practice." In *Handbook of Regional Innovation and Growth*, edited by B. Asheim, R. Boschma, and P. Cooke, 597–608. Cheltenham, UK: Edward Elgar.

Lampreia, Luiz Felipe. 1999. *Diplomacia Brasileira: Palavras, Contextos e Razões*. Rio de Janeiro: Ed. Lacerda.

Lecours, André. 2002. "Paradiplomacy: Reflections on the Foreign Policy and International Relations of Regions." *International Negotiation* 7, no. 1: 91–114.

Lecours, André. 2008. *Political Issues of Paradiplomacy: Lessons from the Developed World*. The Hague: Netherlands Institute of International Relations 'Clingedael'.

Lecours, André. 2010. "Canadian Federalism and Foreign Relations: Quebec and Alberta." In *Foreign Policy of Constituent Units at the Beginning of 21st Century*, edited by Ferran Requejo, 29–42. Barcelona: Collecció Institut d'Estudis Autonòmics.

Lecours, André, and Luis Moreno. 2003. "Paradiplomacy: A Nation-building Strategy? A Reference to the Basque Country." In *The Conditions of Diversity in Multinational Democracies*, edited by Alain-G. Gagnon, Montserrat Guibernau, and Francois Rocher, 267–294. Montreal: Institute for Research on Public Policy.

Levesque, Rene. 1976. "For an Independent Quebec." *Foreign Affairs* 54, no. 4: 737–742.

Ljungkvist, Kristin. 2014. "The Global City: From Strategic Site to Global Actor." In *The Power of Cities in International Relations*, edited by Simon Curtis, 32–56. New York and London: Routledge.

Loughlin, John. 2007. *Subnational Government: The French Experience*. Houndmills Basingstoke: Palgrave Macmillan.

Lowenthal, Abraham F. 2009. *Global California: Rising to the Cosmopolitan Challenge*. Stanford, CA: Stanford University Press.

Lubin, Martin. 2003–2004. "Perforated Sovereignties in the Americas: The Canada-US Border and the International Outreach Activities of Quebec." *London Journal of Canadian Studies* 19: 19–40.

McHugh, James T. 2015. "Paradiplomacy, Protodiplomacy and the Foreign Policy Aspirations of Quebec and other Canadian Provinces." *Canadian Foreign Policy Journal* 21: 238–256.

McMillan, Samuel L. 2008. "Subnational Foreign Policy Actors: How and Why Governors Participate in US Foreign Policy." *Foreign Policy Analysis* 4, no. 3: 227–253.

Michaud, Nelson. 2008. "Interpreting Quebec's International Relations: Whim or Necessity?" In *The World in Canada: Diaspora, Demography, and Domestic Politics*, edited by David Carment and David Bercuson, 189–205. Montreal: McGill-Queen's Press.

Moore, Scott. 2013. "California's Sub-National Diplomacy: The Right Approach." *Power & Policy Blog*, October 8.

Moragas, Miquel de, and Miquel Botella. 2002. *Barcelona: L'herència Dels Jocs (1992–2002)*. Barcelona: Centre d'Estudis Olímpics–UAB, Ajuntament de Barcelona, Editorial Planeta.

Nganje, Fritz. 2013. "Paradiplomacy: A Comparative Analysis of the International Relations of South Africa's Gauteng. North West and Western Cape Provinces" DLitt et Phil thesis presented at University of Johannesburg. https://ujdigispace.uj.ac.za/bitstream/handle/10210/8644/Nganje_2013.pdf?sequence=1.

Nganje, Fritz. 2014. "The Developmental Paradiplomacy of South African Provinces: Context, Scope and the Challenge of Coordination." *The Hague Journal of Diplomacy* 9: 119–149.

NSW Trade & Investment. 2014. *Annual Report 2013–2014*. Sydney: NSW Trade & Investment.

OECD. 2009. *How Regions Grow Trends and Analysis*. Paris: OECD.

OECD. 2010. *Regional Development Policies in OECD Countries*. Paris: OECD.

OECD. 2014. *Belgium, in OECD Tourism Trends and Policies 2014*. OECD Publishing. http://dx.doi.org/10.1787/tour-2014-10-en.

Oppenheimer, Andres. 2013. "Sub-national Diplomacy on the Rise." *Miami Herald*, October 13.

Palermo, Francesco. 2007. "The Foreign Policy of Italian Regions: Not Much Ado About Something?" *International Spectator: Italian Journal of International Affairs* 42, no. 2: 197–207.

Panara, Carlo. 2010. "In the Name of Cooperation: The External Relations of the German Länder and Their Participation in the EU Decision-Making." *European Constitutional Law Review* 6: 59–83.

Paquin, Stéphane. 2010. "Federalism and Compliance with International Agreements: Belgium and Canada Compared." In *Regional Sub-State Diplomacy Today*, edited by David Criekemans, 173–198. Leiden: Martinus Nijhoff.

Pasquier, Romain. 2006. "The Union Démocratique Bretonne: The Limits of Autonomist Expression in Brittany." In *Autonomist Parties in Europe: Identity Politics and the Revival of the Territorial Cleavage*, edited by Lieven de Winter, Margarita Gomez-Reino, and Peter Lynch, 79–100. Barcelona: ICPS.

Pasquier, Romain. 2009. "The Europeanisation of French Regions." *French Politics* 7: 123–144.

Paul, Darel E. 2005. *Rescaling International Political Economy: Subnational States and the Regulation of the Global Political Economy*. New York and London: Routledge.

Porter, Michael. 1990. *The Competitive Advantage of Nations*. New York: Free Press.

Project Management Institute. 2006. *The Standard for Program Management*. Pennsylvania: Project Management Institute.

São Paulo Government. 2014. *Sao Paulo State: A Global Player*. Sao Paulo. Sao Paulo Government. http://www.saopauloglobal.com/arquivos/biblioteca/36Foreign%20Affairs%202011-2014%20ENG.pdf.

Schiavon, Jorge A. 2010. "Sub-State Diplomacy in Mexico." In *Regional Sub-State Diplomacy Today*, edited by David Criekemans, 65–98. Leiden: Martinus Nijhoff.

Shen, Simon Xu Hui. 2014. "Local Governments in Japan and Roles Played in Sino-Japanese Relations." *East Asia* 31: 49–65.

Soldatos, Panayotis. 1990. "An Explanatory Framework for the Study of Federated States as Foreign-policy Actors." In *Federalism and International Relations: The Role of Subnational Units*, edited by Hans J. Michelmann and Panayotis Soldatos, 34–53. Oxford: Clarendon Press.

Stevens, Andrew. 2012. "Shintaro Ishihara: Former Governor of Tokyo." http://www.citymayors.com/mayors/tokyo_mayor.html.

Storper, Michael. 2013. *Keys to the City: How Economics, Institutions, Social Interactions, and Politics Shape Development*. Princeton: Princeton University Press.

Tatham, Michaël. 2013. "Paradiplomats against the State: Explaining Conflict in State and Substate Interest Representation in Brussels." *Comparative Political Studies* 46, no. 1: 63–94.

Tavares, Rodrigo. 2013. "Foreign Policy Goes Local: How Globalization Made São Paulo into a Diplomatic Power." *Foreign Affairs*, October. http://www.foreignaffairs.com.

Tomás, Mariona. 2005. "Building Metropolitan Governance in Spain: Madrid and Barcelona." In *Metropolitan Governance: Capacity,*

Democracy and the Dynamics of Place, edited by Hubert Heinelt and Daniel Kubler, 47–62. London and New York: Routledge.

UN-Habitat. 2008. First Announcement: The First Session of the World Urban Forum. Harmonious Urbanisation: The Challenge of Balanced Territorial. http://mirror.unhabitat.org/pmss/getElectronicVersion.aspx?nr=2446&alt=1.

United Nations (DPADM) (2008). "Contribution of Decentralized Cooperation to Decentralization in Africa." http://www.euroafricanpartnership.org/old/contributi/DCStudy-publication-7_08.pdf.

US Department of State. 2015. *2015 Quadrennial Diplomacy and Development Review: Enduring Leadership in a Dynamic World.* Washington, DC: US Department of State.

Vanthillo, Ties, and Ann Verhetsel. 2011. "Paradigm Change in Regional Policy: Towards Smart Specialisation? Lessons from Flanders (Belgium)." *Belgium Journal of Geography* 1, no. 2: 2–16.

Vion, Antoine. 2007. "The Institutionalization of International Friendship." *Critical Review of International Social and Political Philosophy* 10, no. 2: 281–297.

Wang, Jian. 2006. "Localising Public Diplomacy: The Role of Sub-national Actors in Nation Branding." *Place Branding* 2: 32–42.

Wells, Louis T., and Wint, Alvin G. 2000. Marketing a Country: Promotion as a Tool for Attracting FDI, Foreign Investment Advisory Service/Occasional Paper-13, The International Finance Corporation and The World Bank, Washington, DC.

Western Cape Government. 2013. *International Relations Strategy.* Cape Town: Western Cape Government.

Weyreter, Martina. 2003. "Germany and the Town Twinning Movement." *Contemporary Review* 282, no. 1644: 37–44.

Wolff, Stefan. 2007. "Paradiplomacy: Scope, Opportunities and Challenges." *The Bologna Center Journal of International Affairs* 10: 141–150.

World Economic Forum. 2014. "The Competitiveness of Cities: A Report of the Global Agenda Council on Competitiveness." http://www3.weforum.org/docs/GAC/2014/WEF_GAC_CompetitivenessOfCities_Report_2014.pdf.

Yang, D. 1991. "China Adjusts to the World Economy: The Political Economy of Chin's Coastal Development Strategy." *Pacific Affairs* 64, no. 1: 42–64.

Index